Servants, Shophands, and Laborers
in the Cities of Tokugawa Japan

———————————————

Servants, Shophands, and Laborers in the Cities of Tokugawa Japan

Gary P. Leupp

PRINCETON UNIVERSITY PRESS

PRINCETON, NEW JERSEY

Copyright © 1992 by Princeton University Press
Published by Princeton University Press, 41 William Street,
Princeton, New Jersey 08540
In the United Kingdom: Princeton University Press, Chichester,
West Sussex
All Rights Reserved

Library of Congress Cataloging-in-Publication Data

Leupp, Gary P.
Servants, shophands, and laborers in the cities of
Tokugawa Japan / Gary P. Leupp
    p. cm.
Includes bibliographical references and index.
1. Domestics—Japan—History. 2. Manual work—
Japan—History. 3. Sweatshops—Japan—History.
4. Master and servant—Japan—History I. Title.
HD8039.D52J34 1992 305.5'62'0952—dc20 91-45134

ISBN: 0-691-03139-8
ISBN: 0-691-02961-X (pbk.)

We are grateful to the Japan Foundation for its support

The author thanks the University of Arizona Press for permission to
cite the poem "On your long journey . . . ," from Patia R. Isaku,
Mountain Storm, Pine Breeze: Folk Song in Japan (Tuscon, 1981)

This book has been composed in Linotron Sabon

Princeton University Press books are printed on acid-free paper
and meet the guidelines for permanence and durability of the
Committee on Production Guidelines for Book Longevity of the
Council on Library Resources

First paperback printing, 1994

Printed in the United States of America

3 5 7 9 10 8 6 4 2

For Mari

_____

CONTENTS

LIST OF TABLES

PREFACE

THIS BOOK grew out of a University of Michigan doctoral dissertation in which I attempted to achieve two goals. I wanted, at minimum, to describe a stratum in Tokugawa society that had been largely ignored by Western historians: urban workers, such as domestic servants, manual laborers in construction and transport, and manufacturing hands. Secondly, I hoped to demonstrate that *wage labor*—and hence capitalist relations of production in the specific Marxian sense[1]—had developed to a significant extent in Japanese cities during a period commonly described as "feudal." The latter point seemed of particular importance in that Japan's historical trajectory has so closely paralleled those of the Western capitalist countries in the period since 1868.[2] Perhaps, I hypothesized, the Tokugawa period was to Japanese history what the Tudor period was to British history—a period of proletarianization, of changes in class structure ultimately even more crucial than technological change or foreign impact in giving rise to capitalist society.[3]

Japanese historians had, since the 1930s, written volumes on the question of Japan's transition to capitalism. But they had largely focused upon agrarian conditions, or on the topic of (principally rural) "manufactures."[4] In pursuing this latter question, so far as I could tell, they had been far more interested in such issues as scale of operations and nature of management than the character of the workforce involved.[5] Study of urban labor in the Tokugawa period had in general been neglected.

While initially fascinated by the problem of urban workshop laborers, I decided to begin my study with a description of domestic servants and commercial shop employees. These workers, while by no means wageworkers in Marx's sense of "capital-positing, capital-producing" laborers, were, by the late seventeenth century, typically short-term, contracted employees, paid in cash wages. Their transformation from unpaid, lifetime, hereditary retainers, while not itself constituting the transition from feudalism to capitalism, nonetheless seemed to *mirror* such a transition.[6] And since they were always far more numerous than true wageworkers, it seemed proper to start off with them.

I proceeded, then, to examine casual manual laborers in such fields as construction and transport. In their case, I thought, the wage-labor relation begins to appear: a free day-laborer, for example, hired by a private master-carpenter to haul lumber around a construction site, is probably involved in a specifically capitalistic exchange. As an employer this carpenter, unlike the scullery maid's master, directly profits from the labor power of his employee.

Finally, I planned to discuss manufacturing workers who, in mass-producing commodities destined to produce a profit for their employer, most clearly represent an exploited, pre-industrial capitalistic workforce. However, in order to meet self-imposed dissertation completion deadlines, I compromised with a rather cursory discussion of this stratum; thus the manufacturing chapter became the weakest part of my dissertation.

The present work is less ambitious than that earlier study. I have jettisoned the manufacturing chapter entirely, in order to use it as the basis for a separate volume. Along with the chapter, I have also abandoned much of the argument about nascent capitalism in Tokugawa Japan. My concern here is less to show the emergence of specifically capitalistic forms of labor exploitation than to describe how human relations were radically affected by the tremendous expansion of the money economy during the Tokugawa period.

In researching this work, I have benefited from the suggestions and advice of many scholars. During the early stages, Peter J. Arnesen provided welcome encouragement and was extraordinarily generous with his time and counsel. Hitomi Tonomura helped me see the project through, contributing valuable criticisms and comments. Wakita Osamu of the University of Osaka supervised my research in Japan during 1985–1987, helped me develop my *mondai ishiki*, and allowed me many hours of his time. I especially treasure his friendship and his advice.

Among the others who have read and commented upon the entire manuscript, early chapter-drafts, or other preliminary work, I would like to thank Herbert Bix, Robert Cole, Geoffrey Eley, Cissie Fairchilds, Roger F. Hackett, James L. McClain, Evelyn Rawski, Gilbert Rozman, Saitō Osamu, and G. William Skinner. Kozo Yamamura made useful criticisms as a Princeton University Press reviewer.

I am indebted to Hayami Akira for his direction in locating extant urban population registers of the Tokugawa period, and to Hayashi Reiko, Inui Hiromi, and Yoshida Nobuyuki for various research leads. Usami Hideki of Kyoto University's Machifure Kenkyū Kaisho kindly provided me with photocopies of Kyoto population registers. Maruyama Shigeru of the Takayama Kyōdokan, and archivists at the Kyoto Shiryō Kaikan and Nagasaki Kenritsu Toshokan were also gracious in allowing me access to such registers in photocopy or manuscript form.

For his friendship and empathy as the "other" foreigner studying the Tokugawa period at the University of Osaka during my stay there, I must express my gratitude to Tao Demin of Shanghai's Futan University. Tsude Hiroshi and Murata Michihito I thank for their help, companionship, and patience.

I gratefully acknowledge support for several fellowships received during my research: a Foreign Language-Area Studies grant from the

U.S. Department of Education, a Fulbright Foundation fellowship which made possible two years of study at the University of Osaka, and a fellowship from the Social Science Research Council and the American Council for Learned Societies. I would also like to express my thanks to my copy editor Marylyn Marshall, and to Molan Chun Goldstein and Margaret Case of Princeton University Press for their professionalism and endless patience.

My parents I thank for their support during what must at times have seemed an endless project of doubtful ultimate benefit. Above all, I thank my wife Mari. Without her love, assistance, and cheerful adaptability to graduate student life in two cultures, this study would not have been possible.

Servants, Shophands, and Laborers
in the Cities of Tokugawa Japan

———————————

INTRODUCTION

THE NAMELESS figures are familiar to any student of the cities[1] of Tokugawa Japan (1603–1868). The apprentice-clerk leaning over his abacus, calculating the day's profits in his master's dry-goods shop. The fire-brigadesman with his long hooked staff tearing down wooden houses in the path of a spreading blaze. The blue-liveried maidservant in the theater audience, enjoying a holiday from work. The well-muscled porter or palanquin bearer, naked but for loincloth and sweat-drenched head-towel, scurrying down the Tōkaidō highway. The daimyo's footboy, gorgeously outfitted, accompanying his lord in a ceremonial cavalcade. The scowling packhorse driver arguing with his customer about his fee or the qualities of his animal. The carpenter atop the half-finished tenement sharpening his adze in the morning twilight.

Such were the ordinary working people who lived and toiled in the castle towns and commercial centers of the period. Stock figures in the characteristic genres of *chōnin* (bourgeois) culture,[2] they appear in countless woodblock prints, in the domestic dramas of the *kabuki* theater, in the satirical mini-poems called *senryū*, in humorous anecdotes, novelettes, diaries and household records.

These humble folk also appear, in their less cheerful aspects, in the edicts, legal records, and political-economic writings of the samurai authorities. Their names, and often their occupations, are recorded in the population registers compiled by the Tokugawa regime. The shogunate, its officials, and the various daimyo, while employing multitudes of these workers for their own purposes, also viewed them as objects for control. In registering and regulating them, the authorities developed what amounts to early modern "labor policy," leaving to posterity a rich historical record on that wonderfully durable, hand-molded Japanese mulberry paper.

The many images we derive from these sources constitute a vast, colorful, illustrated scroll of underclass life in Tokugawa cities. But surprisingly, Western historians have not yet applied much of their research energy to this topic. While several generations of English-language scholarship on the period have produced fine monographs on Tokugawa merchants, samurai and peasants, they have only touched upon this stratum in passing. Japanese historians, such as Wakita Osamu, Yoshida Nobuyuki, Minami Kazuo, Nakabe Yoshiko, Ōtake Hideo, Ōishi Shinzaburō, Kitajima Masahiro, Ishii Ryōsuke and Maki Hidemasa, have of course devoted far greater attention to the urban lower classes, but their work has been largely an exercise in legal history, and the exegeses of such texts as the Collected Edicts (*Ofuregaki*) issued by the shogunate.

Yet the topic of the lower classes in Tokugawa cities is significant for at least two reasons. The numbers of servants, shophands and casual laborers in themselves command attention. In the great cities, such socially marginal groupings as day laborers, domestics, porters, palanquin bearers, stevedores, manufacturing hands, peddlers, beggars and outcastes constituted a vast *population flottante*.

Matsumoto Shirō, for example, has estimated that 60 percent of the Edo commoner population consisted, by the end of the period, of day laborers, palanquin bearers, domestic servants, beggars, prostitutes, or entertainers.[3] In Osaka, the "Kitchen of the Realm" and the second largest city, the picture was similar. Saitō Osamu suggests that some 18 percent of the population were servants (*hōkōnin*) during the Genroku period (1688–1704),[4] and Yasuoka Shigeaki regards 30 to 40 percent of the residents during the early eighteenth century as day laborers, handicraft workers, domestics and their families.[5] In the imperial capital of Kyoto, last of the great "Three Cities," a huge labor force, including many connected with the textile industry, swelled the proletarian population. In 1700, hired weavers in the Nishijin district alone may have numbered around 21,000, constituting some 6 percent of the total registered urban population.[6]

Smaller castle-towns might also boast substantial worker populations. In Okayama, for example, 28 percent of the registered households during the mid-seventeenth century belonged to day laborers, while 14 percent belonged to servants in merchant households.[7] Data from half a century later suggests that 21 percent of the Okayama population consisted of servants of the samurai.[8] In Hiroshima in 1768, 13 percent of the registered population were listed as either servants or "artisans" (*shokunin*)— the latter category no doubt including some manual laborers.[9] In Okazaki in 1801, some 17 percent of the registered households belonged to day laborers; in Yamaguchi in 1844, the corresponding figure was 39 percent.[10]

In a commercial town such as sake-brewing Tondabayashi, 60 percent of the urban total might be employed as wage earners or servants.[11] Surely this flotsam and jetsam helped determine the tenor of urban life as much as the swashbuckling samurai and sedulous burghers who figure more prominently in the history texts.

The quality as well as the quantity of these Tokugawa workers is of historical importance, since they provided the stuff from which one of the most remarkable industrializations of world history occurred. As a Japanese economist recently put it, "Meiji Japan's greatest inheritance from the Tokugawa period was an abundance of skilled labour."[12] Thomas C. Smith, noting that labor "posed no major problem" in Japanese industrialization, paid special tribute to village Japan: "For upward of two hundred years the agricultural labor force had been unwittingly preparing for the transition to factory employment."[13] The industrial labor force of the Meiji era, however, drew not only upon the peasant workforce, but upon the pool of workers already resident in the cities.[14] Moreover many of these urban workers, recruited into newly introduced Western industry, practiced skills with indigenous roots.[15] Even structures of labor organization developed during the period remained influential into the present century.[16] Thus the break between the Tokugawa urban workforce and the industrial proletariat of more recent times was probably not so sharp as is commonly supposed.

This is not, then, a general study of "the urban poor." Such a project would require, among other things, discussion of the legions of impecunious samurai—parasitic or productive, masterless or employed—who comprised much of the urban population. They are beyond the scope of this work. Nor do I deal with the "laboring poor" in general, in the sense Jeffrey Kaplow defined this term in his fine work on eighteenth-century Paris.[17] I do not, for example, devote much space to the myriad types of peddlers and hawkers who haunted the streets and market-places; they *worked*, to be sure, and perhaps even produced what they vended, but I regard them as petty merchants rather than laborers. Nor can I include skilled, independent artisans. In this study, I confine my attention to urban workers. I am concerned only with those who perform work *for others* (masters, employers, the *han* or barony, the shogunate) in relationships inherently weighed in favor of the latter.

Chapter 1 surveys the sweeping social changes that accompanied, or slightly predated, the establishment of the Tokugawa regime. It describes how conditions of peace, spectacular urban growth, massive public construction projects, and the *sankin-kōtai* system affected traditional labor forms, and how the shogunate moved to ban slavery, fix employment tenures, and regulate workers through registries and other institutions.

Chapter 2 deals with servants, describing their demographic features, types and duties, and the "feminization" of service apparent during the course of the period in the great commercial city of Osaka. In Chapter 3, I discuss master-servant relations: the ideal as depicted in Confucian tracts, sermons, and legal documents, as well as the realities indicated by criminal records, household documents, loyalty awards and other documents. I describe an increasingly impersonal, monetary class relationship and argue that wages, as opposed to room and board, tips, gifts, and traditional bonuses, became the major form of compensation during the period.

Chapter 4 treats the topic of servants in society, their image in literature and drama, their relations with other classes, their literacy and social
mobility. Chapter 5 is devoted to day laborers, describing their numerous
types, methods of organization, regulation of hours, work quality, and
wages. In Chapter 6 I discuss how the shogunate and various baronies
developed methods to control these workers, including devices designed
to discourage begging and inculcate a positive attitude towards work.

Chapter One

LABOR AND THE PAX TOKUGAWA

CONFLICTS IN THE SOCIAL ORDER

Throughout the Tokugawa period, and for centuries prior to it, Japan was a feudal society—feudal, at least, in the sense that this term is used by many Marxist (and most Japanese) historians.[1] Japan, that is to say, was a society in which the essential mode of production was "the exploitative relationship between landowners and subordinated peasants, in which the surplus beyond subsistence of the latter, whether in direct labour or in rent in kind or in money, is transferred under coercive sanction to the former."[2]

The overwhelming majority of the population had been tied, by laws dating to the eighth century, to their ancestral fields as self-sufficient agriculturalists.[3] And although the ancient laws had fallen into abeyance long before the establishment of the first *bakufu* (shogunate) in 1192, shoguns and local magnates had always attempted to maintain the peasantry in a state of diligent subjection. The Tokugawa shogunate, founded in 1603, was no exception. The famous Keian Edict, issued by this regime to all villages in 1649, specified a regimen of ceaseless toil for this class. Agriculture, it declared, must be carried out "with the greatest diligence" morning, noon, and night. "Peasants must rise early and cut grass before cultivating the fields. In the evening they are to make straw rope or straw bags. . . . The husband must work in the fields, the wife must work at the loom. Both must do night work."[4] Peasants were ordered to "eat millet, vegetables, and other coarse foods" rather than the rice they grew, and they were not permitted, at least by law, to waste time and resources on such pleasures as tea or sake-drinking, tobacco, or sightseeing. A wife, however good-looking she may be, was to be divorced should she show an interest in such diversions. Ruling-class attitudes were given classic expression by the finance superintendent of the 1730s who asserted, "With peasants and sesame seeds, the more you squeeze them the more you get from them."[5]

Typical of the codes issued by local daimyo is that of Tosa in 1612, which threatens peasants who do not pay their rice tax with "prompt and severe punishment," and contains harsh clauses against abscondence.

> It is a very serious crime to desert to another province. Those who assist in the getaway are equally guilty. Both ears and nose must be cut off. If, at a later time, the runaway is caught and brought back, he will be punished by

death, and so will those who helped him. . . . If a person is a fugitive, his offense is less serious if he hides within the borders of this realm. But fleeing to
another province must be absolutely forbidden.[6]

One must note that such laws were in fact often observed in the breach;
during the Tokugawa period, peasants in fact not only smoked and
drank, but migrated in vast numbers.[7] But in theory, the agriculturalist
was a serf, and the heavily armed ruling class—the *bushi* or samurai—
sought to exact from this serf all the products of his labor, aside from
those needed to satisfy his most minimal needs. Thus the fundamental
conflict within this system was the same as that in medieval Europe: a
struggle over the level of tribute.[8]

The respective views of the lord and peasant concerning this issue were
summed up by the perceptive social critic Ogyū Sorai, writing about
1720. In words that might have applied equally well to pre-Tokugawa
centuries, Ogyū observed:

> The lord of the fief is convinced that his sole function is to collect taxes
> while the peasants see him as doing nothing else. The former seeks to collect
> as much tax as possible, while the latter seek to pay as little as possible.
> Both sides are concerned with nothing else but this struggle over taxes. As
> a result, the lord of the fief and the peasants look upon each other as sworn
> enemies.[9]

This "struggle over taxes (*nengu*)" assumed many forms, most dramatically peasant rebellions, which first occurred on a significant scale in the
fourteenth century. Ten major uprisings during this century were followed by more than one hundred revolts between 1428 and 1500. In the
sixteenth century, peasant leagues energized by radical religious beliefs
established fortified communities able to hold their own against the various warring daimyo. And in the course of the Tokugawa period, some
2,700 peasant protests occurred, their incidence rising from four per year
during the seventeenth century to twenty-two per year in the last decades
of the old regime.[10]

No national peasant revolt, comparable to the those occurring in England in 1381, Hungary in 1514, or Germany in 1524–1525, ever took
place, but the specter of agrarian rebellion clearly terrified the ruling
class. The fact that the samurai authorities of the various domains (*han*)
generally hesitated to increase the assessed tax base during the Tokugawa
period, even as productivity sharply rose, suggests a fear of peasant resis-
tence.[11] And the harsh punishments meted out by the shogunate to
daimyo believed to have provoked peasant rebellions in their domains
also indicates this consternation.[12]

This, then, was the fundamental contradiction defining the feudal order, but there were other conflicts in society as well. There were always struggles *within* the ruling class over land and the producers attached to the land. Even before the outbreak of the Ōnin War (1467), the feeble Ashikaga shogunate had seen much of its power pass into the hands of rival daimyo pursuing local and national ambitions. By the mid-sixteenth century, the numerous contenders for national power had been whittled down to a comparative handful, and national reunification was in sight. For each would-be national leader, the principal conflict was that between himself and the rest of the samurai class, in particular the great regional hegemons.

The problem of which daimyo house was to wield nationwide power was finally resolved at Sekigahara, a low pass midway between Kyoto and Nagoya, in a battle involving about 160,000 troops in 1600. In this fateful confrontation, Tokugawa Ieyasu and his allies triumphed over a coalition of hostile daimyo, effectively ending more than a century of civil war. Three years later, the figurehead emperor in Kyoto offered Ieyasu the title of *shōgun* (military governor), and the Tokugawa Shogunate was formally constituted. This, the third such military regime in Japanese history, was the most enduring and successful. It brought an end to interdomainal conflict, establishing a Pax Tokugawa *within the ruling class* which remained unbroken for two and a half centuries. But while, one might say, it resolved for the duration the contradiction between the barons, it brought the country no respite from the chronic challenge of peasant unrest. Indeed, this fundamental conflict was exacerbated by developments under Tokugawa rule.

Methods of Control

The Tokugawa order rested upon policies developed by the early shoguns to insure continued feudal control of the peasants and a high degree of central control over the various daimyo. This order, often called the *bakuhan* system since it allowed the *han* to survive alongside the bakufu, permitted the daimyo to rule their own domains so long as they observed fundamental laws of the shogunate. They were not, for example, to countenance Christian practices within their domains, maintain more than one castle, mint coins, or forge military alliances among themselves. They were not to seek foreign trade or contact, or construct ships capable of navigation on the high seas. They were to accept other miscellaneous bakufu encroachments upon domainal independence: most of their mines were to fall under bakufu management, and along the great national highways, all villages were to fall under bakufu supervision. Daimyo were also obliged to participate in major bakufu construction and reclamation projects, drawing upon their own resources.[13]

The single most burdensome imposition placed upon the daimyo came to be known as the *sankin kōtai* ("alternate attendance") system.[14] This system, presaged by policies dating to the Kamakura period, was only formalized by the third Tokugawa shogun, Iemitsu, in 1635. From this point, all daimyo were obligated to spend half their time in the military capital of Edo, "in attendance" upon the shogun. Meanwhile, their families remained in the shogun's city as permanent hostages. Earlier, the hegemon Hideyoshi had required that his vassal daimyo reside in Fushimi or Osaka for three to five years at a time, leaving their close kin in one of these castle-towns as hostages. While in attendance, the daimyo were prodded to disgorge their treasuries in conspicuous consumption and ceremony, and in projects assigned them by the shogunate. The concept would have been familiar to Louis XIV, who, gathering the greatest French nobles about him at Versailles, consummated their ruin with ostentatious courtly duties.[15]

Meanwhile the bakufu strategy for the containment of the samurai class in general, of which the daimyo were merely the most powerful representatives, rested on a policy of forced urbanization. The *heinō bunri* ("warrior-peasant separation") policy was designed to sever the links between the samurai and peasant classes and thus reduce the threat to central power posed by warriors developing local power-bases. Similar schemes had been carried out by daimyo on a local basis since the mid-sixteenth century, and in 1591, Hideyoshi had issued his famous edict fixing the status of cultivators and warriors, barring the latter from residence in the villages and obliging them to reside in castle-towns (*jokamachi*). The Tokugawa regime continued the separation policy, and while it was implemented only gradually, by 1700 it had converted the vast majority of samurai into urban residents.[16]

A second major motive in these efforts was to reduce peasant discontent. Hideyoshi's edict had been preceded three years earlier by an order to all domains to collect peasant weapons in a nationwide "sword hunt" (*katana-gari*). Ostensibly the weapons confiscated were to be melted down and used in the casting of a great Buddha, but as the contemporary work *Tamonki nikki* charged, "the real explanation is that this order is to prevent uprisings."[17] So long as peasants possessed weapons, the line between them and the samurai remained unclear. Samurai challenging their superiors might recruit retainers from the cultivators, or provoke rebellions by abusing peasants placed under their control. First local, then national hegemons thus hit upon the solution of physically separating the two classes, attempting, indeed, to freeze them into fixed castes.

The *heinō-bunri* policy was not implemented without social costs. Lower-ranking samurai of the cities and towns often grew restless, and particularly during the seventeenth century frequently turned their energies to gang violence.[18] But this element was gradually contained, and ultimately the warrior class as a whole was converted into a literate bureaucracy capable of managing the vast apparatus of the *bakuhan* system.[19]

Both the *heinō bunri* policy and the *sankin-kōtai* policy (which was in essence *heinō bunri* writ large) were designed principally to control the samurai. They were, as suggested above, brilliantly successful in temporarily resolving the conflicts within the ruling class. While lower-ranking samurai sometimes produced urban disorders, no daimyo rebelled against the shogunate until 1863, nor were there violent clashes between the 260 *han*. But in resolving this conflict in the feudal system, the bakufu aggravated the more fundamental one. Peasants became more restive than ever before; as noted, the incidence of peasant revolts rose dramatically through the period. The very strategy of urbanizing the military class produced extraordinary growth of the market, and consequently, new tensions in the village community.

The boom in urban construction from 1580 to 1610 was, according to John Whitney Hall, probably unparalleled in world history.[20] Up until the late sixteenth century Japan could rarely boast of more than one or two large cities. Nara, the eighth century capital, and its successor Heian (Kyoto) may have each reached a population of 100,000 at their respective ancient peaks, and the military capital of Kamakura probably could have counted several tens of thousands of residents in the thirteenth century.[21] But wars and disasters in the late medieval period had partly depopulated these ancient centers; Kyoto's population may have fallen to a mere 40,000 by 1500.

Thereafter, however, a handful of towns came to exceed perhaps 30,000 each by the mid-sixteenth century: Sakai, Uesugi, Tennōji, and Uji-Yamada. By around 1590, Sakai's population had reached nearly 70,000, and this city along with Kyoto (Heian), Fushimi, and Osaka, all located within a radius of about forty miles, may have supported an urban population of around 400,000 souls.[22] But the next century was the great age of castle-town growth. Between 1580 and 1610, at least twenty-five major towns of this type were founded,[23] some attracting huge populations even in their formative decades. Osaka's population may have exceeded 400,000 by 1634, and Edo's total, while unknown, probably surpassed this figure. Sendai's population grew to over 60,000 within a generation of the town's establishment.

By 1700, Edo numbered roughly a million, Osaka well over 400,000, Kanazawa and Nagoya approached 100,000, and Sendai, Okayama, Kagoshima, Hiroshima, Nagasaki all numbered around 60,000. Other urban centers aside from castle-towns also experienced rapid growth. Kyoto may have had 400,000 residents by 1634. Remote Aikawa, the gold and silver-mining center on Sado Island, may have numbered 100,000 by the middle of the century, although decline was quickly to ensue.

Most of these populations remained fairly stable through the remainder of the period, and meanwhile new towns appeared. By the nineteenth century there existed some thirty or forty towns with over 10,000 inhabitants each, and few villages were located more than twenty miles from one such center. Yazaki Takeo maintains that by the eighteenth century 15 percent of all Japanese lived in "towns."[24] Others have suggested even higher figures. It appears certain, at any rate, that by 1700 Japan was probably more urbanized than any country in the world, with the exceptions of England and Holland.[25]

The great cities, and Edo in particular, served during the early Tokugawa period as tremendous engines of economic growth. But this growth had destructive as well as constructive aspects: "Urban influences," as Thomas C. Smith has noted, "seem universally a dissolvent of older agrarian forms."[26] As urban centers grew, they formed vast markets for timber, textiles, foodstuffs and other goods. Some peasants were able to adapt to the growing market, becoming in time successful rural capitalists. Others were not as fortunate; they found themselves obliged not only to the tax-collector but to village money-lenders. Many were forced to mortgage their land to wealthy peasants; losing it entirely, they became wage laborers. Thus the peasant class became increasingly differentiated (Japanese scholars refer to this process as the *bunkai* or "disintegration" of the peasantry) over the course of the period.[27]

T. C. Smith has described changes in village class relations during the Tokugawa period in some detail.[28] However, the processes he describes, and links to the widening market, were prefigured by changes in the nature of *urban* labor. These changes were associated not so much with an expanding market but with the conscious feudal policies mentioned previously. For the bakufu to reign in the samurai and oversee the successful implementation of the *heinō bunri* and *sankin kōtai* policies, it had to overlook the traditional ban on peasant migration and to recognize the formation of a free labor market in the cities.[29] Serfdom remained the fundamental law; the harsh anti-abscondence laws remained in the law books of the various domains; the main highways were at times closely policed to check for absconders; roundups of vagrants were periodically undertaken in the big cities; "people-returning" (*hitogaeshi*) programs occasionally reduced Edo's lower-class population.[30] But the bakufu needed workers to build and service the mansions of the hostage samurai, and to perform all the tasks associated with its ambitious program of urban construction. Traditional means of organizing workers were simply inadequate for the tasks.

The Traditional Labor Force: Lifetime
Servants and Corvee Workers

Little is known about urban labor prior to the Tokugawa period, but it is probably safe to think in terms of three categories of workers: artisans, servants, and less-skilled manual workers. The term artisan (*shokunin*) appears in the sense of a skilled worker as early as the late fourteenth century; it was applied to Kyoto dyers and other craftsmen.[31] In an age when the division of labor was very rudimentary, artisans within the same trade appear to have viewed one another as equals. They were often, although not invariably, grouped into *za*—closed craft or commercial organizations which, like the guilds of medieval Europe, were chartered by powerful patrons, enjoying monopolistic privileges and tax exemptions.[32] Many of these were attached to noble families, great temples, or warrior houses, producing on their behalf. The artisans themselves, according to Toyoda Takeshi, were "semi-free" by the Heian period.[33] By medieval times they were free in the sense that they could enter into relationships with employers at will, and might also migrate as they pleased.[34]

Certain za, organized by leaders called *ko no kōbe* (elders), specialized in providing labor services. Others were directed by captains called *zatō* (za master) or *sata-nin* (officer). Typically small, za might number anywhere from two or three to fifty or sixty members; probably few had a well-developed hierarchy.[35] Aside from the master artisans in these guilds, there must have been apprentice workers; but the terms *detchi* (apprentice), *tedai* (clerk), and *totei* (artisan's apprentice) were still uncommon. These gain currency only in the Tokugawa period. Perhaps most of those in training were the sons or relatives of masters, receiving instruction from these craftsmen.

Domestic servants, up until the early decades of the Tokugawa period, had typically been referred to as *fudai* or *hikan*. These terms are synomous, and were applied to employees of both samurai and commoner households. Marius Jansen regards samurai-household fudai in sixteenth-century Tosa as semi-free indentured servants,[36] and this description jibes well with the description given by the Confucian scholar Ogyū Sorai. In his *Seidan* (*Essay on Politics*, ca. 1730), Sorai wrote that fudai had existed from ancient times in both China and Japan. They were equivalent to a type of servant called *bukyoku* (Ch. *buqu*) which had served Chinese martial households during the Tang period. Distinct from slaves (*nuhi*) who could be bought and sold and who were barred from marrying ordinary people (*heimin*), these servants could marry as they pleased. They were, nevertheless, considered members of their masters' households, "and even their distant descendants did not leave" their hereditary employers.[37]

Sixteenth-century house laws issued by major warlords throw further light on the nature of fudai and hikan. Takeda Shingen's code (1547) is considered the most important of these. In this code, "fudai-hikan" seems to be employed as a single term. The most pertinent clauses concerning such servants are as follows:

(15) When a fudai-hikan takes employment with another person, the former master, upon encountering [the servant] is not permitted to seize him. The former master should explain the situation to the new master, and request that the servant be returned. If the former master has properly informed the new master about the whereabouts of the servant, and if the new master, while agreeing to his return, allows him to escape, he will be obliged to replace him with another.

Slaves [nuhi] and base menials [zūnin] who have not been retained more than ten years are not covered [in this statute], [and questions concerning their employment should be handled] in keeping with the Shikimoku [law code]. . . .

(18) When a hikan is involved in a quarrel or commits a theft, his master is of course not liable. However if, while the authorities are investigating the case, the master, maintaining that no crime has been committed, allows the guilty party to flee, one-third of the master's property will be confiscated. If he has no property, he will be exiled. . . .

(53) It is henceforth forbidden for a fudai-hikan, without informing his master, to take the authority upon himself and give his son and fields to another master. When, however, he has given his eldest son to his master, the master cannot forbid him to give the younger children to another master.[38]

The "Hundred Article Code" issued by by the Tosa daimyo Chōsokabe Motochika in 1597 contains the following:

With regard to regulating fudai status: Men and women who have served their masters for ten years without having been discharged will be considered fudai. Similarly their children will naturally be considered fudai also. A male child will go with his father, and a girl goes with the mother. Even though a servant may have been told by his master that he is dismissed, unless there is written evidence of this no other master is to take him as servant. If a master violates this rule the servant's former master should report this and claim his servant again according to law. It will then be his responsibility to decide whether to put the man in service again or to put him to death. If a servant ran away and his whereabouts were unknown, no matter how many years ago it was he should (if discovered) be reported and returned to his master. Furthermore: But if such a servant's whereabouts in a neighboring area were known by his master for more than ten years without his having taken any action, this will not apply. Similarly, as to fudai attached to fiefs: if a proprietor has gone to another province, even though he return, if he does not receive reinstatement of his original fief, he will not regain his powers over the fudai.[39]

Both of these examples seem to refer to fudai serving members of the samurai class, who might be applied to domestic chores, agriculture or military duties. The texts indicate that while such workers were distinguished from slaves, they were viewed as their masters' property. The law codes imply that masters often struggled over ownership of fudai, who themselves at times attempted to change masters.

Very few records of pre- or early-Tokugawa merchant or artisan households have survived, but those which have suggest that their employees also served on a lifetime basis. The *Terashima Tōemon Yuisho-gaki* (*The Testament of Terashima Tōemon*) dating from the Bunka Period (1804–17) provides a brief history of a prosperous Osaka tile-making family which had provided much of the roofing for Osaka Castle. Referring to the household's employees during the Genna period (1615–23), the document mentions "many hikan" as well as "artisans." Referring to present conditions, in contrast, it employs such terms as *tedai* (clerk) and *komono* (shopboy).[40] The letters of Imai Sōkyū (1520–93) provide additional information. Imai was a great arms and medicine trader who served as intendant (*daikan*) of the thriving port of Sakai under Oda Nobunaga, the national hegemon of the period 1568–82. His letters contain references to "casters" (*shushi*) further defined as hikan, but no intimation that free, short-term workers were in his employ.[41]

The term *hōkōnin* ("servant") seems to be of less antiquity than "fudai." Appearing from the fourteenth century, it originally meant a worker in a noble house, but by the early sixteenth century it also was used for military retainers.[42] A famous edict issued by Hideyoshi in 1586 indicates that the term had come to include persons who had little military function, but who served as domestics and personal attendants: *chūgen* (valets), *komono* (pages) and *arashiko* (lackeys).[43] It was not until the first century of Tokugawa rule, however, that the word was applied to commoners' servants in official documents.[44]

Manual workers fall into several categories: slaves, corvee laborers, and free laborers. Slaves were primarily criminals and prisoners, while those serving corvee duty (*buyaku*) were typically male peasants between ages fifteen and sixty performing a kind of tax obligation. The latter would have been numerous in early castle-towns; in large part it was they who built the fortresses. Among free manual workers, carpenters and those practicing such related professions as thatchers, sawyers and plasterers were much in evidence. These workers tended to live in close proximity to others in the same trade, but wards exclusively reserved for specific occupational groups were not common in the late medieval period.[45] Workers were nevertheless subject to various controls, particularly in castle-towns where they labored at the will of the local lord. The Chōsokabe code cited above specifies the wages to be paid for skilled, average and unskilled workers in more than a dozen occupations. Within such groups as carpenters, a fairly complicated division of labor seems to have existed, and medieval *emaki* (picture scrolls) clearly show headmen directing operations.[46] Possibly an apprentice system existed; the scrolls show boys helping out in the work, although they may simply have been workmen's family members.[47]

Casual laborers hired on a short-term basis were not widely known before the seventeenth century. Under Toyotomi Hideyoshi, who ruled the country from 1583 to 1598, the hiring of day laborers had in fact been strictly prohibited.[48] Writing about 1730, Ogyū noted that, "Until about seventy or eighty years ago the employment of day-laborers was unheard-of."[49] His disciple Dazai Shundai (or Dazai Jun) observed the same in his *Keizairoku* (*Economic Record*) published in 1744. Dazai pointed out that in the past, in both China and Japan, public works (*doboku*) had been carried out by corvee labor (*yoyaku*); lords and kings had never needed to pay out silver and gold as compensation to artisans and workmen, but had simply provided them with their daily meals.[50]

THE IMPACT ON LABOR OF THE PAX TOKUGAWA

The early Tokugawa shoguns, and the hegemons immediately preceding them, pursued policies that radically altered the nature of urban labor. They attacked the za. While some of these survived into the Tokugawa period, this type of organization suffered a decline from 1585, when Toyotomi Hideyoshi abolished them in the city of Kyoto. Soon, other lords followed suit, and the za were banned in such cities as Nara, Koriyama and Wajima. The motive behind this policy was to promote trade in the interests of ever-larger, better-unified feudal units.[51] It also probably allowed workers greater independence and mobility.

The Tokugawa shoguns favored a shift from corvee labor in construction projects to free labor. The projects undertaken by the shogunate and various domains demanded an enormous quantity of labor power.[52] Daimyo lavished funds on their fortresses, and the castle-towns that grew up around them also required legions of quarrymen, carpenters, thatchers and other workers. Traditionally the unskilled workers involved in such projects had been conscripted peasants, but in utilizing such a labor force, the ruling class risked jeopardizing the rice crop. During the formative decades of the Tokugawa shogunate, members of the ruling class came to appreciate the advantages of free labor. For example, the Higo daimyo

Hosokawa Tadatoshi, supervising part of the construction of Osaka Castle in 1636, suggested, in a memorial to the shogun, that hired wage laborers, rather than corvee laborers, ought to be used; the latter, after all, had to engage in rice production, the ultimate source of wealth in early-modern Japan. As peasants seeking wage work were flowing into all the urban centers, it seemed to make more sense to hire them than to oblige the daimyo to recruit conscripts from their own domains.[53]

Indeed, the advice of men like Tadatoshi was heeded; from the mid-1630s, wage laborers came to replace corvee workers in castle-town construction projects.[54] A century later, Dazai Shundai referred to a fairly recent transition in noting:

> It is rare nowadays to use peasants as corvee labor. For such [tasks] as public works, workers in the capital are hired for wages [chinpu o yatote tsukau]. . . . Nowadays lords do not employ people of their provinces, but hire them for wages in Edo. Wage-work [chinpu] is, by the current custom, referred to as *day labor* [hiyō]. For virtually every type of work, people are hired for money. So the people do not suffer, but on the contrary, they prosper. *This is different from the old practice.*[55] [emphasis added]

Another important policy of the new order was the ban on the "trade in human beings" (jinshin baibai). This was no great innovation, since slavery of certain types had been banned periodically since the sixth century. Hideyoshi, angered by the sale of Japanese by Europeans, had outlawed "trade in persons" (hito no baibai) in 1587.[56] Such laws, however, had had a very limited scope. They apparently never precluded the sale of children by their parents, an action often taken as a last resort by those hard-pressed to pay their taxes. Nor did they weaken the institution of hereditary service. They seem to have been designed primarily to prevent kidnapping (kadowakashi) and the involuntary sale of persons by anyone other than their household head.

Whatever its limitations, Hideyoshi's ban, like its precedents, was soon allowed to lapse. The *Zoku sen Kiyomasa-kō* (*Continued Record of Lord Kiyomasa*) records that during the latter part of the Keichō era (1596–1615) "there was no law on the purchase and sale of people" (hito no urikai no hatto kore naki). Indeed, it recounts an episode in which Katō Kiyomasa, the daimyo of Higo, compensates a party for the loss of two female kyōgen (comic drama) entertainers killed by a Katō retainer. The Higo lord simply purchases two female kabuki performers and gives them to the aggrieved party as restitution for his loss.[57]

In 1616 the Tokugawa shogunate issued its first ban on the trade in human beings. Maki Hidemasa believes this step was taken because the authorities regarded such barter as "an infringement of the administration's direct control of the people."[58] It probably also represented the new

regime's desire, as part of its overall consolidation, to more fully implement existing laws, including those against slavery. A new sensibility concerning the subject may have been another stimulus: Maki suggests that
opposition to slavery may have mounted with the influence of Christianity, which at its height in the late sixteenth century counted one-tenth of
all Japanese as believers. It seems however more likely that Portuguese
enslavement of Japanese (to serve on ships) aroused renewed hostility to
the trade in human beings.[59]

The shogunate ban added a new element to the traditional, if largely
ignored, prohibition: by specifying service terms, it left open the possibility of slave-like relations spanning a fixed number of years. Japanese
scholars generally believe that the ban on trade in human beings applied
exclusively to indefinite or lifetime purchase and sale of persons (*hito no
eitai baibai*). This interpretation seems to square with the documentary
evidence; in a legal case during the Jōō era (1684–87), for example, a man
was charged with purchasing a young woman "for an indefinite term"
(*nenki o kagirazu*). The implication is that such a purchase for a specified
number of years was permissible.[60] To understand the real nature of slavery in the period, we must therefore examine the limits placed on service
tenures of all types.

The first law limiting service terms (*nenki*) was issued in Edo in 1616:
"The service term is limited to three years. Stipulation: if [the term] ex-
ceeds three years, both parties involved [will be considered] at fault."[61]
Apparently applying throughout the domains directly governed by the
shogun, the regulation was repeated four times during the next nine
years. In 1625, however, the term was extended to *ten* years. After 1675,
then, an extension of service tenures "by mutual consent" (*sōtai shidai*)
was officially sanctioned, resulting in a temporary revival of *de facto* lifetime service arrangements. Soon prohibited anew, the indefinite extension of master-servant relationships beyond ten years was definitively recognized in 1698.[62]

Although the 1698 law repeated the ban on trade in human beings, and
stipulated that service relations were to be contracted by mutual agree-
ment, it left open the possibility of involuntary servitude. It did not prevent the long-term sale of family members by household heads; moreover, given the legal inequality of masters and servants (described in
Chapter 3), it could not prevent masters from retaining servants against
their will beyond their contracted term. Therefore some have viewed this
regulation as a "great social retrogression."[63] Nevertheless, by this time
rather short service terms were in fact becoming the norm, and so there
was no real revival of slave-like relations.

The reasons for this changing course of policy are not altogether clear.
The original imposition of a service term was no doubt intended to extend

the regime's power over the population, and was connected with the goal of eliminating the sale of human beings. Why was the term of three years chosen? Maki believes it was suggested by laws, observed from medieval times, pertaining to pawned goods such as swords or tools: these articles, once pawned, could not be sold for three years.[64] Thus laws pertaining to property may have been used as models for laws that ultimately encouraged the transition from unfree or semi-free labor to modern wage-labor. What is being sold in the service relationship is not a human being as a chattel, but labor power for a fixed period of time.

The substitution of a ten-year limit for the earlier term may also reveal the influence of medieval practices: runaway slaves retained for ten years by a new master could not be forced back into the former master's household.[65] However, the ten-year term no doubt suggested itself as a round figure, and it suited the needs of employers such as merchants and artisans whose servants had to undergo a long apprenticeship. For them, the earlier tenure limit had proved impractical.

The suspension of the ten-year limit came after a year of heavy, nationwide flooding, which had ruined crops and with them, countless peasant families. Under the circumstances, the survival of many households depended upon their ability to place offspring into service. Both these households and prospective employers probably preferred to enjoy the option of drawing up contracts for long-term or lifetime service, and so the shogunate temporarily lifted the tenure limit. Within a few years, conditions had returned to normal, and the limit was reimposed; nevertheless, famine, flooding, and crop failures were recurring problems, and so the regime came to condone tenure extensions.[66]

While our understanding of the motives behind these regulations remains imperfect, we can at least see a clear pattern: the term grew longer. The most problematic of early Tokugawa laws concerning service terms, however, seems to have worked at cross-purposes with those I have already discussed. This is the ban on one-year terms (*ikkii kinshi*) first issued in Edo in 1609 and repeated every few years until 1661 (see Table 1.1). While the other laws fixed maximum terms for service, this ban forbade those of one year or less.[67]

Japanese scholars have devoted much attention to this anomaly, debating both the scope and the motives behind the one-year prohibition.[68] While it has been suggested that the law was applied throughout the domains directly controlled by the shogun, the most up-to-date research of Maki Hidemasa argues that it was enforced only in Edo. No comparable laws were issued in Kyoto or Osaka. Legal historians have also debated whether the ban applied to all servants, or only to samurai servants, but since such servants as *chūgen*, *komono*, and *wakatō* are specifically mentioned in the text of these regulations, and they at any rate constituted the

TABLE 1.1
Early Shogunate Laws Affecting Labor

	One-year Service Banned	Sale of Persons Banned	Tenure Limits
1609	x		
1610	x		
1612	x		
1613	x		
1616	x	x	3 years
1617		x	3 years
1618	x	x	3 years
1619	x	x	3 years
1619		x	("many years" service banned)
1625	x	x	10 years
1626			10 years
1627	x	x	10 years
1627	x		10 years
1633		x	10 years
1637		x	("many years" service banned)
1638		x	10 years
1642		x	
1655	x	x	10 years
1658		x	10 years
1661	x	x	10 years
1663		x	10 years
1666		x	10 years
1674		x	10 years
1675			("many years" service permitted if "mutual consent")
1682		x	10 years
1698		x	limit lifted
1699		x	limit lifted
1711		x	("mutual consent")
1711		x	10 years
1716		x	("many years" service banned)
1716		x	("eternal" terms banned)

Source: Maki Hidemasa, Koyō no rekishi (Tokyo, 1977), 65–67.

overwhelming majority of Edo servants during the first half of the seventeenth century, I believe it is safe to follow Maki's interpretation. The law
was aimed at samurai manservants.[69]

Three reasons for the ban have been suggested. Minami Kazuo, among
others, has seen it as an effort to stabilize the employment system at a
time when traditional fudai relations were crumbling.[70] No doubt some
members of the ruling class were uneasy about the situation, and regretted the decline of the traditional master-servant relationship characterized by mutual loyalty and long-term commitment. However, the text
most commonly invoked in support of this thesis, Ogyū Sorai's *Seidan*
(*Discourse on Government*), was written a century after the first one-year
term ban, after fudai had all but disappeared in Edo; the work (quoted
below) is a critique of conditions circa 1730, and should not be taken as
a reflection of ruling-class views one hundred years earlier. Moreover, the
imposition of maximum service terms (applicable to samurai and commoner households alike) issued soon after the first one-year term ban
seem designed to eradicate the fudai system.

Two additional reasons for the ban on one-year terms seem more significant than the object of fostering more enduring master-servant ties.
One was of a military nature: in the event of war, samurai servants would
be expected to serve as auxiliaries. The regime thus understandably
sought to regulate their movements and ensure that the necessary numbers were available for duty on short notice.[71]

The other reason has been offered by Tokoro Rikio. The ban, he notes,
was issued during a period when peasants were flooding into Edo as beggars or in search of unskilled work. Many entered samurai mansions as
domestics and attendants. The prohibition therefore probably indicates a
broad concern with managing unruly migrants. If they were forced to
remain with a given household over one year's time, they would be easier
to register and control.[72] This explanation seems particularly persuasive
when one reads contemporary Edo laws dealing with the registration and
lodging of servants and laborers, which show an acute concern with mon-
itoring the movements of the city's newcomers.[73]

For most of the period between 1616 and 1661, then, at least samurai
servants, and perhaps other Edo servants as well, were by law supposed
to work on contracts for no more than three years but more than one
year. Even so, there are edicts that indicate the regime permitted exceptions to the one-year ban during this period. A 1625 regulation dealing
with a visit of the shogun to the Nikkō mausolea ordered that "one-year
servants must serve under last year's guarantors (*ukenin*),"[74] and another,
dated 1636, states that "one-year servants for this year must be summoned in the standard manner" to accompany Iemitsu's procession from

Edo.[75] A half-dozen similar edicts are included in the Kanpō-era (1741–44) edition of the *Ofuregaki*.[76]

Another group of laws that would have worked against the ban on one-year service were those that established *dekawaribi* (roughly translated, "servant replacement days"). So far as we know, the first of these was fixed in Kyoto in 1610. The second day of the second lunar month was chosen as the date for servants to be hired or dismissed. Repeated in 1615, the replacement day was introduced to Edo three years later. While the date was changed several times (to the fifteenth day of the second month in 1653, then the twentieth day of the second month in 1659), from 1668 it was fixed as the fifth day of the third month. In 1672 not only the cities in the shogun's domain, but all villages as well, were ordered to observe this servant replacement date.[77]

Although it is not mentioned in the edicts, from at least the Genroku period (1680–1704) there existed in practice a second servant replacement date as well. On the fifth day of the ninth month, servants hired on six-month terms (*hanki* or "half-season" terms) could be hired or dismissed. The popular writer Ihara Saikaku refers to this shorter term in describing the employment term system as it functioned in the 1680s. Stressing the convenience of the system for both parties, he wonders

> What genius, way back when, decided on the "half-term" system? If the master is dissatisfied, he reflects that the term is only half a year, so he is able to tolerate the situation. The mistress slyly keeps the girl on, in all fairness, until the next employment term comes around, then sends her on her way.[78]

"And if a servant," for her part, "has wound up with a heartless master," she may think, 'Well, it's only half a year,' and get through the days." The replacement date seems to have been maintained throughout the period; in Kawatake Mokuami's kabuki play *Seishin Izayoi*, written during the last years of Tokugawa rule (1859), a mistress tells her husband, "Hakuren, our maid is most impertinent. Let us dismiss her in the third month."[79]

Maki believes that while during most of the seventeenth century a general ban on one-year service terms was in force in the city of Edo, the ban was waived in certain circumstances. In such cases, the replacement date insured that most servants would be hired or dismissed at the same time. Compiling its population registers shortly after this date, the regime could maintain an accurate record of servants' whereabouts.[80]

Probably the principal intent of the replacement day was to encourage service tenures of reasonable duration, and to guard against the further expansion of the vagrant population by unemployed servants. This at least seems to have been the motive behind similar laws in sixteenth-century German cities. In Munich and Strasbourg servants were permit-

ted to change jobs on only two days, six months apart, while in Nuremberg there was only one such hiring day per year.[81] In rural England, from
the seventeenth to nineteenth centuries, a contractual year beginning on
Michaelmas (September 29) or Martinmas (November 11) was common,
and while not fixed by law, it was observed by over ninety percent of
employers, at least in husbandry. Kussmaul explains that this service term
was useful in that "it differentiated job-seeking servants, legitimately
abroad in the country at year's end, from vagrants." Here too we see a
concern with managing the problem of vagrancy and begging.[82]

But if the replacement date was of use to the regime, it might also have
been useful for the principals involved, as Saikaku's story suggests. It allowed a dissatisfied servant to painlessly escape an unpleasant situation,
or a peeved employer to terminate a servant with few hard feelings, and
did not preclude the possibility of a servant leaving during the one year or
six month period originally contracted. As I discuss in Chapter 3, a servant could leave on plea of illness (real or feigned) or family problems,
among other possibilities. Or she might be dismissed for a breach of contract or serious misbehavior (becoming pregnant, for example). But most
servant flaws—a somewhat short temper, an abrasive personality, clumsiness with the sewing, lack of culinary gifts, general ignorance—would
not alone constitute grounds for dismissal. Observing such defects, an
employer would simply make a mental note to "dismiss in the third or
ninth calendar month."

By the end of the seventeenth century, the shogunate, having experimented with minimum and maximum terms, in effect abandoned all such
attempts. Ten-year terms could now be extended indefinitely, but on the
other hand, six-month terms were also permitted and even shorter tenures were very common. Nevertheless, at least in the Edo and larger cities,
these efforts of the shogunate to regulate service terms had enduring effects. The ten-year term became the norm for apprentices in commercial
and artisanal households, but most domestic servants were contracted to
work for one-year terms.[83]

The most significant result of seventeenth-century legislation was the
decline of fudai or lifetime service. Unfortunately, the lack of population
data does not allow us to chart the decline of such service in the cities the
way T. C. Smith has traced it in the villages.[84] Fragmentary documentary
evidence, however, generally suggests that by the early eighteenth century
it had nearly vanished in Edo and was fading out elsewhere as well.

"In recent years, . . . short-term servants (dekawari hōkōnin) have become numerous," Ogyū observed in his Seidan, "and fudai have disappeared from samurai households. Few even remain in peasant households
in the countryside."[85] His leading pupil, Dazai Shundai (1680–1747),
also described the disappearance of fudai as a recent trend, deploring the

dekawari system for its novelty as well as its alleged impersonal character. As a Confucian savant, he characteristically notes that the new system has no continental analogue or precedent:

> In China there is no class similar to that of the house servants of these times, who are called *dekawari* servants. . . . The present dekawari servants are men who may be said to be employed by the year. That is, they change their masters each year, and therefore their employers do not show them much kindness, and the employees show very little fidelity to the masters. Especially is this so in Edo, where a great many runaways and worthless fellows congregate and become dekawari servants and thus pass through life, and where there are a great many who run away.[86]

"If possible," he appeals, "let this state of affairs be changed, and as in ancient times, let the servants be employed for a long time!"

Lifetime service probably survived the longest in samurai households, where it was most clearly articulated as an ideal. Yamamoto Tsunetomo's *Hagakure* (*Hidden by Leaves*), a collection of samurai philosophical homespun written in Hizen around 1700, routinely refers to samurai manservants as hikan.[87] Some urban census registers continue to record commoner household servants as fudai even late in the period; in Fuchū (Echizen) in 1815, the only two servants in a recorded population of about 2,000 were listed as *fudaimono*.[88] The census registers of Ichi no chō and Ni no chō, two wards in the alpine castle-town of Takayama, also typically list servants as genan fudai or gejo fudai throughout the period from 1779 to 1864.[89] In Nagasaki's Okeyamachi ("Barrel-makers' Ward"), very few servants are recorded as genin or gejo but many are given as *kanai* (lit., "in the house"). In modern Japanese, this term means "wife," but in these registers it cannot have that meaning and probably serves as a synonym for fudai.[90]

It is possible, however, that such terms as hikan, fudai and kanai may have lost their original meaning and have gradually been applied even to short-term servants. Early seventeenth-century registers for Hiradomachi, another Nagasaki ward, do not refer to kanai or fudai but list servants as genin and gejo. Since Hiradomachi and Okeyamachi were both mixed artisanal-merchant wards, their conditions probably would have been quite similar.[91]

Clearly the trend was away from lifetime service, even in tradition-bound Kyushu. The *Shūmon tefuda aratame jōmoku* (*Regulations for the Investigation of Religious Sects and Investigation Tags*) which served as a fundamental legal document of the Satsuma barony, specifies that servants of samurai, shrines and temples were to be recorded simply as "servants" (genin) on the identification tags they were obliged to bear. Such terms as hikan, *kerai* (retainer), and *uchi* ("household," i.e., "household

TABLE 1.2
Types of Servants in Kasama, 1705

	Total		Manservants		Maidservants	
	no.	%	no.	%	no.	%
fudai (lifetime)	12	4.3	5	2.9	7	6.5
nenki (long-term)	156	56.3	85	50.0	71	66.4
ikki (one-year)	84	30.3	56	32.9	28	26.2
other	25	9.0	24	14.1	1	0.9
totals	277		170	61.4	107	38.6

Source: Calculated from Hōei ni-nen Kasamamachi machikata kenbetsu aratamechō, in Hayashi Reiko et al., Ibaraki ken shiryō, Kinsei shakai keizai hen, I (Tokyo, 1971), 133–173.

servant"), all of which suggest lifetime master-servant ties, were to be avoided. (The surviving text of this document dates from 1852, but these clauses may have been entered as early as the seventeenth century.)[92]

EMPLOYMENT TERMS IN A KANTŌ CASTLE-TOWN: KASAMA

While no data series survive to illustrate the decline in lifetime service over the following century, figures from Kasama, the castle-town of a rich barony in Hitachi province, provide at least a frozen picture of employment types in an urban center in 1705. The Machikata kenbetsu aratame-chō (Townspeople's House-frontage Registry) for Hōei 2 (1705) records a commoner population of some 1,800 and describes the servant population in great detail, not only providing ages but also carefully specifying servants as lifetime, long-term (nenki), or year-contract (ikkii) employees. Only about 4 percent of the 277 servants were listed as fudai (see Table 1.2).[93]

Of these fudai, three of the men, and two of the women, were over sixty (the eldest being an eighty-five-year-old Haru employed by a carpenter's family).[94] They probably had been with their present employers for most of their lives, entering service before the process described by Ogyū had progressed very far. Two of the fudai men, however, were in their mid-twenties, and one female fudai was only four years old! (She may have been the daughter of the other fudai in the household, twenty-nine-year-old Satsu.)[95] A relatively small number of people were thus still entering, or being placed, in lifetime service.

There does not seem to be any clear relationship between lifetime employment and employers' specific professions. In Kasama, cultivators (chisaku) formed the largest occupational group, with 114 out of 483 households. They also constituted the largest employer group. Only four of their fifty-two employees were recorded as lifetime servants. The nineteen rice-wine dealing households employed nine servants in all, but only one fudai. The few others served merchants of various types, or in one case, a professional dancer (see Table 1.3).

TABLE 1.3
Kasama Servants, by Employer Type

	House-holds	Total Servants	One Year	Long-Term	Fudai	Other
rice-wine shops	7	74	1	53	6	
cultivators	113	53	19	41	2	3
dyers	7	13	6	5	2	
blacksmiths	7	13	1	3	9	
village headmen	3	13	1	11		
grain dealers	13	12	9	3		
rice-wine dealers	20	9	3	4	1	1
oil shops	4	8	5	3		
fish shops	15	6	2	4		
Shingon clergy	5	5	3			2
ginned cotton dealers	3	5	1	3	3	
carpenters	11	5	1		1	3
brewers	4	5	5			
cotton dealer	1	4	1	1	2	
kitchenware shops	4	3	2	1		
wholesalers	2	3	1	2		
village group-chiefs	2	3	1	3		
confectioners	5	2	1	1		
tailors	5	2	2			
doctors	2	2	1	1		
kitchenware dealers	1	2		2		
pan shop	1	2	2			
Mountain Aide	1	2				
bean-curd shops	8	1	1			
tobacco shops	5	1	1			
salt dealers	4	1	2			
bucket shops	3	1			1	
salt shops	2	1	1			
sundries dealers	2	1				
musical instruments shop	1	1		1		
Mounted Officer	1	1			1	
paper shops		5	2	3		
dancer		1		1		
sundry shops	5	7	3	4		
unrecorded or unclear	33	13	5	7	2	

Source: See Table 1.2.

The Kasama data suggest a decline in lifetime service, but also show that long-term service (for contract periods of up to ten years) was more common than one-year-term service. Half the manservants, and two-thirds of the maidservants, were recorded as long-term servants. Those I have listed as "other" were mostly apprentices (including one female totei employed by a cotton dealer); these, too, would probably have served on long-term contracts.

Even so, the fact that one-third of all the manservants, and over a quarter of all maidservants, were employed on yearly contracts may indicate that a transition to shorter tenures was underway. Construction and transport tasks were performed by men hired on a daily basis; day laborers (hiyōtori) constituted 33 of the 483 total households of the town and formed the second largest occupational group after cultivators. With seven dyer households, Kasama boasted a modest dyeing industry based largely upon workers serving on one-year contracts. But it was a town of casual laborers and service professions, rather than a manufacturing center.

The Formation of an Urban Proletariat

The policies described established the *legal* basis for the appearance of a new social class: an urban proletariat. The latter (to paraphrase Marx) is a class free in a dual sense: free from the land, unencumbered by property, and free to dispose of its labor power.[96] But such legal changes as the ban on trade in human beings and limits of service terms alone could not ensure that this new laboring class would assume significant proportions. Had changes in the life of the villages not produced townbound migrants in the tens of thousands, this proletariat might not have outlived the urban construction boom that tapered off soon after 1700.

As noted previously, T. C. Smith has described the process of class differentiation within the peasantry, attributing it to the expansion of commerce and the "slow growth of capitalism" over the course of the period.[97] While acknowledging the stimulus provided by urban markets early in the Tokugawa period, he stresses the "rural-centered" nature of subsequent economic growth.[98] Gilbert Rozman, in contrast, has depicted Edo as an engine for this growth throughout the period.[99] Clearly there was a dialectic at work between the rural changes provoked by urban growth, and urban changes fostered by the arrival of rural migrants. Scholars have, however, too often viewed the emergence of new class relations in the villages in isolation; Smith, for example, does not mention that several of the major changes he describes were in fact anticipated by urban developments. Lifetime servants, for example, had become uncommon in major cities by the late seventeenth century, largely as a result of the shogunate policies. Most of the evidence for the decline of lifetime service in agricultural villages, however, is derived from the eighteenth- or early nineteenth-century documents.[100] The ten-year service limit, the one-year employment term, the very habit of referring to servants as hōkōnin—all seem to have spread from samurai and urban merchant or artisan households to the society of the villages.

Meanwhile peasants, primarily the propertyless poor, flocked to the urban centers; Rozman suggests that the net immigration into the city of Edo alone averaged ten thousand per year during the period.[101] "Edo," complained Ogyū Sorai, referring to the most impoverished of these newcomers, "is the dumping-ground of the domains."[102] A large class of urban poor—thieves, beggars, peddlers, vagrants, itinerant entertainers—is of course not uncommon in history. It is far less common, however, in preindustrial societies, for labor power to become "commodified,"[103] for a free labor market to emerge, for proletarians to become transformed into *wage laborers*. Such transformations represent fundamental changes in class relations, indeed the emergence of capitalism. The Japanese case is perhaps unique in that the feudal ruling class, in resolving its internal conflicts, played so great a role in generating revolutionary change.

Chapter Two

MASTER AND SERVANT POPULATIONS

IN TOKUGAWA Japan as in preindustrial Europe, servants (*hōkōnin*) of various types formed a vast social stratum.[1] Many historians have discussed their roles in village communities of the period,[2] but they were also a major presence in the urban societies which have been less well-studied, at least by Western scholars.[3] In Edo, up to 10 percent of the total urban population were servants of the samurai throughout the period.[4] Prior to the Tenpō Reforms of the early 1840s, which forced many migrant laborers out of the city, about 6 percent of the recorded urban population were transients employed as domestics on short-term contracts during the agricultural off-season.[5] Even on the eve of the Meiji Restoration (1868), an affluent commercial ward such as Hongokuchō Ni-chōme might register 35 percent of its residents as servants.[6]

In Osaka, Japan's commercial capital, the servant contingent was probably larger and undoubtedly grew over time, as indicated by Inui Hiromi's studies of extant census registers (*ninbetsuchō*). In Dōshōmachi San-chōme, a prosperous medicine-peddling ward near the castle, those listed as *genin* or *gejo* rose from 23 percent to 37 percent of the ward total between 1700 and 1800. During the same century, in Kikuyachō, a modestly affluent commercial ward bordering the theater and pleasure district of Dōtonbōri to the south, the figure rose from 18 percent to 24 percent. In Miikedōri Go-chōme, meanwhile, servants grew from 13 percent to 23 percent of the ward population between 1700 and 1813.[7] As Table 2.1 shows, the servant figures remain high throughout Osaka to the end of the period.

Scattered Kyoto census data suggest that in most wards the servant

TABLE 2.1
Servants as a Percentage of Osaka Ward Populations, 1860

Dōshōmachi 3 chōme	47%
Hiranomachi 2 chōme	42
Kikuyachō	35
Kobikimachi Minami no chō	29
Miikedōri 5 chōme	16
Sadoyachō	15

Sources: Inui Hiromi, "Osaka chōnin shakai no kōzō," in Tsuda Hideo, ed., *Kinsei kokka no hatten* (1980), and *Minami-gumi Sadoyachō shakuyaninbetsuchō*.

TABLE 2.2
Servants as a Percentage of Kyoto Ward Populations, Late Tokugawa Period

	Year	%
Koromonotana Kitachō	1837	59.8
Koromonotana Minamichō	1837	31.3
Tochinukichō	1837	28.1
Taishiyamachō	1841	16.9
Shijō Tateuri Nakanomachi	1863	18.9
Gojōbashi Higashi Ni-chōme Higashibori	1863	33.1
Hanagurumachō	1867	10.0
Hakuratenchō	1868	21.6
Kameyamachi	1868	17.1

Sources: Akiyama Kunizō and Nakamura Ken, Kyotō 'chō' no kenkyu (1972); Saitō Osamu, "Shōka hōkōnin to zatsugyōsha: kinsei toshi rōdōshijo ni okeru nijūkōzō no keisei," in Keizai kenkyū, 3 (1985); Taishiyamachō shūmon ninbetsu aratamechō; Hanagurumachō shūmon ninbetsu aratamechō.

population seldom dipped below 10 percent of the total, often reaching 20 or 30 percent, and in some areas reaching over half the total (Table 2.2). In the upper-class commercial ward of Koromonotana Kitachō, the figure was generally around 60 percent between 1787 and 1837.[8]

Small towns might also boast large servant populations. In 1680, 16 percent of the registered total in Hachiman-machi, a temple-centered community of seven thousand near Lake Biwa, were servants. In 1724, the figure was 13 percent.[9] In the renowned textile manufacturing center of Kiryū, in Kōzuke province, 22 percent of the registered residents were servants in 1757, and 19 percent in 1819.[10] Castle-towns large and small, meanwhile, supported legions of samurai household servants. Huddled around the elegant castle in alpine Matsumoto, the servants of upper and middle-ranking samurai numbered 1,254 (15 percent) out of a total of 8,206 residents in 1725. This gives us a very conservative estimate of the number of samurai household servants, since many of those recorded as lower-ranking samurai would have also functioned as domestics and personal attendants.[11] The two groups together represented 44 percent of the castle-town's population (Table 2.3).

Samurai servants were particularly numerous in the wards immediately surrounding the fortress of a castle-town. Tanaka Yoshio's figures for Kanazawa are illustrative. In the thirty-five wards encircling Kanazawa's stronghold, those recorded as footsoldiers, valets (chūgen), or pages (komono) constituted, on average, 37 percent of the inhabitants. In twenty of these wards, these groups comprised over 30 percent of the total, and in one (Iwanechō), they made up the entire population. If we

TABLE 2.3
Population of Matsumoto, Kyōhō 10 (1725)

Household Type	Family Members	Servants	Total Household Members
commoners			2015
samurai			
upper ranks[a]	1118	1111	2229
middle ranks[b]	1376	143	1519
lower ranks[c]		2324	2324
retirees and those on public support			119

Source: Harada Tomohiko, *Harada Tomohiko ronshū, dai-ni kan: toshi keitaishi kenkyū* (1985), 229.

[a] *karō* (intendant) to *chūkoshō* (middle page) ranks

[b] *jushi* (attendant) to *koyakunin* (minor official) rank

[c] *fudai ashigaru* (hereditarily retained footsoldier) to *kobito* (page) rank. This group, while listed in the servants' column, may have included other types as well.

add temporary migrant laborers (*dekaseginin*) to these groups, we find that in these thirty-five wards menials, domestics, and footsoldiers add up on average to 61 percent of the residents.[12]

Servants seem to have constituted at least as large a proportion of urban populations in Japan as in early modern Europe. Domestic servants alone, according to Cipolla, made up about 10 percent of the entire European population during the fifteenth to seventeenth centuries.[13] From 9 to 12 percent of eighteenth-century French urban populations were servants,[14] while in London perhaps 20 percent were servants in 1695.[15] These multitudes were employed, not by a wealthy elite, but by a large proportion of urban households. From the early sixteenth- to mid-nineteenth centuries, about one-third of all English households supported in-servants; the figure was probably higher among urbanites.[16] One-quarter of craftsmen and tradesmen's households alone maintained live-in servants and apprentices.[17] A Florence census for 1551 shows that 46 percent of all households employed at least one servant; in Nuremberg some decades earlier the figure was more than one-third.[18]

The size of service staffs varied greatly between social classes. Of the Florentine households supporting servants, half employed only one, while 11 percent maintained staffs of six or more servants. In eighteenth-century England, the lesser gentry were apt to hire from five to ten servants,[19] but the wealthier would typically content themselves with thirty or more. Staffs of one hundred were not uncommon.[20]

In Japan, employers of servants also constituted a large proportion of

TABLE 2.4
Required Numbers of Valets and Coolies to Be Retained by Daimyo, 1712

Kokudaka	Valets (chūgen) and Coolies (ninsoku)
10,000 –	30
50,000 –	100
100,000 –	150
200,000 –	250 – 300

Source: Shihōshō, eds., Tokugawa kinreikō, vol. 4 (1932), 528–29.

all households, in cities and towns as well as the villages. In the castle-towns, where samurai generally accounted for about half the population, *buke yashiki* (samurai mansions) provided many service positions. The several residences each daimyo was obliged to maintain in Edo were staffed by hundreds of domestics and attendants, many of whom were at least nominally part of the domain's military apparatus. The daimyo of Mōri han (Chōshū), for example, employed 820 valets (*chūgen*) in the 1740s.[21] In 1712 the shogun ordered each daimyo to retain a minimum number of valets and coolies (*ninsoku*), depending on the annual productivity of their various domains (Table 2.4). Like the *sankin-kōtai* system itself, this order was designed to impose a financial burden on these lords.[22]

Meanwhile, the highest of the shogun's direct retainers, the *hatamoto* or bannermen, were ordered to maintain a fixed complement of retainers, ostensibly for reasons of military preparedness, but in fact to ensure that they, too, assumed a debilitating financial burden. Well over 60 percent of these retainers seem, in fact, to have had no military functions but served as mere domestics.[23]

If the regime hoped to encourage the employment of huge numbers of servants, the better to control the samurai, members of the warrior class themselves needed little prodding to employ at least a few attendants. Like their ruling-class counterparts in the West, they retained servants in order to conspicuously assert their status.[24] Samurai of even the humblest rank would suffer indignity if they were forced to venture into society unaccompanied by a servant (*muboku*).[25] When an unescorted samurai appears in a kabuki drama, for example, he is nearly always either ruined, on a clandestine mission, or deliberately concealing his identity while disporting himself in the licensed quarters.[26] Even low-ranking samurai could afford to employ a page to carry spare sandals and an umbrella, at least at the beginning of the period.

Meanwhile, a bannerman with a rice stipend of one thousand *koku* (one *koku* equals 4.96 bushels) could support six or more pages.[27] Iwase

Yoshizaemon, a 1700-*kokudaka* bannerman whose accounts have survived, employed a staff of nineteen, including a steward, two "samurai," four valets, one page, seven chambermaids and wetnurses in 1773. His descendent's household seventy years later still maintained this number of servants.[28] But samurai households made do with far more modest staffs. The Matsumoto data (Table 2.3) show that among the highest-ranking samurai in the castle-town, the numbers of servants almost perfectly matched masters plus their family members. Among households in the second stratum, there was only one servant per 2.75 family members.

There is considerable literary evidence that, as samurai became relatively impoverished over the course of the period, they were forced to prune their service staffs. Even during the late seventeenth century, a rear vassal (*gokenin*) of the shogun, with a cash income of twelve ryō, would have had to choose between employing a servant and taking a wife; unless the spouse brought a substantial dowry with her, he could not have afforded both.[29] From the beginning of the eighteenth century, servantless rear vassals became especially numerous.[30] The Chōshū scholar Murata Seifu wrote in the 1770s that for samurai receiving stipends of less than one hundred *koku* of rice, servants were "out of the question."[31]

Nevertheless, honor required, and the law stipulated, that samurai above a certain rank were to employ attendants. When summoned to official functions or fulfilling such ceremonial obligations as New Year's greetings, a footboy or valet was as indispensable a part of the samurai's gear as his short and long swords. Eventually poorer samurai came to rely upon hired part-timers to perform the servant role. The sudden appearance of numerous samurai attendants around New Year's was lampooned in such satirical verses as the following:

> Dekiai no bushi urikireru matsu no uchi
> Hiyatoi no tomo neagari no matsu no uchi
>
> New Year's, when ready-made samurai are sold out
> New Year's, when the price of day-laborer attendants goes up

Or:

> Hera hera bushi o meshitsurete gyokei nari
> Matsu no uchi fudai onko no tsukiya nari
>
> He who slovenly attends the samurai to his New Year's greetings
> Is the favored rice-husker who has served for years[32]

Both verses refer to impoverished samurai temporarily hiring humble laborers to serve as their lackeys, outfitting them with rented costumes for the occasion.

TABLE 2.5
Employers of Servants as a Percentage of All Households in Osaka Wards

Kikuyachō		Dōshōmachi San-chōme		Hiranomachi Ni-chōme		Kobikimachi Minami no chō		Miikedōri Go-chōme	
Year	%	Year	%	Year	%	Year	%	Year	%
1639	22	1659	31						
1659	23	1684	33						
1682	40	1700	29						
1715	34	1710	41						
1730	30	1729	43						
1751	35	1752	61						
1766	35								
1781	31	1780	74	1779	71	1780	38		
1800	50	1800	67	1800	72	1800	36	1806	39
1819	52	1819	84	1820	68	1820	51	1831	59
1841	67	1841	78	1840	76	1840	55	1861	50
1860	60	1860	83	1860	68	1860	45	1868	30

Source: Inui Hiromi, "Ōsaka chōnin shakai no kōzō."

Commoners, meanwhile, boasted their own share of servants and of employing households. Table 2.5 shows ninbetsuchō data from selected commoner wards in Osaka. In the two best series, which provide data from the mid-seventeenth century, the rise in the percentage of employers is quite remarkable. In Kikuyachō, only 5 of 23 households (22 percent) employed servants in 1639, but the figure rises to 50 out of 82 (61 percent) by the end of the period. In wealthier Dōshōmachi San-chōme, employers increase from 73 out of 232 (31 percent) in 1659 to 75 out of 90 (83 percent) in 1860.

Unfortunately no other data series for Osaka are available for the early period, but we know that in Hiranomachi Ni-chōme the percentage of employing households hovered around 70 percent over the last century of the period, while varying from 35 to 55 percent in both Kobikimachi Minami no chō and Miikedōri Go-chōme between 1780 and 1860 and 1800 and 1860 respectively. These latter three wards show no clear trend concerning the growth or decline of servant employment, but the Kikuyachō and Dōshōmachi registers suggest that over the whole period the practice of employing servants spread in Osaka.[33]

In Kyoto, the evidence is more sketchy but similarly varied (Table 2.6). Since few good data-series survive, it is impossible to know whether or not these figures represent a growth in servant employment in the imperial capital. Hayami Akira has studied the ninbetsuchō for Shijō Tateuri Nakanomachi, a mixed ward of merchants, craftsmen, physicians, and scholars off Shijōdōri, one of the main avenues of the metropolis. Despite

TABLE 2.6

Employers of Servants as a Percentage of All Households in Kyoto Wards,
Late Tokugawa Period

	Year	Employers of Servants (%)
Koromonotana Kitachō	1837	71
Koromonotana Minamichō	1837	47
Tochinukichō	1837	50
Taishiyamachō	1841	27
Shijō Tateuri Nakanomachi	1863	33
Gojōbashi Higashi		
Ni-chōme Higashibori	1863	58
Hakuratenchō	1868	36
Kameyamachi	1868	21
Hanagurumachō	1867	19

Source: See Table 2.2.

large gaps, these registers more or less span the period. They show that while 32 of 43 households (74 percent) employed servants in 1697, the figure stabilized at between 60 percent and 70 percent through the first half of the eighteenth century. When the sequence resumes, in the early nineteenth century, only 27 of 64 households (42 percent) have servants, and by the closing years of the period, a mere one-third are employers (Table 2.7).[34]

Akiyama Kunizō's research on Koromonotana show contrasting patterns in the two merchant wards, North and South, bearing this name. They occupied adjacent one-way streets in the northern part of the capital. Fourteen and twenty-one households inhabited Koromonotana Kitachō and Koromonotana Minamichō respectively in 1787; of these, 9

TABLE 2.7

Employers of Servants as a Percentage of Households in Shijō Tateuri
Nakanomachi, Kyoto

Year	%	Year	%
1697	74	1739	63
1702	67	1743	67
1703	57	1747	72
1710	65	1808	42
1711	68	1849	38
1715	64	1861	33
1737	69	1863	33

Source: Hayami Akira, "Kyōto machikata no shūmon aratamechō: Shijō Tateuri Nakanomachi."

TABLE 2.8
Employers as a Percentage of All Urban Households in Two Kyoto Wards,
Late Tokugawa Period

Hanagurumachō		Taishiyamachō	
1813	—	1813	26%
1819	13%	1823	16
1829	15	1833	21
1839	22	1841	27
1848	13		
1858	24		
1867	19		

Sources: Taishiyamachō shūmon ninbetsu aratamechō; Hanagurumachō shūmon ninbetsu aratamechō (Kyōto Shiryō Kaikan).

(64 percent) and 15 (71 percent) had servants listed in the registers. Fifty years later, while the former ward's employer population had increased to 71 percent, the latter's had declined to 47 percent. It is a tiny sample, and only the data from these two years have been analyzed, but at least this example cautions us against assuming universal growth in the habit of employing servants.[35]

Data for Hanagurumachō and Taishiyamachō (Table 2.8) reveal no clear trend over the limited span of time covered by the registers. These, too, were commercial wards in the north part of the city, each with a population from two hundred to three hundred people constituting from fifty to eighty households. In both cases, the figure for employers fluctuates between about 15 and 25 percent.[36]

Data for Edo is unfortunately even more scarce. Virtually nothing survives prior to the last years of the shogunate, and the figures available show another wide differential. In Yotsuya Denmachō Shin-itchōme and Kōjimachi Jūni-chōme, employers of servants accounted for 5.2 and 2.8 percent of all ward households respectively, while in Kanda Matsudachō they made up 6.0 percent two years after the Restoration. In Nihonbashi Hongokuchō Ni-chōme, on the other hand, 41.7 percent of all households had servants in 1869. Nihonbashi, of course, was the center of wholesale merchandising in Edo.[37]

Saitō Osamu has ventured the intriguing thesis that Osaka and Edo represent two opposed types of cities in Tokugawa Japan. In his view, a system of long-term employment (labor "internalized" in a business operation) developed in such prosperous commercial centers as Osaka, whereas centers of consumption promoted the "casualization" of employment. Cities in the former category boasted many firms that nurtured employees through a long apprenticeship, while those of the latter type

TABLE 2.9
Employers of Servants as a Percentage of All Households in Osaka Wards, According to Class

Kikuyachō			Dōshōmachi San-chōme			Hiranomachi Ni-chōme			Kobikimachi Minami no chō			Miikedōri Go-chōme			Sadoyachō (all tenants)	
Year	H	T	Year	H	T	Year	H	T	Year	H	T	Year	H	T	Year	All
1639	22%	8%	1639			1779	92%	66%	1780	83%	30%	1806	90%	37%	1832	51%
1659	33	19	1659	70%	26%	1800	100	66	1800	75	28	1831	100	57	1842	59
1682	57	35	1684	70	28	1820	100	62	1820	85	46	1861	100	46		
			1700	72	24	1840	100	72	1840	79	49	1868	93	24		
1713	43	33	1710	53	38	1860	85	65	1860	92	37					
1730	75	24	1729	79	36											
1751	86	27	1752	86	55											
1766	90	26														
1781	88	23	1780	94	70											
1800	87	46	1800	89	64											
1819	67	49	1819	94	82											
1841	80	65	1841	91	75											
1860	83	53	1860	100	80											

Sources: See Table 2.1.
Note: H = householders; T = tenants.

employed legions of caterers, construction workers, day laborers, and servants on such short tenures as to escape registration.[38]

The data for Edo (at least, for wards other than Nihonbashi Hongoku-chō Ni-chōme), indicate to Saitō that the shogunal capital was a city of the second type. He suggests—on the basis of admittedly sketchy information, principally ninbetsuchō, which exclude the samurai—that monthly or daily workers came to preponderate in the shogun's city.[39] He does not, however, discuss the employees of the half-million warriors in the shogun's city. Surely the mansions of the daimyo, hatamoto, and perhaps lower strata of samurai internalized many of their employees. When we read that the three Kaga han mansions in Edo employed a staff of one thousand servants,[40] or that the shogun's seraglio dismissed over 3,700 maidservants as an economizing measure in 1651,[41] we must recognize that a substantial portion of the unregistered population were employed as domestics and attendants by the samurai mansions.

If the spotty urban census data do not allow us to draw many firm conclusions concerning trends in servant employment in the great cities over the Tokugawa period, one point is clear: the householders (iemochi) and caretakers (yamori) who constituted the chōnin proper were always more apt to employ servants than were their tenants (shakuyanin, tanagari). The Osaka registers (Table 2.9) indicate that employers of servants in both groups increased through the period. By the mid-nineteenth century, however, from 80 to 100 percent of the chōnin population were likely to have servants, while only 50 to 80 percent of the tenant population could afford this luxury.

In Kyoto, too, the proportion of employers among chōnin was higher than among tenants (Table 2.10). The series for Hanagurumachō shows employer chōnin numbering from 25 to 75 percent depending on the year; tenant employers vary from 6 to 12 percent. In Taishiyama, from 36 to 60 percent of the chōnin had servants, while this was the case with only 10 to 20 percent of the tenants. In Shijō Tateuri Nakanomachi, where the proportion of employers of both classes fell through the period, 67 percent of all chōnin households, as opposed to 30 percent of tenant households, supported servants in 1863.

These commoner employers, like samurai employers, maintained staffs of radically varying size. Some had vast retinues of servants. Early in the era, Ōkubo Nagayasu, the son of a comic performer who became Ieyasu's advisor on agriculture and mining, traveled about with several hundred servants and concubines.[42] In the Tenpō period (1830–1844) the Edo townsman Sanemon, an associate of the reformer Mizuno Tadakuni, employed thirty maidservants, thirty-three manservants, and six concubines.[43] Large businesses might employ staffs numbering in the dozens:

TABLE 2.10

Employers of Servants as a Percentage of All Households in Kyoto Wards, According to Class

Hanagurumachō			Taishiyamachō			Shijō Tateuri Nakanomachi		
Year	House-holders	Tenants	Year	House-holders	Tenants	Year	House-holders	Tenants
						1697	100	68
						1743	100	61
						1808	50	42
			1813	36	20			
1819	25	8	1823	41	10			
1829	25	12	1833	44	15			
1839	62	12	1841	60	17			
1848	57							
1858	75	8				1863	56	30
1867	44	6						

Sources: See Tables 2.7 and 2.8.

in 1690 the Mitsui Echigoya shop in Edo employed forty-five clerks and twenty-three "children," and late in the period Edo's Matsuzakaya employed over one hundred workers in five different shops.[44]

Mixed or commercial wards might typically boast one or two establishments employing more than ten persons listed in the registers as maidservants or manservants. In 1697, Hachimonjiya Yozaemon, a householder in Shijō Tateuri Nakanomachi who headed a family of five, employed a staff of eighteen.[45] One Monya Jihei, of Hanagurumachō, listed twelve servants in the 1858 register.[46] In Hiranoyamachi Ni-chōme in 1800, six out of seventy-two employers had staffs of over ten servants.[47]

Usually the establishments supporting such large staffs were retail shops, manufactories, or tea-houses. Six of Yozaemon's manservants are further described as clerks. Jihei's dozen employees are all female; the name of the shop suggests they were textile workers of some sort. Literary evidence, however, attests to the fact that affluent urbanites might surround themselves with domestics. Saikaku gives the impression that a middle-class woman would have felt lost without the services of her little staff of chambermaid, parlormaid, and seamstress.[48]

The Kikuyachō ninbetsuchō data illustrate the changes that occurred in the scale of service staffs in a modestly affluent ward over the course of the period. In 1659, one Kagiya Chōemon employed three manservants and three maidservants. He was the largest employer of the forty-three

TABLE 2.11
Average Number of Servants per Employer Household in Three Wards

		Dōshōmachi		Shijō Tateuri	
Kikuyachō (Osaka)		San-chōme (Osaka)		Nakanomachi (Kyoto)	
1659	2.10	1659	2.86		
1713	1.98	1700	3.14	1697	2.84
1751	2.59	1752	3.75	1743	2.84
1800	2.04	1800	2.69	1808	1.74
1860	3.16	1860	3.47	1863	2.30

Sources: Inui (see Table 2.1); Hayami (see Table 2.7).

ward households.[49] Kawachiya Shingorō had a staff of six manservants and three maidservants in 1736, making him the largest employer out of 143 household heads.[50] Later in the century, staffs exceeding ten became fairly common among chōnin, but smaller staffs remained the norm.

Table 2.11 indicates that the average employer household in each of the three wards for which relatively extensive data survive maintained a staff of two to four live-in servants. However, further analysis of the data shows that one-servant households were always by far the most common. In 1697, for example, 50 percent of the employers in Kyoto's Shijō Tateuri Nakanomachi retained only one servant; in 1713, 57 percent of the masters in Osaka's Kikuyachō; and in 1700, 32 percent of the employers in Dōshōmachi San-chōme retained only one servant. In each case, two-servant households constituted the next largest category: 19 percent, 15 percent, and 26 percent respectively. The situation had changed little by the end of the period. In 1863, 48 percent of the Kyoto ward's masters employed one servant, while in 1860 28 percent of the employers in Kikuyachō and 41 percent of those in Dōshōmachi San-chōme did likewise. The next largest category continued to be two-servant households: 22 percent, 22 percent, and 17 percent respectively. Households employing more than ten were not rare, but rarely accounted for more than 5 or 6 percent of all employer households.[51]

The majority of tenant employer households, in particular, could normally afford only one or two servants. Such employers as Matsuya Kiemon, of Kikuyachō, and Yorozuya Shōbei, of Shijō Tateuri Nakanomachi, were exceptional individuals. In 1736, two manservants and four maidservants lodged with Kiemon, his wife, son, daughter and aunt in their rented lodgings.[52] Kiemon's contemporary, Shōbei, with his family of six employed four servants, including a clerk, in 1743.[53]

Thus, in the major cities, if not in every urban ward, masters and servants were an ubiquitous part of life. Before examining such structural aspects of the servant labor force, particularly about their ages and gender ratios, let us inquire what service meant, what servants did, and what they symbolized in a highly status-conscious society.

SERVANT TYPES AND FUNCTIONS

The Japanese terms *hōkō* and *hōkōnin*, like their English counterparts "service" and "servant," contain a degree of ambiguity.[54] Originally a hōkōnin was a feudal retainer who provided military services, and in some contexts the word continued to convey this sense well into the Tokugawa period.[55] More commonly, however, it suggested the range of occupations that "servant" implied in early modern Europe. In England, practically any working dependent—apprentice, gardener, personal attendant, wet-nurse, tutor, secretary, or chief clerk—was viewed as a servant.[56] So, too, in Japan hōkōnin included not only valets, chambermaids, nursemaids, and footboys but shop clerks, apprentices, some casual laborers, concubines, and even prostitutes.

Service, in theory, was based upon loyalty—loyalty to the master and to his household as a sacred entity. But hōkō had a far broader meaning as well. Samurai often interpreted their responsibilities towards their lord as part of a greater obligation to society. Thus the Ise Confucian scholar Saitō Setsudō (1797–1865) argued that a samurai had a moral duty to the ten or twenty farming households necessary for his maintenance to perform his duties well.[57] In merchant households, meanwhile, hōkō in theory involved not only service to one's master, but obedience to the law, and to the Tokugawa regime that had pacified the country; concern for the welfare of society; and the notion of *shokubun*—work as gratitude to society.[58]

In reality, service did not always live up to such ideals, but it did underpin the feudal social order even as its character came to reflect that order's decline. The master-servant relationship idealized in the hōkō concept was to be found, not only among samurai and tradesmen, but at every level of urban society. If Kyoto courtier households (*kuge*) typically employed stewards, valets and chambermaids, even the members of outcast communities established at the outskirts of a town might employ a servant or two.[59] Persons described as hōkōnin worked in temples, shrines, inns, and bath houses as well as in private homes and mansions. The two most important servant categories, however, are *buke hōkōnin* (lit., "military-household servants") and servants employed by those commoners, tenants and householders alike, who enjoyed higher status than the *eta*-type pariahs.

Let us begin with the samurai-household servants. Table 2.12 lists the

TABLE 2.12
Samurai Household Servant Types: Manservants

Manservants (genin, genan)	Alternate Terms	English Equivalent
wakatō	saburai, samurai	steward
	yonin	steward
	uchitonin	chamberlain
	sobayōnin	chamberlain
chūgen	arashiko	valet
	orisuke	footman
	kachi, aruki	lackey
komono	kachi, koshō, kobito kozamurai	page
zōritori	kozōritori	footboy
kagokaki	kumosuke	palanquin bearer
rokushaku		menial

types of samurai manservants roughly in order of rank. The second column gives alternative terms, while the third gives the English words I have chosen as rough equivalents. It is extremely difficult to define these people with any precision, for several reasons.

One is the problem of their status: were they themselves considered to be samurai? Samurai were members of the hereditary military class. They possessed the right to bear both short and long swords, which they were, in theory, entitled to employ in striking down any commoner for "insolence." They were allowed to adopt surnames, exempted from general registration, and regulated by a special body of law. Commoners might adjudicate minor matters in their villages or wards, but government was in general a samurai affair. While degrees of rank and income among them were as numerous as those among the French nobility, the samurai as a whole constituted the ruling class.

Most Japanese authorities agree that samurai-household servants held at least a quasi-samurai status.[60] They might, as noted, be drawn from the ranks of commoners, and since their duties might in many cases be virtually identical to those performed by commoners' servants, they must be distinguished from the pedigreed members of the military class. On the other hand, while in service they enjoyed privileges generally denied to commoners. They were (unfortunately for the historian) exempt from general census registration, although they might be listed in a separate record of military personnel. They were entitled to bear a short side-sword, and in some cases might adopt a surname. Most significantly, they were bound by samurai law while in service, although upon their departure they would derogate to commoner status and escape the often severer strictures of military household law.

It would be dangerous to conclude, however, that these servants always held a lower status than the samurai proper. A comparison of *wakatō* (stewards) and *ashigaru* (footsoldiers) illustrates the point. In theory, footsoldiers were the lowest-ranking samurai, while stewards were the highest-ranking samurai household servants. But the status of footsoldiers was also ambiguous. They often, for example, shared their quarters with domestic servants and were recorded along with the latter in domainal logs.[61]

Conversely, stewards in high-ranking households, although denied full recognition as samurai, might, like the chamberlains of European courts, be men of far more power and influence than ordinary footsoldiers. The ambiguity of this position is revealed by the fact that some scholars regard stewards and footsoldiers as of the same status, while others treat "steward" and "valet" (*chūgen*) as synonyms. Even the term *samurai* was sometimes used as a synonym for "steward" early in the Tokugawa period.[62]

If, at the upper levels of samurai household servants, the distinction between servants and samurai proper is unclear, at the bottom levels the distinction between quasi-samurai servants and civilian menials becomes problematic. Edicts (*ofure*) and other legal documents frequently group stewards, valets and pages together; these were viewed as part of a single category of samurai household servants.[63] Footboys, palanquin-bearers and menials, however, are less often listed with these other types, and some of them may not have received such perquisites as the right to bear arms.

A second problem is the existence of two types of "samurai-household servants." One type was in fact not employed by individual households but by the shogunate or by the various domains (*han*). The shogunate, for example, maintained between 540 and 560 valets who served under three headmen (*chūgen-gashira*) and accompanied the urban police on their rounds in Edo.[64] Every domain, on its roster of samurai, included personnel with such titles as "valet" or "page" who were actually fully recognized as samurai officials, and provided, like other feudal retainers, with rice stipends.[65]

The other type of samurai servant was employed by an individual samurai to perform miscellaneous domestic services and to attend him in public. These must have been far more numerous than the sort recorded in the account books of samurai personnel. Ordinarily they were employed on short terms and paid in money wages. They were thus quite different from

those who worked as officials and bureaucrats, but in the historical record, the two types are not always easy to distinguish.

Finally, the duties of samurai household servants varied widely according to locality and the practices of individual households. Terminology
used for these servants was also idiosyncratic: Kitajima Masamoto lists
about fifty different terms used for "valet" and "page" in different parts
of the country. While various types are equated in Table 2.12, some domains distinguished, for example, official corps of koshō from kobito or
komono.[66]

Despite these problems, we can hazard some general definitions of
samurai household servants. Stewards were usually trusted, long-term
employees who managed the other servants, as well as the finances, of the
samurai household. Valets, pages and footboys served as personal attendants and lackeys. These four types clearly constituted a hierarchy; the
encyclopedic work *Teijō zakki* (*Teijō's Miscellany*, comp. 1763–1843)
states that "Valets (chūgen) are below stewards (samurai) and above
pages (komono). They are so called because they rank between stewards
and pages."[67] (The Sino-Japanese characters used for writing "chūgen"
are "middle" and "space.")

The duties of the three lower types were, however, probably similar. As
noted, only a handful of these held residual military implications. On
ceremonial occasions, such as the march of the daimyo to and from Edo,
or from Edo to Nikkō to pay respects at the Tokugawa mausolea, they
would serve as an armed escort. They might also take turns guarding the
master while he slept. But for the most part the duties of samurai servants
resembled those of domestics in commoner households. As messengers
and agents, they would represent the master in his absence. They might
even serve as go-betweens in love affairs. Manservants would most typically be called upon to draw the well water, clean and cook the rice, and
chop firewood.[68] A pageboy might, in his master's absence, be assigned
such menial chores as clearing away spider webs and cleaning the water
pipes:

kozamurai   the page
kumo to gesui de   spends his days
ni wo kurashi   with spiders and drains[69]

The traditional samurai antipathy to handling money notwithstanding,
they often did the household shopping. They might grow garden vegetables, and make items for household consumption such as rope, *zōri*
thongs, straw sandals and other footwear.[70] But other tasks were of a
purely personal nature, such as cutting the master's hair and nails and
attending him in his bath.[71] Servants also had some responsibility for the
upbringing of the lord's children, in which capacity they were expected to
combine deference with firm discipline.[72]

Footboys (*zōritori*, lit., "sandal-bearers") performed various tasks, but indeed many of these centered around the master's sandals. Wood-block prints of the period often depict samurai accompanied by boys dutifully carrying spare sandals; in Tokugawa society, various courtesies were associated with footwear. Not only were sandals removed upon entering a room, but clogs would be removed in favor of sandals when a pedestrian passed in front of a social equal or superior wearing sandals. Such customs suggest that some of the footboy's functions were quite practical. "It is the general custom throughout the kingdom," wrote the Jesuit missionary João Rodrigues (in Japan for most of the period from 1577 to 1620),

for any person of quality, from the highest ranking to the lowest, to be accompanied by a lad who takes his sandals at the entrance of the rooms in houses; the boy also carries clogs in case of mud and an umbrella against the sun or rain. He gives his master the sandals on his coming out of the house or room when he has to tread on the ground. If the owner of a large house comes out to meet his guest in one of the courtyards or sometimes in the street, he also is accompanied by a lad with the same duty of seeing to the sandals. This is a very base office.[73]

It was, however, also a highly ceremonial office, similar, perhaps to that of the pampered blackamoor in early modern Europe. It was the elegant appearance of these boys that mattered most. Clothed in padded silk garments, sporting a short sword at the side, they would, according to one account, accompany their lords only in fine weather. They would not attend their masters during stormy weather, on days when the sun was intense, or on rough roads—the better to protect their refined appearance.[74]

Palanquin-bearers and the menials who worked in the kitchen or stables constituted the lowest type of servant, but where staffs were too small to permit such specialization, these duties would fall to pages or valets. The case of Fukuzawa Yukichi, the noted educator born in 1835, illustrates the range of tasks that might fall upon a servant. Born of a samurai family, he lived with a samurai gunnery teacher's family in Nagasaki from 1854. His status was that of a *shokkaku* or guest without obligations, but in return for his room and board he was in fact obliged to serve the household in various capacities. His duties included reading aloud to the master, whose eyesight was failing; teaching the Chinese classics to the master's son; renegotiating the master's debts; washing the master's back in the bath; taking care of the mistress's cats and lapdogs; and when the hired manservant was ill, drawing water from the well and sweeping the house. "I had," Fukuzawa reminisced in his *Autobiography*, "taken in hand every kind of work from the highest to the lowest."[75]

Table 2.13
Samurai Household Servant Types: Maidservants

Maidservants (gejo)	Alternate Terms	English Equivalent
koshimoto	jochū, kozukai	chambermaid
nakai	ocha-no-ma	parlormaid
uba	moto-uba	wet nurse
daki-uba	komori	nursemaid
monoshi	saihojo	seamstress
meshitaki	tsukaimono	scullery maid
	hashitame	
	shimo-jochū	

Samurai-household maidservants might be ranked more or less as shown in Table 2.13. Such employees' tasks were generally similar to those performed by their counterparts in commoner households, which I will describe here. An important distinction of samurai household maidservants, however, was the fact that they might attain a certain political importance. Ladies-in-waiting (such as chambermaids) in important military households might, for example, serve as envoys in delicate political negotiations. Ieyasu himself often used them as spies and diplomats.[76] High officials such as Tanuma Okitsugu and Mizuno Tadakuni took care to bribe and curry favor with the maidservants who surrounded the shogun.[77] In the domains, too, maidservants might exert considerable influence. Not a few lords won out in succession struggles through the timely intervention of a loyal wet nurse.[78]

Maidservants in humble samurai households, however, were preoccupied with the less glamorous pursuits of cooking, sewing, baby-sitting, or wet-nursing. Sugimoto Etsu, a woman of samurai origins from the castle-town of Nagaoka in Echigo province, described the lives of her family's maidservants during her childhood in the last years of the Tokugawa period. The picture is no less credible for its naive charm.

The half-dozen maidservants employed by the Sugimoto household worked in a large hall with a clay floorboard. Half of this was covered with *tatami* matting, and here the servants spun thread, ground rice and prepared meals. In the middle of the floor was a fireplace, a clay-lined box sunk in he floor.

> Here the air was filled with the buzz of work mingled with chatter and laughter. In one corner, a maid was grinding rice for tomorrow's dumplings; another was making padded scrub-cloths out of an old kimono; two others were tossing from one to the other the shallow basket that shook the dark beans from the white, and a little apart from the others sat Ishi whirling her spinning wheel with a little tapping stick.[79]

TABLE 2.14
Servants in Commoner Households: Manservants

Manservants (genin, genan, gonsuke)	Alternate Terms	English Equivalent
bantō		head clerk
tedai	wakaishū	clerk
detchi	deshi	apprentice, attendant
kozō	totei, bōzu	shopboy
komono	kodomo	houseboy, shopboy
zōritori	kozoritori	footboy
meshitsukai	shimobe, kaboku	menial

Since these servants were not listed in the general population registers, and in domainal rosters might not be distinguished from low-ranking officials, we cannot provide accurate data on their numbers. However, the case of Matsumoto was perhaps typical. The record cited in the preceding note indicates that at least 15 percent of the castle-town's population were domestic servants of the samurai.[80] Most of these were probably pages and footboys.

Hōkōnin employed by the commoner classes, like their counterparts in samurai households, also performed a wide range of duties. We might think of these servants as falling into several general categories: those who performed shop-related chores, those involved in housework, and those hired for personal attendance upon the master or members of his family. Such distinctions are admittedly arbitrary, since a given servant in a merchant household might well draw the well water, wait on customers, and accompany his employer to the theater, umbrella in hand, all in the same day. Some types of servants are particularly difficult to categorize. Komono in townsmen's employ, for example, seem to have been equally applied to domestic and business activities.[81]

Nevertheless, Tokugawa period literature, census registers and household records permit us a fairly comprehesive view of commoners' service staffs. We can roughly rank the various positions and, at the risk of some distortion, attach English equivalents. Table 2.14 shows the most common manservant types. There are problems with this list, as with our list of samurai household servants. If a term like komono was inherently vague, even workers listed under relatively specific headings may not have performed the tasks that present interpretations of such terms might suggest. "Detchi," for example, seems like a straightforward term indicating an apprentice or clerk-trainee in a commercial establishment, but it could be stretched at times to simply connote "valet."[82]

If the meaning of certain terms is not completely clear, the order of rank also presents problems. Although head clerks, apprentices and shopboys clearly formed a hierarchy, there was no clear system of rank among the lower types of servant. Various households also used distinctive terms for domestics and shophands, and might invent numerous subcategories.

Such problems notwithstanding, it is possible to describe most of these service positions by tracing a rather ideal career history of a boy, hired at age eleven or twelve, in a prominant Edo dry goods shop. Our model is the Isedana dry goods shops of Odenmachō, which flourished from the Tenna period (1681–83).[83] All of the male employees of these shops were recruited from Ise at age eleven or twelve, appointed as shopboys (*kodomoshi*), and assigned to miscellaneous tasks.

These would have included such responsibilities as sweeping the shop floor, watering down the dust at the doorway, polishing the tobacco trays used by customers, running errands, and gradually learning how to handle the abacus, scales and other tools utilized in the trade. After three years of this regimen, the youth underwent an examination of his use of these tools, and if successful, he would take a more active part in dealing with customers. Four years later, he would be appointed *kodomogashira* or "shopboy chief" and supervise his younger colleagues. The following year, the seventeen- or eighteen-year-old would, after undergoing the *genpuku* ceremony, graduate into *wakaishū* (tedai) status and begin handling receipts and expenditures.

Now his responsibilities took a quantum leap, and he was made to feel it. "If even one bolt of cloth was missing," writes Kitajima, "he would have to search for it, without sleeping, for five days to a week."[84] Eight years later, after his first vacation (a generous six months back in Ise), the clerk would be promoted to *hanbai-in* (salesman). After six more years, another vacation was granted, and if the employee had talent, at age thirty-five or thirty-six, having spent eighteen years with the firm, he might be appointed head clerk. A few years later, retiring from this post, he would be permitted to establish a branch shop under the company's trademark-curtain (*noren*), and at age forty-five or six, with his master's approval, take a wife.

This is indeed an ideal success story; the story, according to Kitajima, of only 5 or 10 percent of Isedana employees. The vast majority thus never acquired positions of commercial responsibility, and probably spent their time at menial tasks. One of the stories in *Saikaku oritome* depicts a lacquerware shop in Osaka where the apprentices clean the lanterns, polish the tobacco pipes offered to customers, and clean the grooves of the sliding doors.[85] A clerk might even be assigned management of the kitchen staff.[86]

In addition to those who fit into this hierarchy of shop employees, there were manservants whose duties were primarily domestic. Footboys (zōri-

tori) were, in commoner as well as samurai households, personal attendants—probably something of a luxury for most merchants. The terms
shimobe ("low menial") and *kaboku* ("household menial") also generally
connote domestic servants. Where census registers distinguish genan
from komono, tedai and other employees, it is quite probable that these,
too, were retained for the most part to perform household chores or to
wait upon the master and his family.

Unfortunately, population registers shed little light on the nature of
commoner servants. It is often unclear, for example, how many manservants were primarily shop workers, and how many were domestic hands.
Census registers normally recorded servants under the broad categories
of "genin" (a gender-neutral term which however invariably connotes
"manservant") and "gejo" or maidservant. Other terms, like komono,
detchi, and genan also occur, but the meaning of these terms, as we have
shown, can be vague. If, as is probable, servants were listed under titles
suggested by the household head, the manner of recording them might
also reflect personal and local idiosyncracies.

The registers for Osaka's Kikuyachō, for example, always record
the overwhelming majority of manservants simply as genin. In 1750, 76
out of 98 manservants in the ward were recorded under this heading, the
rest being listed as apprentices. Meanwhile, Shijō Tateuri Nakanomachi's
record for 1743 lists 35 genin, 16 clerks, and 2 apprentices.[87] One is
inclined to assume that the genin were domestics rather shop workers, but
data from other Kyoto wards raise doubts. Registers from Kita Koromonotana-chō, Minami Koromonotana-chō, and Taishiyama, for example,
rarely record manservants as genin. They appear, rather, as genan,
komono, and detchi. While one might assume that here genan signifies
domestic servant, it seems strange that there are so few of them. In Kita
Koromonotanachō, surely the most prosperous of the wards, only 3 out
of 50 manservants are listed as genan in 1832; in the adjoining ward of
Minami Koromonotana, none of the 26 are so listed. In both wards, the
great majority of employees are komono—i.e., perhaps houseboys, perhaps shopboys. The following year's data for Taishiyama show a radically different pattern: here 29 out of 37 manservants are listed as genan,
all the others being komono.[88]

The records of *hyōshō* (monetary grants bestowed by the shogunate
upon worthy commoners for exemplary filial piety or other virtues) shed
a bit more light on the question of manservant types.[89] These documents
provide some of the best biographical material on Tokugawa-era commoners, including servants, and since there are few extant census register
series from Edo, the records of Edo grantees provide us with one of our
best sources for that city. Of the 309 recorded Edo recipients during the
period (all between 1735 and 1843), thirty-three are listed as servants

TABLE 2.15
Servants in Commoner Households: Maidservants

Maidservants (gejo, osan)	Alternate Terms	English Equivalent
koshimoto	shimyō, kamijochū	chambermaid
nakai	jochū	parlormaid
meshitaki		scullery maid
monoshi		seamstress
uba		wet nurse
komori	daki-uba, mori	nursemaid

(hōkōnin). For most, additional occupational information is also given. Fourteen are listed simply as genan, thirteen as "menials" (meshitsukai), one is a "branch manager" (shihainin), another a clerk, and two are maidservants.

Genan and meshitsukai almost certainly mean the same thing; the first compilation, the Kōgiroku (1789) uses the former term but makes no allusion to meshitsukai, while the three other sources that include Edo commoners use meshitsukai but not genan. And since here, as in the census registers, some hōkōnin are specifically described as shop employees, we can probably conclude that the others were domestics. Twenty-eight domestics out of thirty-one male hōkōnin appears to be a very high proportion, and perhaps reflects the fact that employees concerned with service to the master's person were naturally more likely to receive loyalty awards than those assigned tasks in his shop.

The list also includes an additional thirty-seven individuals, all described as tenants, whose biographical sketches indicate a service background. This group seems to have included more shop workers, since many of them are credited with sustaining or recovering the master's trade along with various acts of personal devotion. Yet only a handful are explicitly described as shop employees, including six apprentices.

Commoner households' maidservants (Table 2.15) are more easily described than their manservants. The women generally served as domestics and personal attendants. True, some were employed as tea girls to wait on customers, and many women listed simply as gejo in the registers were actually textile workers.[90] But where only one or two maidservants were employed, their duties usually would have involved housework.

By the end of the period, most chōnin households would employ at least one maid-of-all-work, whom they might refer to as a meshitaki. The term itself means "rice-boiler" and suggests kitchen responsibilities; both Saikaku and Kiseki refer to the meshitaki's "right hand bearing the scars of the kitchen-ladle."[91] But she might perform numerous other duties aside from cooking. A Genroku-era description of her functions includes baby-sitting, chopping firewood, and operating a *kara-usu*.[92] In more affluent homes, specialized employees such as nursemaids (*komori*) and seamstresses (*monoshi*) would provide some of these services.

Parlormaids could command a bit more prestige, since their duties were more closely associated with the employer's person. The ever-observant Saikaku gives a succinct definition of their functions:

> The duties of a parlormaid include, first of all, accompanying the mistress in her vehicle [*norimono*], wearing short sleeves. Since she is hired to deliver formal greetings, she must be able to recite long messages well, and when the mistress has guests, she must prepare a few refreshments, and keep bringing on the trays.[93]

He equates parlormaids to servants who in samurai mansions are called *ocha no ma*.

Heading the maidservant hierarchy, chambermaids were most intimately associated with their employers. Among other things, they attended to the master's bedding. Saikaku suggests that while previously young girls had been preferred, in the late 1680s those in their late teens or early twenties were favored; since they were "strong as ten" of the girls, they were better equipped to lift the quilts into the closets each morning. They also appeared more dignified accompanying a palanquin.[94]

Thus scullery maids, parlormaids, and chambermaids constituted a clear order of ranks. There were also servants whose relative status was less clear, such as seamstresses or girls hired to watch the children. Wet nurses (*uba*; sometimes pronounced *onba*, or referred to respectfully as *ochi no hito*) seem to have had a fairly high status within the household. Their association with the master's family was of course particularly intimate, and those employed by wealthier households often continued on as nannies (*dakiuba*, or "hugging nurse") after the infant had been weaned. Parents were often happy to allow a nurse to suckle her own infant along with their child, resembling in this respect upper-class households in Old Regime France.

Just as in France the *frère* or *soeur de lait* was considered the "ideal future servant" for the master's child, so in Japan, by ancient tradition, the *menotogo* ("nurse-child") was regarded as a foster sibling of the employer's infant. The two children might even become lifelong companions, although particularly in wealthy families, a fundamental status distinction between them would be observed.[95]

Two facts about the treatment of wet nurses seem particularly evident:

they were especially well fed, and their behavior was carefully supervised. Saikaku alludes to both phenomena when he writes, "These servants

> are not allowed to enter the employment hostel [for illicit liaisons] for even a short time, and they are forbidden to wear ornamental hair pins or berets [to protect the baby]. They are only permitted to wear soft silk against their skin, and even their food is special: for breakfast each morning, aside from flying-fish and mackeral with their white-rice gruel, their diet changes every day.[96]

The attention to the nurse's moral conduct as well as to her diet was probably intended to ensure the quality of her milk. In both China and Europe, certain foods were felt to heat the milk and to make it difficult to digest; these were to be avoided.[97]

Concern with nurses' sexual behavior probably had two aspects. It doubtless reflected the belief that an immoral nature could be passed on to the suckling infant. This too was a fairly universal belief.[98] Even so, it does not appear that employers were always terribly particular in choosing nurses, perhaps because they would always have been in short supply. Klapisch-Zuber writes that in Florence, "Girls who had been seduced, 'bestial' Tartar slave women, or mothers who had abandoned their children all made good nurses if their milk was abundant enough."[99] Saikaku gives a similar picture for seventeenth-century Japan:

> When you look at the people who take up employment as wet nurses these days, they are generally either people whose marriages have broken up, or servant girls who, unable to get boyfriends, go chasing after men [and get pregnant]. Eventually they bear the children in an employment hostel, abandon them and—as luck would have it—able to produce milk, work as wet nurses.[100]

Thus concern for the moral qualities of the wet nurse was not very profound, at least in bourgeois households. They did, however, desire to ensure that the women remained chaste while in their employ, because they felt that the milk of a pregnant woman was somehow impure. There was no custom of putting infants out to rural households to be weaned by married peasant women. Masters could maintain fairly tight control over the private life of a live-in nurse.[101]

The wet nurse's duties were taxing, allowing her little free time or privacy. According to Saikaku, she was expected to watch over the infant all night, noting the number of diaper changes. Three times a day, she applied the Five Medicinal Fragrances. If she attended to her own affairs even for a moment, her employer "will not wait until morning to dismiss her."[102] As I point out in Chapter 3, these women had quite a reputation for mischief.

These, then, are the major maidservant types. In the final analysis, however, a clear definition of most maidservant, or manservant, categories is impossible. Literature reveals the great variety of household tasks that maidservants of any designation might be asked to perform in a day's work. Laundry was a laborious process, particularly with bedding and kimono. "Washing a kimono involved taking it to pieces, washing and starching them separately, on frames, and reassembling, changing round the pieces to distribute wear."[103] The process of cooking rice over an open hearth to a suitably sticky consistency required skill and attention. The fetching of well water, for bathing, cooking, and the washing of pots and vegetables, were daily chores. So was the collection or purchase and cutting of firewood, and the dispensing of wastewater at refuse heaps in each ward. (Not a few servants, perhaps, were charged with violating ward regulations against dumping from second-story windows.)[104]

But the ability to handle such rudimentary tasks was the minimal requirement of a maidservant; she would be far more attractive if she could play the shamisen and koto, sing folksongs, apply moxa treatment, cut hair, shampoo, and massage. Thus each household developed its own expectations of its employees and sought to take advantage of their talents and assets. The Numano household of Wakayama is a case in point. This family had operated the Moriya Pawnshop, in the ward of Hashichō in the castle-town, from the Tenshō era (1573–92). Since its head also often served as an elder (toshiyori), the house had considerable prestige and wealth and employed numerous servants. Luckily, some details concerning Numano maidservants survive in the form of a "Maidservants' Wage Advance Notebook" (Gejo kyūgin kashi hikaechō) kept by the mistress of the household from 1838 to 1858.[105] This extraordinarily rare document—perhaps the only one of its kind extant—lists details about eighty-four women, divided into chambermaids (shinmyō), parlormaids, scullery maids, and nursemaids (mori). Most entries offer only sketchy data, but others record the servant's name, age when hired, place of origin, employment agency, agency commission, dates of hire and dismissal, yearly wage, dated payments, gifts and tips, and various (often unflattering) observations concerning the maids' personalities.

The document clearly indicates that all categories of maidservant performed miscellaneous chores as the occasion demanded. All might be called upon to sew or to work the shimobata loom, do the laundry, or boil medicines. (Special tips were bestowed for a successful performance of the two latter tasks.) Nursemaids had responsibilities unrelated to the children: the thirteen-year-old Kiku, hired in Tenpō 15, reportedly could "not do anything." "Will use for trivial chores," writes the mistress. "Will wait until she learns how to do something."[106]

A parlormaid might be called upon to do the cooking. One "Satsu from

Kuroe" apparently failed at the assignment and, after having been scolded on that account, quarreled with other maids and was dismissed in 1840.[107] Scullery maids seem to have been expected to pitch in with the sewing. Several entries note with irritation that a scullery maid "absolutely cannot sew"; another Satsu was apparently a particular disappointment. "She is here to sew, but she is not very good at it," her mistress complains.[108]

Yet job distinctions existed, and the Numano mistress did not hesitate to promote or demote her employees. The notebook records the demotion of two parlormaids to scullery maids (one of whom quits rather than accept her new status), and the promotion of one scullery maid to parlormaid. The distinction must have been one of duties and status, since the wage difference was minimal.

The Numano household invariably employed several maidservants simultaneously, but in one-maid merchant households the employee might encounter a regimen similar to the following.[109] Up at dawn, she would open the shutters, as the shop would be open for business at six a.m. After drawing water from the nearby well, shared with the other households of the ward, she would light a fire under the kettle in the open hearth and begin to prepare rice for the first meal of the day. As the other household members stirred, she would store away their bedding, or if the weather was fine, air the quilts. She would then sweep the tatami mats before returning to the kitchen to prepare bean-paste soup and wash the breakfast vegetables in a wooden sink.

After serving breakfast to the male members of the household, she would dine separately with the women and girls, then perhaps haggle with a beggar or peddler at the door before setting off to the vegetable market or the fish market. Later she might help prepare the second, final meal of the day, served in the late afternoon. Perhaps she would wash the pots and dishes before doing a bit of sewing, keeping an eye on the children while her mistress attended to the laundry. If the master was entertaining a guest, she might attend the two, conscientiously pouring their sake as their cups emptied. In the evening, after lighting the candles or lanterns, she might massage the master or mistress before preparing the bath which she, the lowest member of the household, would be able to enjoy only after the others had soaked in the bath water. Perhaps then, after playing a tune on the shamisen, she would spread out the family members' *futon* bedding, make sure that all fires were extinguished, and finally rest her own head on the wooden concave block, padded with hempen cloth, used for a pillow.

Such were a servant's practical chores. As noted, however, servants were valued not only as workers, but as ornaments, status symbols reflecting a household's wealth and prestige. Samurai in particular com-

TABLE 2.16
Wages for Valets in Edo, 1829, According to Stature

Stature	Daily Wage in Silver
5 shaku 8 sun–6 shaku (176cm +)	10 monme
5 shaku 6 sun 5 bu–5 shaku 8 sun (171cm +)	up to 7 monme 5 bu
5 shaku 5 sun 5 bu–5 shaku 6 sun 5 bu (168cm +)	up to 5 monme 5 bu
under 5 shaku 5 sun 5 bu	up to 2 monme 5 bu

Source: Minami Kazuo, "Edo no chūgen kyūkinkō," Nihon rekishi, 204, 5 (May 1965).

peted, as their means allowed, to hire dashing attendants and to outfit them in the most striking liveries. In so doing, they indulged in what Veblen termed "conspicuous consumption," sometimes lavishing funds on servants' garments and glittering ceremonial weaponry, while allowing at least some servants "conspicuous leisure," idleness connoting affluence and the supportive capacity of the master's house.[110]

Idleness was also associated with beauty; only the leisured, sheltered from manual labor and the elements, could attain the genteel grace of a high-born woman's chambermaid or the elegance of a daimyo's footboy. Such servants could command the highest wages. In Akasaka, a samurai ward in Edo, valets called orisuke boasted a particularly high reputation; according to the Meiwa shi (History of the Meiwa Era, 1764–71), Orisuke was originally the name of a handsome manservant, but gradually became synonymous with "chūgen": "Universally admired for their good looks, [Akasaka valets] were called 'Orisuke' or 'Akasaka yakko [varlets].' These have become the popular names for them."[111]

Wage structure, too, reveals the preference for manservants who might cut a fine figure in public. A work published in 1829 gives the contemporary wages for valets contracted to serve between about five o'clock in the morning to five o'clock in the evening (Table 2.16): the taller, the better![112] (The statuesque manservants most preferred must have been rare indeed. As late as 1900 army conscripts averaged 158.5 centimeters [5 feet, 3 inches] in height.)[113]

Budgets set some limits on the quantity and quality of samurai-household servants. Sumptuary legislation then imposed limits on their finery: just as early modern European rulers set restrictions on how much trunk hose an apprentice might sport, or how ample a ruff a maidservant might flaunt, the shogunate banned excessively ostentatious servant liveries.[114] The Tokugawa kinreikō (True Record of the Tokugawa) records a 1615 ban on silk for samurai-household menials: "If there are pages or foot-boys wearing silk, the garment will be stripped from their bodies and their master will pay a fine of two silver pieces."[115] Such an amercement might have exceeded the servant's yearly wage. (Compare the Tudor proclamation of 1562, in which masters are fined 200 marks for conniving with their servants to defy sumptuary laws.)[116]

Another prohibition, issued in 1635, specifies that pages and servants should on all occasions be clothed in cotton.[117] Such shogunate rules were applied in the various domains as well.[118] Maidservants did not escape these regulations, and were singled out in an instruction issued in Edo in 1724: "Especially maidservants should be firmly instructed so that there will be a clearer distinction between superiors and inferiors."[119]

Although the commoner class was surely less preoccupied with display than the samurai, literary and legal evidence leaves no doubt that commoners, too, were anxious to maintain appearances. In his *Seken musume katagi* (*Portraits of Young Women in the Modern World*, 1717), Ejima Kiseki satirizes the vain concerns of spoiled young wives. In one story a mistress, observing that "people in the neighboring wards peek in" to the family's compound, orders all the chambermaids to be dressed in fresh summer kimono.[120]

Mi no date ni	She does the hair
gejo ga kami made	even of the maidservant
yutte yari[121]	just for her own sake

So runs the senryū, suggesting that the mistress is more concerned with how her maid's image reflects on her, than with the maidservant's own feelings.[122]

Such concerns about image were not an exclusively female conceit. In *Kōshoku ichidai otoko* the hero Yonosuke reveals the same preoccupation with asserting status.[123] A Miyajima prostitute guesses that he is a petty trader, while in fact he is a wealthy wholesaler. With some irritation, Yonosuke replies that she ought to have been able to judge his true status by the style and size of his medicine case (*inrō*), the quality of his hands and feet, and the attributes of his attendant. The latter, Katsunojō, "impresses everyone. How unperceptive of you to underestimate the man he accompanies!" If servants' qualities were not apparent in their masters, surely a master of refinement was revealed in his choice of attendants!

The shogunate, needless to say, was vigorously opposed to such pretensions, especially on the part of mere commoners. Donald Shively's excellent essay on sumptuary legislation (*kenyakurei*) throws a great deal of light on this subject. Edicts (*ofure*) from at least 1648 in both Osaka and Edo limited the types of silk cloth commoners' servants might wear and regulated which items of apparel (down to underwear articles unlikely to be detected) could be made from specific materials. Like sartorial laws in early modern Europe, however, these edicts were probably ineffective. Literary evidence suggests the codes were widely ignored, as does the fact that they frequently were repeated and elaborated. In 1656 a law against "presumptuous appearances" was issued, and then in 1668 a wide-ranging list of prohibitions included restrictions on use of formal dress tunics (*kamishimo*) and woolen coats. "Servants," the announcement specifically warns, "and also artisans of lower status should wear coarser clothing."[124]

This law was soon repeated, but the real rash of sartorial legislation came in the 1680s, after a famous event involving a wealthy merchant of Asakusa Kurobune-chō named Ishikawa Rokubei, his ostentatious wife, and eight gorgeously dressed chambermaids in their employ. The several accounts agree that on a day in 1681, as the shogun Tsunayoshi was making his first official visit to Ueno, he noticed the conspicuous party among the crowd paying their respects and inquired about who they were. Learning that the beautifully dressed ladies were mere commoners, the shogun, outraged at their arrogant display beyond their station, ordered Rokubei's property confiscated.[125]

This episode was perhaps not the cause, but two years later seven edicts dealing with clothing were issued, with at least four more to come in the period between 1688 and 1690, and a comprehensive list of bans for Edo townsmen in 1718. Some of these included specific clauses concerning servants, like the 1683 law specifying cotton or ramie cloth for manservants, maidservants and scullery maids (*hashitame*), or a 1719 prohibition of chōnin servants wearing silk.[126] The repetition of such laws became a fixed feature of conservative reform movements up to the Tenpō era (1830–43). Thus the bakufu endeavored, with little apparent success, to prevent the use of servants as items of conspicuous consumption.[127]

What of the age structure of the servant population? Literature informs us that a samurai's valet would typically be a man in his twenties; a page, a youth in his late teens; and a footboy, a preteen as young as nine or ten. In a merchant house, meanwhile, a clerk would normally be over eighteen years old, while boys as young as ten or twelve might be taken on as houseboys or apprentices. (Conditions apparently resembled those of Renaissance Europe. The minimum age for entering apprenticeship in various trades in seventeenth-century Venice varied from ten to sixteen, the term usually lasting five years.)[128] Maidservants such as scullery maids and housemaids would typically be in their teens, while chambermaids would be slightly older.

Unfortunately actual data on servants' ages, particularly for the early Tokugawa period, is not abundant. Census registers are not as helpful as one might hope; the Osaka records do not list ages, and while the Kyoto records typically do, they often provide only insignificant samples.[129] The

TABLE 2.17
Ages of Manservants, Mid-Tokugawa Period

	Nakamachi (Fukushima) (1731) Number (%)	Kasama (1705) Number (%)
to age 10	—	2 (1.2)
11 – 15	12 (11.8)	6 (3.6)
16 – 20	26 (25.5)	30 (18.1)
21 – 25	31 (30.3)	23 (13.9)
26 – 30	12 (11.8)	29 (17.5)
31 – 35	4 (3.9)	21 (12.7)
36 – 40	4 (3.9)	19 (11.5)
41 – 45	5 (4.9)	15 (9.0)
46 – 50	4 (3.9)	8 (4.8)
51 – 55	1 (1.0)	7 (4.2)
56 – 60	1 (1.0)	4 (2.4)
61 – 65	—	2 (1.2)
66 – 70	1 (1.0)	—
71 or older	1 (1.0)	—
total	102	166
mean	25	31
median	23	30
mode(s)	17	19, 27, 30, 31

Sources: "Hōei ni-nen Kasamamachi machikata kenbetsu aratamechō," in Hayashi Reiko et al., eds., *Ibaraki ken shiryō. Kinsei shakai keizai hen*, vol. 1 (1971); Fukushima-shi shi hensan iinkai, eds., *Fukushima-shi shi: Kinsei shiryō*, vol. 2 (Fukushima, 1968), 317–33.

largest samplings I have found for the mid-Tokugawa period are those of the castle-town of Kasama (1705) and the ward of Nakamachi in Fukushima (1731).[130]

The life expectancy of those surviving infancy was only about fifty years, and so naturally the typical servant was young. As Table 2.17 shows, in both these communities manservants were overwhelmingly between fifteen and thirty years of age. In Kasama, however, the male servant population was relatively mature, the mean age being over thirty-one, while in Nakamachi the mean was slightly over twenty-five.

Modal figures suggest a close relationship between age and function. Nine seventeen-year-old boys were employed in Nakamachi, but only three nineteen-year-olds, while men in their early twenties constituted the largest group in service. In Kasama, men in their late twenties and early thirties filled a disproportionate number of positions, but here nineteen-year-olds were in equally high demand. Demographic factors no doubt account for some of these imbalances, but plainly certain jobs were regarded as appropriate for particular age groups.

TABLE 2.18
Ages of Maidservants, Kasama (1705)

	Number	%
to age 10	1	.9
11 – 15	11	10.2
16 – 20	16	14.8
21 – 25	20	18.5
26 – 30	18	16.7
31 – 35	11	10.2
36 – 40	10	9.3
41 – 45	9	8.3
46 – 50	3	2.8
51 – 55	5	4.6
56 – 60	1	.9
61 – 65	—	—
66 – 70	1	.9
71 or older	2	.9
total	108	
mean	30	
median	26	
mode(s)	38	

Source: Hayashi (see Table 2.17).

In Kasama (see Table 2.18), the disproportionate number of manservants between ages fifteen and twenty can be partly explained by the presence of nine apprentices. Presumably a number of these quit during their late teens, being replaced with others. Only four apprentices over age twenty appear, and two of these were "temple apprentices" obviously pursuing some kind of religious calling. Employers did not seek adult men as apprentices, and thus a youth too old for such service, without yet having acquired a skill, would perhaps have found it more difficult to secure employment.

The figures for maidservants' ages in Kasama resemble those for their male counterparts, in that roughly half of them fell into the sixteen to thirty age group. However, the age structure of these women was quite different in several respects. Proportionately twice as many maidservants were children under age fifteen. Although a somewhat smaller proportion were in their late teens, a significantly greater proportion of maidservants were serving during their early twenties. Indeed, while manservants aged twenty to twenty-five were fewer than boys in their late teens or men in their late twenties, maidservants were most likely to fall into the twenty to twenty-five year age group.

The mean age of maidservants was only about one year less than that

TABLE 2.19
Ages of Numano Household Maidservants

	Number	%
10 – 14	1	1.33
15 – 19	15	20.00
20 – 24	34	45.33
25 – 29	19	25.33
30 – 34	5	6.67
35 – 39	1	1.33
total	75	
mean	23	
median	22	
mode	22	

Source: "Gejo kyūkingin kashi hikaechō," in Wakayama-shi shi hensan iinkai, eds., *Wakayama-shi shi*, vol. 5 (1975), 173–98.

of manservants, but the modal age of thirty-eight is much higher. All this suggests that the demand for females of different ages to work as servants was quite consistent, and that the nature of their work was such that age was no great factor in attaining a post. Kyoto figures from later in the period compiled by Hayami Akira, and Meiji figures on Kikuyachō published by Inui Hiromi, support these interpretations.[131]

In the Numano household of Wakayama, there was a clear preference for maidservants in their early twenties. Of the eighty-four women who appear in the *Maidservant Wage Advance Notebook*, ages are given for seventy-five (Table 2.19). Of these, 71 percent were in their twenties, with average figures clearly linking age with job status: eighteen years for nursemaids, twenty-two years for scullery maids, twenty-four years for parlormaids, and twenty-five years for chambermaids.[132]

It is curious that girls younger than fifteen were so rarely employed in Meiji-era Kikuyachō and by the Numano family, while they made up a large part of the servant population in Kasama and in the Kyoto wards studied by Hayami. Prosperity may well have been a factor; Kikuyachō was a wealthy commercial district, and the Numano ran a flourishing pawnshop business. Wealthy households may have preferred adult to adolescent servants not only because of their greater competence, but for their display value.[133] Saikaku, as noted earlier, opined that women in their twenties looked more elegant accompanying a palanquin.

They would also have been more expensive to employ. Children, indeed, were in most cases probably not paid. The youngest maidservant in the Numano household (age thirteen) is the only one who received no wage. (The next youngest servants, however—both nursemaids age 16—

received seventy-five monme each.) This fact no doubt explains the common, if obvious, misconception that servants generally received no wages. Children's compensation was largely in the form of training, room and board, whereas adults were in a position to demand money for their services.

Clearly a large percentage of the total service labor force, male and female, consisted of children. Males sought service positions (or were placed in them by relatives) very early in life but tended to quit their posts early. In Edo's Ise shops, as already noted, only a small percentage of boys who were signed on as shophands graduated beyond apprentice status.[134] Moreover, since employees hired in their late teens (after the *genpuku* coming-of-age ceremony) were at a disadvantage,[135] one would expect most commercial houses to support a high percentage of adolescents; indeed, in many shops these hires were referred to simply as "children" (*kodomo*).[136]

That such youngsters did not receive money wages does not, of course, argue against a trend towards wage labor in Tokugawa society. I will offer ample evidence of wage payments for older servants, calculated to the very day. The fact suggests, however, that the structure of the service occupations in Japan was quite different from that in contemporary Europe, where children formed a smaller proportion of service staffs.[137] Servants in Japan were probably at an even greater psychological disadvantage vis-à-vis their masters than were their European counterparts. The fact that many indeed knew very little of life adds poignancy to the house code references to employees as the master's "children," but it also implies that many servants would have been especially vulnerable to abuse, exploitation, and the loneliness of early separation from their families.

Nevertheless, this age structure proves that service was more often than not a temporary occupation, a childhood training process soon outgrown. Then too, the harsher elements of service might be mitigated by ample company. In Kyoto's Tsukinukichō, for example, where servants comprised 28 percent of the recorded population in 1837, they made up the overwhelming majority of residents between eleven and twenty-five years of age. Forty-nine out of the fifty-eight males aged eleven to twenty (84 percent) were hōkōnin.[138]

A final characteristic of the servant labor force remains to be considered: its sexual composition. Women seem to have always made up a large proportion of the servant population. In the castle-town of Matsumoto, for example, 52 percent of all samurai household servants were female in 1725. Here the highest-ranking households were least apt to hire women; 50 percent of their servants were female. But in households of lesser rank, women constituted fully 70 percent of the servants.[139]

Unfortunately, only a few data series have survived to give us a sense of changing sex ratios over time. The best are from Osaka wards, and provide information only about commoner service staffs. But sparse though the data is, it suggests a significant trend—a feminization of service in urban households of the late Tokugawa period, perhaps analogous to the feminization that occurred in service staffs in Bourbon France.[140]

According to Saitō Osamu's research, maidservants as a percentage of total Osaka servants grew from 36 percent in 1686 to 46 percent in the 1860s.[141] Inui Hiromi's researches show that in 1730, only 27 percent of the servants in Kikuyachō were female, but the figure grew to around 35 percent during the last years of the period. In Dōshōmachi San-chōme the figure was 24 percent in 1710, but 43 percent in 1860. This trend seems to be closely connected with the increasing tendency of tenants to employ servants. In their households, the feminization trend is even more marked: in Dōshōmachi San-chōme, for example, maidservants constitute 19 percent of the servants employed by tenant households in 1710 but 51 percent in 1860.[142] It is likely that they were typically set to work, not at shop-related tasks, but at domestic chores. Housework, that is to say, was becoming women's work.

The reasons for this trend are unclear. It may be connected to the slow economic decline of Osaka relative to the towns and villages on its periphery, which caused the city's population to drop from 410,000 in 1756 to 321,000 in 1856.[143] The development of rural handicrafts and manufactures is thought to have acted as a disincentive to urban-bound migration in general, but it may have disinclined more men than women from the prospect of urban service. For example, the total population of Dōshōmachi San-chōme in 1780 was 625 persons, of whom 296 (47 percent) were recorded as servants. Eighty years later, the population had declined by 12 percent to 548, while the servant population of 260 (still 47 percent) had dropped by precisely the same extent. What had changed was the sex ratio: maidservants had constituted 32 percent of all servants in 1780, but 43 percent in 1860.[144]

Hayami Akira has studied this question from the angle of village migrants. His analysis of ninbetsuchō of a village in Mino province show that from about 1815, as a result of rural economic growth, the incidence of labor migration out of the village declined. Even so, village women were spending more and more time in the city of Osaka. Years worked in Osaka, as a percentage of total years in which females worked outside the village, rose from 6 percent in the period from 1773 to 1800 to 25 percent during the period 1851–68. Meanwhile, migration to towns (market centers of up to 10,000) dramatically increased over the last century of the Tokugawa period. Overall, the cases of female urban-bound labor migration rose from 55 percent to 74 percent of all instances of female dekasegi, while male urban-bound dekasegi stagnated or declined.[145]

Thus, women may have migrated to Osaka to fill service positions formerly held by men who were no longer interested in such work. Meanwhile employers seem to have developed new tastes affecting their choice of servants. First, samurai households, then wealthy commoners, seem to have increasingly sought talented women, trained in singing, dancing, the koto and shamisen, who could entertain as well as perform domstic chores. Nishiyama Matsunosuke writes that 1760s and 1770s "girls with vocal talent and some skill on the shamisen could find employment within a day. Those lacking such abilities, on the other hand, did not even need to apply."[146] He refers to samurai mansions in Edo, not to commoner households in Osaka, but upper-class commoner families also sought girls trained in such arts as penmanship and shamisen.[147]

Employers' interest in hiring skilled maidservants contin ued through the latter half of the Tokugawa period. "As for the employment of female servants (*onna hōkōnin*)," complained Uezaki Kuhachirō during the Tenmei period (1781–88), "if they have not studied shamisen, *ko-uta* [folksongs], and dance, they will not be hired."[148] Novelist Shikitei Sanba in 1809 amusingly described how one contemporary "education mother" forced her preteen daughter to prepare for a service position. The girl has writing practice each morning, followed by shamisen lessons, then breakfast; dance practice, then more penmanship, a snack and bath; a koto lesson, more shamisen and dancing, and a little playtime; finally, koto practice to dusk. The father is more indulgent: "It's only to go into service after all. A little bit will do."[149]

All these examples involve Edo, but conditions in the Kansai area appear to have been similar. Shibata Kyūō (1783–1839), a famous Shingaku savant, described how wealthy commoners in Ikeda, a town fifteen kilometers northwest of Osaka, forced their fourteen-year-old daughter to study flower arranging, painting, tea ceremony, and koto.[150] He found the trend disturbing, and advocated more practical education, but the emphasis upon preparation for service positions may have been mostly positive. Hayami Akira suggests that the decline in female infanticide in the latter part of the period was related to the increasing availability of service positions for women.[151]

Service possibilities may have not only increased the likelihood for female survival, but the educational prospects for women as well. Women in general became better educated through the period, and by the time of the Restoration some 10 percent of all girls were receiving formal education outside their homes. (The figure would have been closer to about 30 percent in Osaka and Kyoto.)[152] Girls, like Sanba's example, would learn to write to enhance career prospects, and once in service, they might be allowed to take lessons along with their mistresses' daughters.[153]

Young women, for their part, seem to have perceived the various advantages of service in urban households. Uezaki Kuhachirō, a high-ranking bakufu official, wrote in a 1787 memorial to the rōjū, Matsudaira Sadanobu, that peasants, regarding farm work as drudgery, were apt to send their daughters into domestic service "in order to satisfy their wish to see Edo and the life there. . . . All vie with one another in sending their daughters to Edo.[154] Preparation for an advantageous marriage was a big factor: Lafcadio Hearn wrote during the Meiji period that "a nice girl" does not seek domestic service for the wages, although she receives them, "but chiefly to prepare herself for marriage.[155] The age of women at their first marriage sharply rose during the late Tokugawa period due in large part to the increasing popularity of "life cycle service" among young women.[156]

Chapter Three

MASTER-SERVANT RELATIONS

FOR MOST SERVANTS, the decision to seek urban employment meant a decision to migrate. Of the thirty-three entries concerning Edo servants in the records of *hyōshō* awards, only ten list the grantee's birthplace, but they are suggestive. Only one of these servants had been born in the city, while two were born "outside Edo" and two were from other places in Musashi. The remaining four were from Kai, Mikawa, Ise, and faroff Harima, over four hundred kilometers west.[1]

These were all manservants, but females were apparently even more apt to migrate in search of employment. Of the Numano maidservants for whom birthplace is recorded, only a few had been born in the castle-town of Wakayama; most were from agricultural villages elsewhere in Kii province. Table 3.1 shows data for the three Kyoto wards of Shijō Tateuri Nakanomachi, Hakurakutenchō, and Kameya-chō, along with Osaka's Kikuyachō at the end of the Tokugawa period. It indicates that 68 percent of the manservants in the Kyoto wards, and 56 percent of those in Kikuyachō, had been born in these cities. This was true of only 46 percent of the Kyoto wards' maidservants, and 25 percent of the Kikuyachō maidservants. Inui Hiromi's data, meanwhile, shows that in 1872, thirty-four of sixty-seven manservants in Kikuyachō came from merchant families, while only twenty-one were of peasant background. On the other hand, twenty-two of the thirty-seven maidservants in the ward had fathers engaged in farming, and only five were from merchant families.[2]

There were, no doubt, as many reasons for this migration as there were migrants. Certainly grinding poverty spurred some; during the latter half of the period, the concentration of landownership, particularly in the most advanced areas such as the Kinai, produced a large class of landless peasants (*mudaka*) who, particularly during periods of famine, would flock to the cities and towns seeking relief or employment.[3] On the other hand, some abandoned a reasonably tolerable life for one they simply calculated would be better. Judging from the boom in travel literature during the Tokugawa era, a healthy Wanderlust might have provided the motive in some cases. "Even for a woman," exclaims the heroine of Saikaku's *Kōshoku ichidai onna*, "there is nothing more exciting than travelling about and going into service!"[4]

But if real-life motives were complex, ruling-class perceptions of

TABLE 3.1
Birthplace of Servants Employed in Kikuyachō (Osaka) and in
Three Kyoto Wards, 1868

	Shijō Tateuri Nakanomachi,* Hakurakuten-chō, and Kameya-chō		Kikuyachō	
	Manservants	Maidservants	Manservants	Maidservants
Kyoto City	46	12	1	
Osaka City		1	32	3
Yamashiro	6	5		4
Settsu			7	
Kawachi				3
Izumi			8	1
Omi	9	5	4	1
Mino		1		
Ise	1		1	
Wakasa	2	2		
Echizen	1			
Kaga	1		1	
Tanba	1	1		
Tango	1			
Tajima		1		
Harima			1	
Sanuki			1	
Awa			1	
totals	68	28	57	12

Source: Hayami (see Table 2.7), 541.
* Shijō Tateuri Nakanomachi data for 1863.

urban-bound migration were simple. Arthur Young, writing in 1771 that, "Every one but an idiot knows that the lower classes must be kept poor or they will never be industrious,"[5] would have found no quarrel with officials of the shogunate. One of these urged that peasants be taxed to the breaking point: "Peasants are like sesame seed. The more you squeeze them the more oil you get."[6]

Peasants who arrived in a town looking for service positions were, in the view of such officials, shirking their appointed tasks and looking for a free ride. Ogyū Sorai grumbled around 1720 that "Edo is the dumping-ground of the domains"—the destination, that is, of the most worthless migrants.[7] Gamō Kunpei (1768–1813) protested that Edo's samurai mansions were filled with "many male and female servants, who lead rootless and useless lives."[8] And around 1787 Uezaki Kuhachirō complained of the depopulation of the countryside as a result of the exodus of lazy peasants. "Many small farmers," he wrote,

> regard farm work as drudgery and develop an inclination to leave their villages. . . . Thus, there is a steady increase in the number of people who prefer life in Edo to that in their native provinces. The result is that farm work is largely neglected and the supply of rice falls off. As no restrictions are placed on the free emigration of people to Edo, the city finally is turned into a reservoir of population from all parts of the country.[9]

Women, Uezaki believed, were particularly vulnerable to the titillating appeal of the big city.

> So far as the girls are concerned, their parents send them out to domestic service in Edo, in order to satisfy their wish to see Edo and the life there. At first, these girls sigh for their homes and tearfully regret that they had ever been engaged to work in a strange city, but they soon come to imitate the manners of the Edo people and to detest life in their native provinces. . . . All vie with one another in dispatching their daughters to Edo.[10]

Such references express the assumption, widely held among the ruling class, that urban-bound migration resulted from peasants' selfish desire to better their lot; that it occurred as a result of the pull of the city, rather than the push of intolerable conditions of agrarian life. But the bakufu conception of the proper villager's life, outlined in the Keian Edict cited in Chapter 1, must have strained the endurance of many peasants who, had they experienced less oppressive lives, would not have been drawn to quit their ancestral fields by the lure of urban life.[11]

Whether sought as a positive goal in itself, or as a last resort, service in urban households offered some advantages over village life. Employment in a well-to-do household was widely believed to confer educational benefits, particularly to the young, and parents strove to secure suitable positions for their offspring in hopes that the skills they would learn in service would benefit them later in life. Service was also thought to improve character, as the following bath-house conversation in Shikitei Sanba's *Ukiyoburo* suggests:

> "Our eldest son gives us nothing but trouble. Nevertheless, he's our only boy, for better or worse, and so we've spoiled him and haven't put him into service [*hōkō ni dashimasen*]. Now we're sorry. He's clever and inventive, but that's no help when he can't function among other people. Though he doesn't know the first thing about making money, he does a good job at spending it!"
>
> "Oh well, he's at that age when they all run wild. We told our second son

that being with other people would be good medicine for him, and placed him with the main shop [*hondana*]."

"Oh? He's quite mature then, isn't he? It always holds that unless you eat someone else's food you won't understand other people's feelings. . . . Those who can't leave their parents' arms don't understand what pain and irritation are."[12]

The reference to the "main shop" implies that the youth's family manages a branch shop which has spun off from the operation of a former employer. Such arrangements, in which a branch shop family member received training in his future trade outside his own household, were common.

In the case of females, vocational training as an aim of service was less important than the acquisition of culture and social graces. These might, conceivably, enable the young woman to make an ideal match into a well-to-do (samurai) house. Service positions in samurai mansions were especially sought after, for reasons that Shikitei reveals. Elsewhere in his novel two commoner matrons are soaking in the bathhouse, accompanied by their daughters, and talk turns to the girls' employment. The one mentions how her little girl, now eight years old, has been serving a samurai household since age six (five in our reckoning).

"How nice for her dancing," the other replies, "that you could get her into service while so young!" She would like to place her own daughter into service, but so far has been unsuccessful. Perhaps she has been too choosy:

"If they're not meant to be, those service opportunities will slip away from you. When I think, 'Let's place her here,' the other party thinks she won't quite do. And when they take a liking to her, I have my doubts about *them*! We've gone to interviews [*omemie*] any number of times, but there's always been some hitch. Ha ha ha! What a lot of trouble it is!"

"It's all up to Fate, so you've just got to be patient. But you know, service is a real blessing. They don't call it discipline, but [the experience] improves their manners. At home no matter how often you scold them, you don't really correct their bad habits, but when you get them into a [samurai] mansion, they begin to change completely."[13]

Aside from acquiring better manners and higher culture, women of humble backgrounds might secure fine futures as concubines or wives of ranking samurai. Such an alliance would, of course, considerably boost the status of the maidservant's parents.

Men from the commoner class, as mentioned, might also find employment in samurai mansions. Ogyū Sorai observed (with some alarm) that both footsoldiers and valets were being recruited "from town coolies (*machi ninsoku*)."[14] Thus a vast number of people entered service in both types of urban households. The records of hyōshō awards suggest that about one-third of all Edo commoners, for example, worked as hōkōnin at some point in their lives. Of the 309 recorded Edo commoner grantees, thirty-three (11%) were in service at the time the award was granted. An additional 183 grantees were tenants, and the records provide biographical sketches for 121 (66%) of these. Thirty-seven of the 121 tenants (31%) definitely had service experience.[15]

How did would-be hōkōnin find positions and enter service? By all accounts, the process was not difficult. Given the relatively high urban mortality rates, a constant influx of rural migrants was necessary to maintain city populations, and as the merchant class tended to steadily prosper, there was always a high demand for servants. The bakufu official Tanaka Kyūgu (1663–1729), describing conditions around Edo in 1721, wrote, "Men and women who will work as hōkōnin are scarce. This is especially true of those employed [in the towns] by warriors, but there is scarcity of such people even in the country."[16] Contemporary comment upon the poor quality of samurai-household servants suggests that nearly anyone could under normal circumstances find employment in service.

GUARANTORS AND EMPLOYMENT AGENCIES

Many found service positions through friends or acquaintances from the same village or province who had already settled in a town. Others entrusted themselves to employment agencies which, for a fee, would match them up with employers. In either case, the law required that a friend, relative or professional surety act as guarantor (*ukenin*) to ensure the servant's adherence to the employment contract. The fact that this precaution of involving a third party was felt necessary suggests the increasingly impersonal, if not mistrustful, relationship between masters and servants, a fact which Ogyū Sorai stressed: "Hired servants," he wrote, "are not the same as hereditary servants because they take service with their master on the basis of a certificate from a guarantor."[17]

Servants' contracts were generally accompanied by promissory notes (*tegata*) from these guarantors, who would then be held liable for repayment of wages in the event of the servant's abscondence. A single employee might have several guarantors: a parent or relative would act as "person-owner" (*hito-uke*), a landlord might act as sub-surety (*shita-uke*), and a professional agent (*hito-oki* or "people-placer") would serve as principal guarantor.[18] Members of the servant's Five Family Unit (*go-nin-gumi*) back home also might be involved as sureties of a sort, liable to reprisals if the servant broke the law. Thus the servant seemed hemmed in on all sides by persons vitally interested in ensuring that he met his contractual obligations.

In reality, however, controls were not so thorough-going. Guarantors did not always live up to their responsibilities, and might become difficult to locate in the event of the servant's disappearance. As Sorai notes:

> Hired servants come straight from the country, and of course are not known to the guarantor, but receive his guarantee in return for a small fee. They thus have someone who is responsible for them, but that person is one who has no fixed place of residence, or who may have given [the servant's employer] a false place of residence.[19]

Worse yet, guarantors might actively collude with a runaway servant; Sorai describes cases in which both parties vanish simultaneously. In such cases, the guarantor's landlord was obliged to pay damages, and any property left in the guarantor's lodging was subject to confiscation. The guarantor, however, would usually evacuate the premises, removing his household goods, before any inquiry could begin.[20]

On the other hand, so long as guarantors properly offered compensation for damages incurred by abscondence (and perhaps theft), masters suffered little inconvenience. Masters, Sorai complains, are all too willing to let the matter drop upon receiving reparations—particularly if they discover that their former hire has entered the employ of someone of higher status than their own. Too easily did principles of loyalty and legal obligation acquiesce to crude considerations of profit and loss.

The legal position of the runaway servant may indeed have been quite comfortable: if caught, he would be handed over to a guarantor, rather than his former master, and the guarantor would decide upon his disposition.[21] Thus while the guarantor might seem an impediment to the servant's freedom, he also acted as a shield protecting the servant from possible employer vengeance.

Employment agencies were among the more reliable guarantors. Profitable businesses of fixed location, they could not elude their obligations as easily as small-time employment agents. These operations went by a variety of names: *hito-yado, naka-yado, tanin-yado, koyado, shussen, kuchiireya, kuchiire,* and *keian* being the most common. (The *yado* in these terms connotes "lodging" or "hostel," indicating that the offices maintained rooms to house job applicants for brief periods between employment terms.) Some specialized in particular types of employee, such as wet-nurses, menial laborers or male and female prostitutes available for terms of several months. In 1730 some two hundred agencies specialized in samurai household servants, hiring out men as stewards and valets as well as domestics of lower status.[22]

Charging rent as well as a percentage commission from the servant's advance wage payment, employment agencies thrived at the employee's expense. In Osaka during the Genroku period, a maidservant residing at an employment agency paid one *shō* (1.8 liters) of rice per day as rent. "As the days pass," writes Saikaku,

> she is finally even stripped of [i.e., forced to sell] her padded cotton kimono. If employment is found for her, the agency takes all of her advance pay and a commission of one *mon* per ten of her salary. She goes to work with only the clothes on her back (but no one goes naked)![23]

It was to one's advantage to keep the stay at the agency short.

In concept, these institutions were not dissimilar to the servant placement agencies, statute halls and *bureaux d'adress* of late medieval and early modern Europe.[24] Like some of these, they combined a number of functions; naka-yado, for example, sometimes doubled as wedding halls or cheap overnight lodgings. Like European agencies, they were closely supervised by the authorities, the objects of numerous laws. First officially recognized in Edo during the Genna period (1615–24), they were charged with ascertaining their clients' backgrounds;[25] later they were commanded to ensure the observance of maximum-wage laws and sumptuary provisions dealing with servants.

In 1730 an edict issued in Edo ordered all employment agencies (*hito-yado*) to form associations (*kumiai*) of thirty to forty establishments each. The regime plainly hoped this reorganization would allow for more thorough supervision of the agencies, which were accused of overcharging employers and colluding with servants who absconded.[26]

The Numano maidservant wage notebook gives us a rough idea of how employment agencies functioned in Wakayama in the mid-nineteenth century. Of the eighty-four maidservants listed therein, fifty-nine are recorded as having been hired through kuchiire. The household had dealings with at least six such agencies in the castle-town, but did the bulk of their business with two: Okinu (nineteen hires or 32%) and Tsuchino (twenty-one hires or 36%). Most of the maidservants hired through these agents were new arrivals from the countryside, although a handful were from families residing in the city. The agencies do not appear to have operated on a geographical basis but handled clients irrespective of their place of origin.[27]

The first step in the placement process was the *omemie* or personal interview.[28] Accompanied by a surety plus hito-yado representatives, the applicant would visit a prospective master's house and meet with the potential employer. Females would typically be greeted by the mistress, males by the master. If both parties found the situation promising, the applicant would put in a day or several days' work, retiring to the employment agency in the evening.

The trial period could be an eye-opener for either party. In an amusing tale by Saikaku, a household gives two applicants for a parlormaid position a one-day trial run to determine which of the girls would be more suitable. As it turns out, the homelier of the two is a skilled calligrapher, seamstress and koto-player, while the prettier candidate, favored at first, is not only ignorant of simple kitchen utensils and unable to act as partner to a card game, but is slightly deaf and subject to seizures. She is, of course, sent on her way while the other gets the job.[29]

Apparently none of the Numano maid-applicants were rejected so expeditiously, although most went through a trial workday or two. This, at least, seems the only plausible explanation for such references as the following: "Sawa, twenty-four years old this year. Came twenty-fourth day, seventh month. Can sew, too. Stayed from the evening of the twenty-sixth." Once the decision to employ had been made, both parties would enjoy a cup of sake—the traditional rite sealing a bond of retainership or discipleship—and a commission would be handed over to the employment agency.

In the Numano case, commissions always appear to have been paid at from 3 to 10 percent of the yearly wage recorded in the notebook (and probably specified contractually). Saikaku's account implies that in Genroku Osaka the commission was 10 percent, and exacted from the maid's advance wages (maegane) along with the hito-yado bill for room and board. In Wakayama, a century and a half later, the Numano household usually paid one-third of the commission payment while demanding that the new employee pay the difference. Probably the sum was handed over by the Numano mistress and then recorded as an advance on the servant's wages.

If a servant absconded, the employment agency serving as guarantor was responsible for recompensing the employer for the commission and advance payments. Takizawa Bakin, the famed novelist (1767–1848), provides an example in his diary. In Tenpō 2 (1831, a year in which Bakin dismissed and replaced no fewer than seven servants) he records the following: "Maidservant (yatoi-gejo) Masa has still not returned home tonight. A truly bad person, becoming an irritation. No limits to her misbehavior." He records further that his wife has contacted the employment agency, securing her refund within one day, along with a promise to arrange an interview with a new candidate after three days.[30]

IDEALS AND REALITIES OF THE MASTER-SERVANT RELATIONSHIP

Thus guarantors of various types mediated the master-servant relationship, introducing the parties to one another and helping to reduce the risks involved on both sides. Most assisted servants newly arriving in towns and cities by providing lodging and counseling. As noted, some employment agencies might conspire with servant clients to deceive and bilk employers, but for the most part, the employment agency system worked to the masters' advantage. For example, given servants' legal inequality with their masters, it was far more likely that a hito-yado would grant a master satisfaction upon the abscondence of his servant than provide a wronged employee with support.

Even so, despite ties with sureties and under-sureties, servants were generally free agents, and the experience they underwent in service had far more to do with their personal interaction with their masters than with their obligations to these third parties. Such interaction could be positive and affectionate, negative and hostile, or merely indifferent.

Ideal master-servant relationships were described in law codes, and public notices, prescribed in sermons, household codes and didactic tracts, and celebrated in popular fiction. All of these treated the service relationship as a component of the entire polity, hardly less essential to its smooth operation than correct parent-child relations. Fidelity and obedience to parents and masters were specifically demanded by law, and regarded as expressions of loyalty to the regime. Moreover, just as the Tokugawa state theoretically responded to the masses' obedience with policies of "benevolent government" (jinsei), so masters were exhorted to compensate employees with fatherly humanity. Public posters (takafuda) in Edo, for example, stressed obedience and kindness as the virtues of servant and master respectively.[31]

"The master is a man, and so is the servant."[32] The conviction was ingrained in the popular consciousness. When the clerk Tokubei, in Chikamatsu's Sonezaki shinjū (1703), resisted his master's attempt to arrange his marriage with the declaration, "I too am a man!" the theater audience would have responded sympathetically.[33] So too, readers of Ishida Baigan's Tōhi Mondō (1739) would have nodded approval at his statement that an employer who squanders his shop's profits, which "the clerks earn by the sweat of their brows," in effect sucks his workers' blood.[34] Itō Jinsai's Yamato-zokukun stresses not merely loyalty but "just dealing" in master-servant relations, as duties owed to Heaven.[35] Many employers no doubt took such advice to heart; some even sought their employees' advice and tolerated their remonstrances. Maruyama Masao refers to a pre-Tokugawa tradition "which required the loyal servant to be his own judge of what was really in his lord's interest," just as the conscientious minister was expected to chastise an errant sovereign.[36]

Mitsui Takafusa's Chōnin kōken roku (ca. 1730), translated by E. S. Crawcour as "Some Observations on Merchants," favorably mentions such servants as Hanshichi, a clerk in the household of Yodoya Tatsugorō which had fallen into ruin a generation before. Hanshichi had tried in vain to discourage Tatsugorō's spendthrift habits, even risking his own dismissal to save the business. Mitsui depicts Tatsugorō's fall as the result, not only of his dissolute habits, but his underhanded attempt to get rid of his honest clerk. Hanshichi, Takafusa declares, "was an outstanding example of the old saying, 'Serve no one but the right man.' "[37]

Popular literature offers many examples of servants who respectfully took their masters to task when circumstances required. "The faithful servant whose warnings go unheeded" is a stock character in the writings of Ejima Kiseki.[38] One of the epistles in Saikaku's posthumously published *Yorozu no fumihōgu* (*A Miscellany of Old Letters*) is addressed by nine clerks to their former employer who has retired into the religious life. They profusely apologize for interrupting his retreat, but implore him to return home if only for one evening in order to chastise his son, their current master, whose profligate ways threaten the welfare of the household.[39]

In return for conscientious service, servants had a claim to the master's respect and even affection. As in Old Regime France, where a "patriarchal theory of the household" implied that servants were the "adopted children" of the master, in Tokugawa Japan master-servant relations were ideally modeled after family relationships.[40] The Mitsui house code (*kahō*) of 1722 counsels the company head to treat the servants "like a real father" would (*jitsu no oya gotoku*).[41] (Sons, meanwhile, were during their youth to "be treated like any other employee."[42]) But paternalism could be a double-edged sword; if it allowed the servant some claim to the master's affectionate regard, it also obliged him to shoulder the burdens of the parent-child relationship. In a society that recognized the right of a family head to administer corporal punishment to wife and children,[43] few would dispute his right to beat an employee.

Legally, too, this putative family relationship had its drawbacks. Whereas masters could unilaterally cancel an employment contract, servants did not enjoy this right.[44] The act of filing suit against an employer was seen not only as a serious breach of propriety but as an example of unfilial conduct. Regulations concerning lawsuits issued to Edo commoners in 1633 flatly state that, "Any dispute (*kuji*) arising between a master and his servants (*kaboku*) must, of course, be judged in favor of the master." (The added caveat that, "if the master is found to be culpable in certain respects, then judgement may be rendered in accordance with reason," allows some judicial flexibility but hardly affects the servant's disadvantaged position.)[45] A servant's very action of filing suit invited danger. Other regulations promulgated in 1655 specify the following:

> In suits between townsmen and their servants [*kenin*], those who submit complaints and go to trial do not understand the proprieties of the master and servant relationship [*shujū no rei shirazu*]. When the servant is at fault, he will be imprisoned. Furthermore the complaint is a matter to be entrusted to the master's discretion.[46]

While servants were also at a profound legal disadvantage in early modern Europe, the nature of their handicap was somewhat different than in Japan. Courts in France generally took the word of masters over that of domestics in master-servant disputes, on the premise that masters (fellow gentlemen as were the judges themselves) would not lie. Nevertheless, the act of filing suit was not a criminal action in itself, and was in fact used as a device for servants to publicly embarrass their masters.[47]

Literary and legal evidence thus suggests that servants, while partly shielded from abuses by a humanitarian social ethic, were afforded little official protection. Since they fell under the master's jurisdiction, they were presumed to have no business approaching magistrates with their grievances.[48] The *Osadamegaki*, the definitive law code of the latter Tokugawa period, drawn up under the shogun Yoshimune and issued in 1742, reconfirmed the impropriety of suits against masters or parents, adding that servants falsely accusing masters were to be crucified. Article 65 of this code, however, adds two important qualifications. One was that where suits against masters involved "serious matters affecting the public good" (*kōgi e kakari sōrō omoki shina*) officials might give them a hearing. The other was that, where a preliminary investigation indicated the master guilty of wrongdoing, samurai officials, while not trying the case themselves, might instruct local personalities and leaders to arbitrate the dispute:

> When a master or parent is at fault and the subordinate pleads hardship and requests relief, the headman, five-man group and relatives will be summoned and entrusted to satisfactorily dispose of the matter.[49]

This greater leniency towards servants' suits indicates a growing stress upon "conciliation" in law over the course of the Tokugawa period.

Naturally, the repeated issuance of such laws indicates that servants did, in fact, resort to the courts to resolve disputes with their masters. One semi-fantastic case is recorded in the *Ōoka seidan*, an eighteenth-century work of unknown authorship which celebrates the decisions of Ōoka Tadatsune, a famous *machi-bugyō* in Edo from 1717 to 1736. A certain Yagorō, who worked as a clerk in a dry goods shop, was falsely accused by his master of stealing a load of cotton cloth, and "having no alternative, he went to the town court for help." But the tale, which involves the possibility that a statue of Jizō Bosatsu stole the cloth while Yagorō was sleeping, is plainly entertaining fiction.[50]

Servants convicted of attacking or killing their masters, whatever their reasons, faced the most horrible retribution Tokugawa authorities could devise. Of all crimes, the killing of one's master (*shugoroshi*), was regarded as most heinous.[51] For this offense the regime reserved its most tortuous form of punishment: execution by the slow sawing off of one's head by a bamboo saw (*nokogiribiki*). The *Osadamegaki* prescribe the following punishments for violence against masters:

> Killing of one's master: expose for two days in public, then parade about in public for one day. Saw off the head, then crucify [the headless corpse].
> Wounding one's master: expose in public, then crucify.
> Cutting or striking one's master: death.
> Killing one's former master: expose in public, then crucify.
> Wounding one's former master: parade around in public, then crucify.
> Cutting or striking one's former master: death.[52]

Clearly these punishments, including the humiliations imposed upon the offending servant's corpse, were designed to impress upon the living the grave nature of crimes against the ruling class as a whole. But the manner of retribution was by no means extreme by world standards of the time.[53]

Disadvantaged by the class-biased nature of Tokugawa law, servants also suffered from their inclusion in the corporate responsibility system. This dictated that the household and "joint-responsibility group" (*goningumi*) of an offender shared the blame with the offender himself. When, for example, Takeda Kōunsai, one of the samurai leaders of the Tengu rebellion in Mito, was beheaded in 1865, all of his dependents followed him to the grave. Not only were his wife and infant children executed, but his nineteen-year-old maidservant Kome was beheaded and cast into the river.[54]

However unequal the master-servant relationship, many servants seem to have genuinely loved their employers. The great samurai scholar Arai Hakuseki (1656–1725) recorded that in his early career as a teacher in Edo his two servants refused to leave him and his wife, despite their poverty.

> I did not have the means to support the one man-servant and one maid we kept, but when I told them they must do whatever they thought best, they said that they would work at anything, even if not used to it, and so keep themselves, for they did not want to part from us.[55]

There are many documented instances of servants risking their lives for their masters or mistresses. In one famous case, a fourteen-year-old maidservant of a high-ranking attendant in the Edo mansion of the Suō daimyo attacked and stabbed to death another lady-in-waiting who had humiliated her own mistress into suicide. The daimyo, Matsudaira Yasutoyo, was so moved by the avenger's loyalty that he rewarded her with a dowry. This incident occured in 1723, and was immortalized by the kabuki drama *Kagamiyama Kokyo no Nishikie* (or popularly, *Onna Chūshingura*) written half a century later. (This fictionalized account, however, takes place in the Kaga daimyo's mansion. Playwrights were forbidden by law to stage true-to-life accounts of contemporary events.)[56]

Such behavior, it might be argued, reflects a feudal concept of loyalty more than "affection," or, as the contradiction has been phrased, "cold duty" rather than "warm duty." Indeed, the sacrifice of one's life for one's master—loved or unloved, virtuous or undeserving—was held up as the samurai ideal. Yamamoto Tsunetomo's *Hagakure* vividly reflects this value: "The way of the samurai (*bushidō*) is found in death."[57] But as objects of the death wish of samurai-household servants, love and loyalty might run into conflict. Yamamoto approvingly quoted one Edoyoshi Saburōzaemon, who suggested that the homosexuality widespread among the samurai, idealized in the *shudō* concept, was "both pleasant and unpleasant": pleasant in that it provided the opportunity to die joyfully for one's *comrade*, but unpleasant in that, once dead, one could never give one's life for one's *master*.[58]

Both samurai and commoner masters, for their part, could show benevolence towards their servants. Arai recorded in his autobiography how his father, a retainer of the Kazusa daimyo, dressed his own hair and abstained from warm water baths until late in life "so as to spare the servants trouble."[59] The religious reformer Ishida Baigan (1685–1744), according to the *Ishida sensei jiseki*, was saddled with a useless manservant by well-meaning disciples. "He did not even know how to tie his own *obi*," reads the account, "so our teacher tied it for him. Moreover, in cold weather his feet ached with cracks and sores. Our teacher felt sorry for him and said, 'I will bundle them up for you.' "[60] Arai's father and Ishida may have been men of uncommon moral qualities, and their behavior may have been exceptional. Nevertheless, even so cantankerous a master as Takizawa Bakin, whose diary is filled with venomous comments about his servants, postponed a family celebration when he learned that the infant of his maidservant Okane, who had been sent out to nurse, had died.[61] A particularly kind and indulgent attitude towards servants is reflected in such Meiji works as Sugimoto Etsu's *Daughter of the Samurai*.[62]

Naturally it was in the master's best interest to cultivate warm relations with the servants. The *Hagakure* points out that in-servants should be encouraged by frequent praise.

> If you tell your live-in servants [*kumi hikan*], "Well, you're working hard!" or "That's the hardest chore," or "Here's an old hand," not just [on exceptional occasions] when it's natural to do so, but on ordinary occasions as well, they will devote themselves to you all the more. A single word can be most important.[63]

More than words, perhaps, gifts might win loyalty and affection. But such gestures were not always made with an underlying motive; when servants leaving the household were favored, the presents symbolized the employers' genuine regard. The mistress of the Numano household developed intimate ties to some of her employees, including a parlor-maid named Toyo who, after working only six months, married the shopclerk Jinbei. Showering the couple with gifts, the pawnbroker's wife recorded that "both parties are glad to have her leave in such happy circumstances."[64]

Examples of close master-servant ties are abundant in the records of the loyalty awards mentioned in the previous chapter. Just as in prerevolutionary France, various individuals and societies established prizes to reward faithful servants, while the English Parliament also flirted with such ideas.[65] In Japan, the shogunate awarded cash gifts (*hyōshō*) to commoners commendable on various grounds: charity (*kitoku*), loyalty (*chū-gi*), filial piety (*kōkō*), loyalty and filial piety (*chūkō*), chastity (*teisetsu*), brotherly devotion (*kyōdaimutsubi*), and purity (*keppaku*). The records of such commendations, published for the edification of society, include numerous cases involving servants and provide us with some insights concerning master-servant relations at their most ideal.

A dozen sources survive, officially or privately compiled, describing these awards. The most substantial is the first such work, *Kōgiroku*, compiled on the orders of the rojū (Senior Councillor) Matsudaira Sadanobu, published in 1789. A supplementary volume, updating the record to 1789, was issued in 1801. These two records contain brief descriptions of 8,614 grants awarded between 1602 and 1798, and give details about the meritorious deeds in 894 cases.

Based on these and later sources, Ikegami Akihiko has produced a chart showing the 309 recorded awards bestowed upon Edo commoners between 1716 and 1843.[66] Thirty-three of these were given to people described as servants (*hōkōnin*). The figure probably approximates the servant proportion in society. The awards for loyalty and loyalty/filial piety, however, generally went to servants: thirty-one out of forty-one (75.6%) went to this class, for whom loyalty—in theory—came with the profession.

Maidservant recipients, however, were under-represented. As noted earlier, only two of the thirty-three Edo servants awarded prizes between 1735 and 1843 were listed as *gejo*. (One of these, an Asakusa centenarian named Some, received her prize for charity rather than loyalty.) From the late eighteenth century through the Bakumatsu period, live-in maidservants at samurai and commoner mansions in Edo received fewer awards than other lower-class women such as hired laundresses, hired seamstresses, piecework laborers and day laborers.[67]

The awards were bestowed, and the deeds recorded, to move others to similar acts of virtue. Who could fail to honor Mansuke, the manservant of physician Yasunaka Masuo, a tenant living in Higashi Nakachō in

Asakusa? In 1735, at the age of forty-two, he was awarded a prize (sum unrecorded) for thirty-three years of loyal service. Noteworthy among his virtuous deeds was his evening employment as a palanquin-bearer to help support his aged master. The latter was eighty years old in the year of the grant.[68]

In other cities administered by the shogunate, as well as in the various domains, similar awards were established to encourage virtuous conduct. One such prize, amounting to ten silver coins, was bestowed upon a twenty-nine-year-old servant in Osaka in 1792. Chōbei had rendered exemplary service to his master Yamamotoya Gihei, as the text of the award describes:

> Tenma Kitamorichō. *Servant of Yamamotoya Gihei,*
> *Chōbei, age twenty-nine*

> Chōbei [began] service with Gihei at age twelve [on a] ten-year [contract]. Losing both his parents, he gradually grew to adulthood, performing his service in extremely diligent fashion. He worked every day, from before dawn until after dusk. When, during this past Year of the Serpent, the rice-price rose, his master Gihei's lot was difficult. Realizing the hardship, [Chōbei] himself economized discreetly, in order not to arouse Gihei's concern, and managing all the household affairs by himself, was able to safely tide over [their difficulties].

> Then, when Gihei's elderly father Kinzō was ill, [Chōbei] visited the Konpira Gongen at Masazumi Temple in Tenma Nishideracho one hundred times, earnestly praying [on Kinzō's behalf] and Kinzō recovered from his illness. After that, while Gihei was away in Edo and Kinzō fell ill again, Chōbei exerted himself with great sincerity to [procure] medicine and food and also nursed [Kinzō]. He also, of course, managed the business by himself every day. In addition, when both Kinzō and Gihei were off in Edo, and [Gihei's] younger brother Kanbei went insane, Chōbei nursed him while managing other affairs as well, maintaining [the business] without incident in [their] absence. When this Kanbei later died of his derangement, on the memorial days Chōbei invariably performed the memorial rites.

> Then a year ago, when it was time for Gihei to welcome his [new] wife Soyo, Chōbei was asked why his clothing was so shabby. Since [Gihei's] marriage to Soyo was to take place very soon, [Chōbei's appearance was inappropriate]. Chōbei replied that he had loaned money to his own relatives [pawning his better clothing?], glossing over his master's financial distress as though he knew nothing about it. [He had] performed many charitable deeds.

> Beginning with the husband and wife, Gihei and Soyo, all the people of the neighborhood and ward came to admire these acts of selflessness. Thus, not forgetting his profound obligations [to those who had] raised him from childhood, performing his service diligently, rallying his master's household

out of its distress, seeking its commercial prosperity in everything and thinking of the continuation of the house name, throwing himself into his work
day after day, with no ambitions for his own future, in all things quietly
working only for his master Gihei's sake, he merits commendation.

Since his fame has reached Edo, and since he is a particularly charitable
person, it is ordered that he receive ten pieces of white silver as an award. Let
the content of the above be told throughout the wards of the Three Districts
[of Osaka], as a lesson to disloyal and unfilial persons.[69]

(Kansei 4, Year of the Rat, Fifth Month, Sixth Day)

The closing words clearly state the didactic goal of such awards.

Servants might also win Imperial Grants (*kashi*) for loyalty from the
emperor's court in Kyoto. In the third month of 1726, for instance, the
manservant of an Asakusa rice warehouse clerk received 258 hyō of residential land, and in 1755 one Yasuke, manservant of the Edo townsman
Shihei, received fifty copper mon for his devotion to his master.[70]

Western scholars have made extensive use of wills in discussing master-
servant relations in Europe. Few Edo-period wills (*yuigon*) survive, so
they do not provide a comparable data-base, but some examples of servants as legatees survive. In 1636, the daimyo of Iida, Hori Chikayoshi,
instructed that upon his death sums ranging from ten to two hundred ryō
were to be distributed to the retainers of his household. These would
probably have included domestics.[71] Testaments drawn up by Mitsui
branch heads (*bekke tedai*) show that merchants might also be generous.
Yoshisaki Shinjirō of the main Kyoto shop specified in his will, dated
1750, that each of his four clerks was to receive ten silver pieces upon his
death.[72] Saikaku, as usual, provides fictional illustrations of contemporary practice; in one of his stories, a Kyoto merchant bequeaths two hundred kanme silver to his son, twenty to his wife, and ten each to all his
servants.[73]

Sometimes these bequests were earmarked for business purposes, "entrusted" to the recipient rather than given. Thus Katō Michiki, of Mitsui's main Kyoto shop, willed in 1744 that upon his death, ten kanme
silver be turned over to Shōji Jingorō and two hundred silver pieces to
Fukumi Shōbei. Both of these men were clerks at the Osaka shop, and the
funds were to be delivered "as capital" (*motode toshite*). Other grants of
money, however, were clearly designed as a reward for service rather than
as means to continue in business. The same document stipulates that both
Densuke, meshitsukai in the kitchen of the Kyoto establishment, and the
"young woman Toyo" who worked as a wet-nurse, were to receive ten
ryō in gold. Toyo, the text notes, has performed various services in the
kitchen aside from her other duties.[74]

Homes were only infrequently willed to employees, although such instances may have increased during the eighteenth century. Yasuoka Shigeaki has studied 220 cases of home inheritance in Kyoto's Kannonyama ward during that century, and his evidence shows that whereas only three of 121 cases (2.5%) involved a bequest to clerks or branch heads from 1700 to 1750, eight of ninety-nine (8.1%) involved such employees from 1751 to 1800. Employee bequests to masters also increased, from three (2.5%) during the first half of the century, to four (4.0%) during the latter half. (This second figure includes homes willed to the master's descendents, or in one case, to a dead nephew's master.)[75]

Gaibun no	A shameful thing
warusa nyōbō to	the quarrel between
gejo no ron	mistress and maidservant[76]

At the other extreme of master-servant relationships, mutual suspicion and hostility were also much in evidence. Masters might explode at employees they deemed lazy; mistresses, chafing at their own subordination to harsh mothers-in-law, might vent their frustrations upon their maids; employees, nurturing real or imagined injuries, might respond by petty theft, physical violence or arson.

An interesting document from Tochigi village, Shirakawa-gun, in the Takata han (Echigo), reveals some of the problems servants posed for their masters. It alludes, of course, to rural life, but the conditions it reveals—aside from the third point—probably resemble those in the cities. In 1754 a wealthy peasant named Oshō Nemoto Hachiemon Hidekage obliged his eight manservants and four maidservants to take a series of "Religious Vows for Manservants and Maidservants," which included the following:

1. Holding the Master in high regard, we will not be slipshod in our work.
2. We will not form factions.
3. We will scrupulously attend to the harvest.
4. We will not waste brush and firewood.
5. We will pass along any rumors to the Master.
6. We will practice solid morals, so as not to cause the Master trouble.
7. We will not fight or argue.[77]

The list indicates, of course, that laziness, clique formation, wastefulness, rumor-mongering, immorality, fighting, and arguing were common problems.

The most troubling problem for masters was naturally servant violence—particularly violence directed against them. We do not know how many masters were attacked or murdered by their servants during the Tokugawa period. To slay one's master was, with parricide, the ultimate crime, punishable by exposure followed by crucifixion, but many surviving records identify servants who risked this fate. Shina, the maidservant-mistress of an unemployed samurai (rōnin) named Yoshitomo, of Edo's Bakurōmachi San-chōme, conspired with Yoshitomo's manservant Chōsuke in the first month of 1675. Together they strangled the rōnin, but the crime being discovered, Chōsuke was paraded through the streets, then exposed at Nihonbashi for three days before his crucifixion in Asakusa. At her trial, Shina showed signs of contrition, producing a small knife and attempting to slit her own throat; after some days in prison she, too, was crucified.[78] The Hagakure records several such murder attempts.[79]

Servants of commoners were equally apt to attack their employers. In 1690, a certain Sōzaemon of Saiōjichō in Edo scolded his manservant, who thereafter attacked him in resentment. As punishment, the servant was exposed at Nihonbashi for three days before being crucified in Shinagawa; meanwhile, in accordance with the doctrine of collective responsibility, the heads of his father and brother were displayed above a prison gate.[80]

There are, however, indications that employer violence against employees also entailed serious legal risks. In his Tōhi mondō, Ishida Baigan records a conversation with a merchant who confesses that he has a short temper. This flaw, however, has created problems only once: "when I struck a negligent shop-boy. He was hurt and cried out with the pain. I calmed him but he said he wanted to go home despite his unhealed wound. That caused my parents and the clerks a great deal of trouble." The merchant, indeed, as a filial son, seems more concerned about his parents' reaction to the incident than about the shop-boy's pain.

Their concern is with the law, as Baigan observes: "Think how your parents felt as the shop-boy was bleeding after your blow. They feared not only for his injury but for you too, lest you be executed if the worst happened to him. . . . If the shop-boy had died on the spot, you might have received a death sentence."[81]

An incident in Osaka's Kikuyachō in 1770 also suggests that violence against a servant resulting in serious injury would be punished. The following report was filed on the ninth day of the fourth lunar month, Meiwa 7, by Tanbaya Sōshichi, a tenant of Fukushimaya Tōsuke:

> I have a nineteen-year old maidservant named Soyo. Recently she has had a convulsive disorder, and sometimes has had seizures. Today at around the fourth hour, seeing her aiming a dagger at her throat, I quickly wrested it from her. Examining her, I found a cut of one or two bu, bleeding just slightly. Therefore I called a physician and he treated her. Since there was a bit of a wound, I accordingly reported [the matter].[82]

Why did Sōshichi bother reporting the incident? The attached documents make it clear. On the same day, two officials, from the East and West City Commissioners, come to verify the facts. They interview the physician involved, record his statement, and then interview Soyo herself. "I have done this to myself," she confirms, "and hold a grudge towards no one." She had gone upstairs, then lost consciousness, and remembers nothing except someone taking the knife from her. The officials specifically inquire whether she might be lying; whether her master had not, perhaps, chastised her (and, one surmises, provoked the suicide attempt), but Soyo denies this and asserts that she wants to continue serving in that house. (No doubt the incident left an unpleasant taste in Sōshichi's mouth; the census registers show that Soyo was dismissed later that year.)

Even the members of the samurai class, who according to the *Legacy of Ieyasu* might strike down a commoner for any "impropriety," were in practice held accountable for unreasonable treatment of their servants. Thus in one case, in Edo in 1703, a bannerman was ordered to commit suicide after having killed two maidservants with his own hand.[83] The *Hagakure* mentions a samurai beheaded for ordering a retainer to slay a manservant during a drinking spree.[84] In Kanazawa in 1664 a ranking samurai was exiled for having slain his maidservant-mistress, even though the action was in self-defense.[85]

Servants nurturing resentments towards their masters had other outlets aside from direct violence. Arson as a lower-class crime was much in vogue; in 1722–23 alone, 101 Edo laborers and vagrants were arrested for this offense, and numerous cases of fires set by servants are on record.[86] Many maidservant incendiaries are on record,[87] and even Tokugawa Ieyasu's life was threatened by a fire which, investigators concluded, had been deliberately set in his Sunpu castle by two maidservants. The latter were naturally burned at the stake.[88]

Theft was another common problem, and in some cases served as a means of evening the score with a despised master. The Numano notebook includes a case of a maidservant dismissed for stealing an apron, and literary evidence attests to masters' fear of servant pilfering.[89] Ishida Baigan rhetorically inquired how spendthrift employers could blame their clerks for embezzling.[90] Samurai households were not immune, either. A teenage page (koshō) in the retinue of Saga daimyo Mitsushige (1632–1700) stole a spear from one of the daimyo's retainers and pawned it in order to buy the sexual services of the famous actor Tamon Shōzaemon. Mitsushige had him decapitated.[91]

A dissatisfied servant might even resort to malicious sabotage. A fictional account in *Saikaku Oritome* so sensitively depicts master-servant psychology that it warrants quoting at length:

Then there's the irritable housewife who can't let the slightest thing pass without getting upset. "There's a surplus of scullery maids this summer," she tells her daughter. "I noticed one crying in the rain, wearing an apron over her head [i.e., too poor to afford an umbrella]. Life is so miserable down there in Harima [due to famine] that girls just right for service come crawling out, pleading, 'Just feed me [i.e., they will work for room and board alone]!' You can't find better ones for weaving cloth, operating a grain-hulling mortar, baby-sitting or chopping firewood.

"Those saucy ones who've been drinking the water all over Osaka—whose right hands are scarred from holding the ladle handle—who'll hire them? Such girls will sell their last kimono just to get by, and wind up the type of women who sing night-songs and stroll around in a daze!"

The maidservant listens passively as her mistress makes these spiteful insinuations, then takes the poker to the ears of the kitchen cat.

"Your ears have a function, too," she says, "so you'd better listen, even though this won't be pleasant. The only reason you're employed here—allowed to eat and play all year long—is so that you'll catch mice for them. So long as you don't run off with the dried bonito, you have nothing to fear. If you don't satisfy them, or if they throw something and hit you, you can always seek refuge in one of those huge houses in Kitahama or Naka-noshima. There are houses where they have guests every day and can't find space to discard the wild-goose guts and carp entrails!

"You wear the livery you were born in, so you're just a servant in that they feed you! Talk about fish! All you ask is to sniff the horse-mackeral—the kind they buy in crates of eighty or so—while it fries.

"To whom do you owe your introduction here, anyway? There are ten thousand other houses like this, so you're really not so fortunate to be here after all!"

She makes these insinuations in response to her mistress's [remarks], and afterwards the two are on one another's nerves day in and day out.

"You can't win against masters and illness," says the mistress angrily. "So from now on, even though you object, you won't go to bed so early, but polish the cauldrons and dice the dried greens. You're a good one for such menial chores. Now get busy and mend that tear in the mosquito netting!"

"Even if I just work here one more day," replies the girl, "go ahead and drive me as hard as you like! So long as I'm working, you'll be satisfied!"

But behold the trail of destruction she leaves behind: there are cracks in the big pot, and none of the lathework trays are left intact. The neck of the vinegar bottle is broken, the edging on the nest of boxes has been peeled off, the parasol has been thrown under the verandah, the leather-soled sandals have been hurled up onto the bathhouse roof—and aside from these, the master suffers losses in ways he doesn't even notice.

It's a fact: the lower classes are vulgar, and she who can employ them skillfully is an intelligent mistress.[92]

Despite the concluding sentence, Saikaku's sympathy seems to be more with the maidservant, who expresses her hurt feelings while tormenting the cat, and finds her revenge in malicious destruction, rather than with the callous mistress.

Another fictional account, penned by Takizawa Bakin about 120 years after this, conveys little sympathy for the servant's position but nevertheless, like Saikaku's story, depicts the loneliness and alienation of the child-servant.[93] A spoiled young boy has been placed in an apprenticeship in a merchant household in his hometown. Permitted two holidays per year, he also drops by his parents' house while on errands for his master. As his doting mother welcomes him with special foods, declaring that his master is not feeding him well enough, he begins to complain that his fellow shop-boys bully him, the head clerk physically abuses him, and the mistress forces him to peel radishes.

"That," his mother angrily declares, "was something never mentioned in his contract!" When the boy complains that, while drawing the well water, he slipped on the well planks and bruised his knees, the mother orders her somewhat dubious husband to request cancellation of the indenture contract. In fact, Bakin explains, the boy's knee injuries were acquired while wrestling in a bath house, and the employer was no monster but "a painstaking master who, quite aware of the youth's propensity to cheat him out of the price of many a feast was fondly hoping that time might improve him."

The problematic relationship between nurses and employers deserves special mention. The foul reputation of these servants is perhaps universal.[94] "The most ill-tempered people," went the Japanese proverb, "are packhorse drivers, ship captains, and wet nurses."[95] It was, no doubt, an ill-temper born of misfortune. Stories in both *Seken munezanyo* and *Saikaku oritome* describe how impoverished couples, unable to make ends meet or repay debts, tearfully decide to separate so that the wife can work as a wet nurse.

> When you look at the people who take up employment as wet nurses these days, they are generally either people whose marriages have broken up, or servant girls who, unable to get boyfriends, go chasing after men [and get pregnant]. Eventually they bear the children in an employment hostel, abandon them and—as luck would have it—able to produce milk, work as wet nurses.[96]

Neither type was likely to be very happy in the new job, and a young girl was particularly unlikely to know the first thing about childcare. Worse, nurses aware of their inadequate milk supply might purposely defraud employers. In the same Saikaku story a woman applies for a nursing job, saying she has recently given birth. When only a little milk is forthcoming, she lies that she has quarreled with her husband during the last few days and has not had much to eat. The kind matron signs her on anyway, assuring her that some solid meals will bring the milk flowing again.

She is unaware of the trap being laid and decides on the contract, lending the whole salary in advance, and the woman's precious baby has to suck the nurse's inadequate milk all night long.

The mother, considering the problem, says, "I don't understand the reason for this."

"It must have something to do with the fact that I'm not related to your child. Since the milk won't come gushing out like a water-fall, please hire someone else to replace me. My husband has already used the advance on my salary to purchase a divorce document."

Saying all sorts of contradictory things, she annoys [her employers] miserably. She goes about deceiving tens of households by the same means. The collaboration of her guarantor is also thoroughly despicable![97]

Of all crimes committed by servants, running away was apparently most common. A record from Tsushima, entitled *Toganinchō* (Criminal Register) survives, providing a list of fifty-five servants (genan and gejo) apprehended between 1680 and 1698. The law-breakers were nearly all from Osaka or the Kyoto area, working on ten-year contracts in the castle-town. A range of offenses are recorded in the document, including adultery, murder, and unspecified misdemeanors, but over 40 percent were arrested on the charges of absconding, abetting, planning or leading attempts to abscond.[98]

In Edo, meanwhile, where samurai-household manservants enjoyed a particularly unfavorable reputation, the City Commissioners' (*Machibugyō*) Office was flooded with suits concerning runaway valets. Six hundred complaints were filed in 1718, and 517 the following year.[99] Since wages for this profession were traditionally prepaid, professional con-artists might swindle a number of households. Ogyū Sorai, as already noted, complained that many conspired in such crimes with their guarantors, but since the injured households sought to avoid embarrassment, most employers were inclined to let the matter drop, so long as they were able to receive a refund of the advance wages. They would be particularly disinclined to pursue the matter if they discovered that the departed servant had found employment in a higher-ranking household.[100] The suits filed with the City Commissioners therefore understate the actual incidence of abscondence.

Runaway servants often committed theft or sabotage as they fled. Four of the Tsushima runaways were also charged with theft. (Two, who had committed murder as well, were punished by crucifixion.) The Numano household also occasionally suffered loss. An entry for Kōka 2 (1845) in the notebook refers to an absent parlormaid:

Kiyo requested a bit of time off to return home, from the second day of the tenth month of the Year of the Serpent. We allowed her to return home, but when she wickedly stayed away as late as the twenty-third, I checked her clothes and personal effects and found that she had removed almost everything.[101]

Among the surviving Kikuyachō documents is an official report made in Kaei 2 (1849) concerning one Teisuke, a servant of the Kawachiya paper shop, who absconded with shop funds (*shōhindai*). Arrested, he apparently won his master's forgiveness after his parents offered restitution of the loss.[102] In kabuki plots, too, the runaways typically make off with funds for the road.[103]

If master-servant relationships were inherently problematic, threatening to erupt into violence, the presence of servants could also exacerbate intrafamily conflicts, or provide wayward wives and children with accomplices.[104] Kaibara Ekken (1630–1714) wrote in his widely read *Onna Daigaku* (*The Great Learning for Women*) that a wife, who "lives like a stranger in her husband's home, is easily influenced to have an ill-feeling or ingratitude" and is particularly vulnerable to the damaging influences of her maids:

She should never believe her maid's words at the cost of the affection of her own father-, mother-, and sister-in-law. Any maid who is found to be talkative and vicious must soon be discharged, for she will only do mischief by carrying tales among her mistress' relatives and disturb the peace of her home. Thus care should be exercised in the employment of a maid.[105]

Ishida Baigan mentions problems involving sons and male employees. Shopclerks, for example, might agree to conceal the pleasure-quarter outings of the son of a merchant house, in return for tips.[106] In many ways servants might contribute to tensions among family members while jockeying to advance their own positions. Conflicts among servants themselves, meanwhile, often disrupted the harmony of the household. The Numano notebook provides many examples. The fact that in many cases both nominal and confidential wages were recorded suggests that the mistress feared maidservant jealousies concerning income. Specific instances of friction, such as the following, also appear:

Kōka 1: We had planned to give [chambermaid Tsune] another extension, but since she says she is not getting along with Suma, and asks to be dismissed, it seems she will return home.

Ansei 4, 7th month: The said [chambermaid] Sawa is extremely serviceable, but she is spiteful. She torments the parlormaids, nursemaids and scullery-maids about everything, and quarrels with all the shop-hands. She is greedy, and even though she has been with us for three years, there is no one who doesn't hate her. [Sawa is soon dismissed after telling "a big lie."]

TABLE 3.2
Reasons for Departure of Numano Maidservants

9	misbehavior [*furachi*, *daifurachi*], quarrels
9	incompetence
8	illness (include 1 bad eyes, 1 scabies, 1 nervous disorder)
6	marriage
6	pregnancy
2	abscondence

Source: See Table 2.19.

Ansei 3: [Parlormaid] Yasu "quarreled with other servants and left for home."

Tenpō 12: Satsu from Kuroe was scolded about the poor quality of her cooking, then she argued with Fusa and Yoshi, quarreling about this and that. Satsu dismissed due to her ill temper.[107]

The recorded reasons for Numano maids leaving service indicate the poor quality of relations between mistress and maidservants, and among the maids themselves. In forty of eighty-four cases the reason for departure is clear (Table 3.2). Nearly half (and well over half, if we regard pregnancy as an offense) left Numano employ in unfavorable circumstances.

There is no reason to assume that male hōkōnin enjoyed better relations with their employers. Hayashi Reiko has examined 326 cases of male employment in the Shirokiya Nihonbashi (Edo) dry goods shop between 1837 and 1867, and finds the reasons for termination shown in Table 3.3.[108] More than one-fifth were either fired or fled.

These figures do not speak very well for the quality of master-servant relations. Nor do figures concerning service tenures, particularly when measured against the old fudai ideal or the common textbook description of "lifetime employment" periods spanning, for example, a genan's progress from detchi to bantō. The Numano wagebook, which records the

TABLE 3.3
Reasons for Departure of Shirokiya Employees, Nihonbashi Shop,
Edo, 1837–1867

110	"finished" (34%)
82	illness (25%)
64	death (20%)
26	dismissed (8%)
44	absconded (13%)

Source: Hayashi Reiko, "Edodana no seikatsu," in Nishiyama Matsunosuke, ed., *Edo chōnin no kenkyū*, vol. 2 (Tokyo: Yoshikawa Kōbunken, 1974) 10.

TABLE 3.4
Average Service Tenures of Numano Maidservants (Days)

chambermaids	283
parlormaids	235
scullery maids	318
nursemaids	360

Source: See Table 2.19.

hire and dismissal dates of most of the maidservants, indicates that servants in all four categories averaged terms of under a year (Table 3.4).

Osaka ward registers also tell us much about servant tenures from the early eighteenth century. They indicate that throughout that century, terms of employees in merchant houses averaged only about three years—the same as in England during the time.[109] The ninbetsuchō data on the Hiranoya household of Kikuyachō provide similar results, as shown by examining the histories of all 189 servants employed by this house between 1713 (when it appears in the register) to 1795. They are listed as gejo and genin, or very occasionally as apprentices or wet nurses. In 21 percent of the cases, the months of hire and dismissal are listed, while in the remaining cases, we can only conjecture tenures on the basis of appearance in, and disappearance from, the yearly register. Errors of some months are therefore unavoidable. Nevertheless, the results are similar: a term of 3.0 years was the average for all 189, while the 39 cases for which more exact data exists averaged 2.83 years (Table 3.5). The Hiranoya case does not appear to have been exceptional.[110]

Possibly some of these employees on one-year or relatively short terms simply sought a bit of job experience before moving on to other things. Possibly some, observing no prospect of promotion to head clerk or branch manager, requested dismissal. However, these figures suggest that

TABLE 3.5
Service Tenures of Servants in Hiranoya Household, 1713–1794

Years	All Servants (%)		Manservants (%)		Maidservants (%)	
1.9 or less	82	(43.4)	23	(36.5)	59	(46.8)
2 – 3.9	58	(30.7)	18	(28.6)	40	(31.8)
4 – 5.9	19	(10.0)	6	(9.5)	13	(10.3)
6 – 7.9	11	(5.8)	5	(7.9)	6	(4.8)
8 – (9.9)	9	(4.8)	5	(7.9)	4	(3.2)
10 or more	10	(5.3)	6	(9.5)	4	(3.2)
total	189		63		126	

Source: See Table 2.1.

servants normally did not remain in their positions long enough to build strong, sentimental bonds to their employers.

Thomas C. Smith observed that in the rural brewing industry of this period master-servant relations, while "not utterly devoid of the personal element, . . . had more of self-seeking than mutuality about them."[111] This seems to hold for urban merchant households as well. Indeed in most cases, master-servant relations were probably neither particularly warm nor hostile but simply indifferent. Some contemporary comment on the dekawari system stresses the advantages of impersonal relations with the service staff. Ogyū Sorai, while favoring a return to ancient ways, nevertheless observed that if a servant is unsatisfactory "a year is not too long to put up with him. . . . The replacement of servants every year provides a diverting change which the master enjoys."[112] A later samurai scholar, Kaiho Seiryō, expressed a far more radical opinion in his 1813 work *Keikodan* (*Lessons of the Past*). Approvingly quoting the *Shiji* (*Records of the Historian*) by Han scholar Sima Qian, he declares:

> From ancient times it has been said that the relations between lord and subject are according to the ways of the market place. A stipend is offered for the service of a retainer, and the retainer obtains rice by trading his ability to his lord. The lord is a buyer and the retainer is a seller. It is simply a business transaction, but business transactions are good, not bad. . . . Much parasitism and wasted labor have resulted from the notion that the relation between lord and subject is not a trade relationship.[113]

Ministers and coolies alike "all live in the same way"—according to "simple business arithmetic"! Surely Kaiho's view, which explicitly reduces all the revered Confucian relationships to the simple cash nexus, is exceptional in its apparent modernity, but it betrays the fact that both parties in the master-servant duo had deviated far from the ideal of loyal kindliness enunciated in house codes and bushidō homilies.

Masters employing servants for short periods of time would have little incentive to cultivate their affection, and may have had difficulty in recognizing employees as fully human. The very ubiquity of short-term servants in the wealthier households ensured that these half-strangers would share or observe many of the master's most intimate moments; servants in Saikaku's works are always overhearing their masters disporting with their wives or pages.[114] Attended by their servants in their baths, shampooed by them, massaged by them, receiving moxa treatments from their hands, masters would have had little to hide from the domestics in their employ. But this very absence of modesty in the servant's presence suggests an indifference to the latter's thoughts and feelings.

A number of practices suggest that servants were not viewed by their masters as "significant others." The habit of bestowing servant nicknames (*tsūshō*), for example, was widespread in commoners' households in Japan, just as in early modern Europe, and may reflect a similar attempt to "objectify" the servant. Such names as Gonshichi, Kyūza, Kyūshichi for men, and Tama and Rin (often preceded by the syllable 'O') for women, indicated servile status. In Edo, the names Gonsuke and Osan became virtually synonomous with manservant and maidservant, respectively.[115]

In Europe, some masters used the same name for a succession of employees. "All our footmen were called John," recalled the daughter of a Scottish laird. "My father announced firmly that he couldn't be bothered to learn a new name each time the footman changed."[116] This seems to have been the case in many Japanese households as well. The Harimaya household in Kikuyachō, for example, employed a "Shichibei" between 1728 and 1730, between 1731 and 1734, and again between 1735 and 1736. It is most likely that these were three different people. The Nakami-chiya household, meanwhile, had a servant throughout the period from 1716 to 1782. Here the record gives some specifics. "Third month [1763]. Maidservant Rin dismissed. Maidservant Rin hired." Again: "Third month [1765]. Maidservant Rin dismissed. Maidservant Rin hired."[117]

The Numano wage notebook provides further evidence of nick-naming. From Kaei 4 to Ansei 5 (1851–58), the household employed ten chambermaids. Eight of these, with only brief tenure overlap, were named Sawa (a name that does not occur even once among the sixty-two parlormaids, nursemaids, or scullery maids). Among parlormaids, three Kiku were suceeded by three Kayo from 1853 to 1856, and from 1838 to 1841, there were six named Satsu in a row. Between 1853 and 1858, nine of thirteen scullery maids were named Kiyo.

If a servant forfeited part of his identity in losing his name, he might suffer further depersonalization in having to appear in livery. European servants often regarded the wearing of livery as a demeaning experience; however elegant, it publicly reflected their servile status. Their Japanese counterparts were often dissatisfied with their raiment as well. A senryū, for example:

Itadaite	Dissatisfied
shikise no fusoku	with the livery she receives
shita wo dashi[118]	she sticks out her tongue

The head clerk in one of Saikaku's stories complains that while the manservant across the street—who has been employed three years less than he—receives clothes of Hino silk, all he gets is rough cotton. "I can't even go out in the daytime!" he declares in embarrassment.[119]

Nevertheless, these expressions of dissatisfaction seem directed at the taste (or stinginess) of individual masters, rather than to the practice of wearing livery itself. Light or navy blue was associated with servants and laborers, just as in Europe.[120] But as the protests of moralizing scholars attest, servants' clothing was often hardly distinguishable from that of their masters. There was, moreover, nothing analogous to the hated shoulder-braid that clearly betrayed the status of European servants. For samurai servants, the privilege of wearing a sword and sporting the master's family crest would have been both a source of pride and a means of intimidating commoners.

SEX AND MARRIAGE BETWEEN MASTERS AND SERVANTS

However affectionate, acrimonious or indifferent the relationships between masters and servants, they often included a sexual element. The same was true in Europe, but in Japan the links between sex, marriage, and service were less well-defined than in the West. In the Genroku period one could employ a servant expressly as a concubine (*mekake*) for up to one hundred gold ryō per year.[121] Legally, such a woman's status would be somewhat different from that of an ordinary maidservant, but society did not accord such employees the respect due to wives. Ward regulations (*shikimoku*) required that fees (*shūgi*) be paid to the community fund when a resident married, and some (such as the regulations for Minami Komeyachō in Osaka) suggested that if such a fee were not paid the woman would be regarded as a mere maidservant.[122]

Given such ambiguous status distinctions, it is not surprising that masters took their sexual prerogative for granted. Quantitative data on maidservant pregnancies is lacking, since this period offers nothing equivalent to the *declarations de grossesse* of early modern France, but the Numano data are suggestive (Table 3.2). In six out of the forty cases where the reason for the maidservant's departure is known, she leaves in a delicate condition. It is not clear, of course, that these pregnancies resulted from relations with the master or members of his family, but it is not unlikely, since maidservants were generally expected to remain single while in service.[123] Maidservants were also vulnerable to seduction by manservants and men other than their master and his male relatives. Edicts concerning abandoned children (*sutego*) indicate that they were particularly apt to desert their newborns.[124]

Literary evidence is telling. The old Sakai merchant in Saikaku's *Nanshoku ōkagami* is depicted as eccentric and "old-fashioned" because, "He took no interest in how the maids looked who worked in his kitchen. As long as they were capable of weaving cloth in their spare time, he hired whoever would accept the lowest wages."[125] Ogyū Sorai's reticence, meanwhile, was attributed, in one account, to his high moral standards:

In his bedroom Sorai was extremely strict in his adherence to correct forms. At the outset, he had a maid who was extremely good-looking. Sorai liked her, and had her come to his study and serve there. She began to think in her maid's heart that she had won her master's heart by means of her good looks. One day Sorai by chance took a nap in the middle of the day. While he was asleep, the maid came and covered him with a quilt [as she was] afraid that the cold air would hurt him. Sorai woke up surprised and asked, "Who made you come to my study and put the quilt on me without my orders?" The maid answered, "I did." Sorai was first enraged, but then he regretted his anger. [However,] from this time on he hired girls who were not more than twelve or thirteen years old and not sexually inclined, and no one except those girls were allowed into his study.[126]

"This is indeed," concludes Minamigawa Kinkei, author of the *Kansan yoroku*, "the way I heard it!"

The more representative spirit, however, is suggested by chapbook erotica or by senryū such as the following:

Hinja no ittō	A ray of light among the poor:
danna no rinbyō	the maidservant
naosu gejo	who cures the master's gonorrhea[127]

(It was commonly believed that sexual relations with a menstruating woman would cure venereal disease.) Or:

Haramaseta	The investigation
sengi wa kore de	into her pregnancy
yama wo tome	was discontinued[128]

(The maidservant, it seems, is with child by a family member.)

Master-maidservant relations could lead to trouble, both for the master, who if the relationship is on the sly, makes himself vulnerable to blackmail, and for the wife who must contend with a rival:

Mekake no wa	The concubine coaxes
nedari gejo no wa	and the maidservant
yusurikake	blackmails him

Hitoberashi	Jealous
yorazu sawaranu	she lessens the servants
riuki neri[129]	avoiding trouble

Or to avoid trouble and expense, one might oblige the maidservant to undergo an abortion. Asahi Bunzaemon, the Genroku-era Tatami Bugyō in Nagoya, records in his diary such an episode concerning his own parlormaid.[130]

Since Japan had no firm conception of illegitimacy, the children of maidservants or concubines suffered no particular disadvantage, but the mothers might face persecution from irate wives. Ieyasu's second son, Hideyasu, was born of his wife's chambermaid Nagai. Infuriated, the wife stripped and bound her servant, and would have left her to die in a field.[131] The shogunate, for its part, was not inclined to prohibit sexual involvements between masters and maidservants. It frowned, to be sure, on adultery, but if the maidservant were unmarried, authorities would not interfere.[132]

A manservant, meanwhile, could receive the death penalty for even proposing adultery with the master's wife; if the mistress was a willing partner, both parties could be put to death. The case of Osan, the wife of the official calender maker in Edo, and her servant Mohei, is recorded in the *Nishijin tengu hikki* (*Notebook of a Nishijin Braggart*) and celebrated in several thinly fictionalized versions. Having eloped together, they were captured, and after the husband refused to grant pardon despite pleas from a prominent priest, publicly crucified in 1684.[133] Women of samurai status were even more sternly prohibited from contact with manservants. Those of wealthier households would be surrounded by maidservants, but in the absence of their husbands they were not to so much as invite a priest into the house.[134]

The advice a samurai mother gives her daughter in Chikamatsu's puppet-play *Horikawa nami no tsuzumi* (*Hand-drum of the Waves of Horikawa*) thus seems altogether reasonable:

> When you are alone together with any man you are not so much as to lift your head and look at him. It doesn't matter who the man may be—a servant, a member of the household, a stranger, an old man, a boy—when your husband's away, you must observe the proprieties.[135]

The only person her daughter may look at without risk, the mother adds, is the scullery maid! Even widows were forbidden relations with their manservants. The following law was issued in Edo in 1655:

> If a husband dies without leaving an heir, the widow may remain in the house. If she commits adultery with an employee [*genin*] soon after her husband's death, it is a clear sign that she is ungrateful to her late husband, and is not respectful of her relatives. She must be expelled from the town [*machi*] and the husband's relatives may decide who may inherit the household.[136]

Masters, however, or male members of their families, might actually marry their maidservants, and literature provides examples of conniving maidservants who even attempt to displace their mistresses.[137] The great storyteller Ueda Akinari was adopted into the family of Ueda Mosuke, an ex-samurai oil and paper merchant in Osaka. Refusing a marriage arranged by his foster father, Akinari married the maidservant, Otama, who had been with the Ueda household for five or six years.[138]

The principal wife of a ranking samurai was likely to be chosen politically, but secondary wives might be selected from among the maidservants, or mistresses of servant status might receive promotion. A samurai's attraction to a maidservant might encounter family opposition, however. In 1723 a fourteen-year-old bannerman, Aoyama Tetsunosuke, in love with his foster mother's nineteen-year-old parlormaid (jochū) Ran but ordered to break off the relationship, committed double suicide with his lover in an Edo temple.[139]

Love-suicides of this type were experiencing quite a boom at the time. In 1716, the diary of Asahi Bunzaemon records Bunzaemon's own investigation of a love-suicide in the castle-town. On the eighth day of the third month, while making his rounds, he discovered two bodies in a temple courtyard; his careful report reveals that one Tadashirō, son of Buemon, a merchant in Noribana ward, had killed himself after stabbing his lover Fuji, a maidservant in Buemon's house and daughter of one of his tenants. Both were nineteen years old.[140] There are even recorded cases of masters committing suicide with maidservants, such as occurred in Osaka in 1724.[141]

Alliances between female family members and manservants were even more likely to end in tragedy, however. Seventeenth-century laws prescribed death for the abduction of, or sexual intercourse with, the master's daughter or wife, although the punishment could be reduced to banishment or the crime pardoned at the master's request.[142] A famous case occurred in Himeji, probably in 1659. Aside from Genroku-period dramatized accounts, there are semi-historical sources dating from 1718 and 1760 which describe how Seijūrō, a servant in the Tajima shop on the main street of the castle-town, was beheaded after seducing—and possibly eloping with—his master's daughter Onatsu.[143] Factors other than fornication seem to have been involved (in some accounts Seijūrō kills or injures another manservant), although the literary accounts play up the sexual element. Even so, at the time the seduction of Onatsu would itself have constituted grounds for capital punishment. Time seems to have moderated the attitudes of legal authorities, however. A 1741 edict merely sentences the seducing manservant to "medium deportation" and places the daughter in her parents' custody.[144]

Such cases might involve the most heinous offense imaginable under Tokugawa law. If the manservant slew his lover before taking his own life, he would have killed a member of his master's household—a crime considered more vile even than parricide. In a case in Yonezawa han, in

1692, a manservant committed love-suicide with his master's daughter. Applying the concept of collective responsibility, officials executed the servant's father and brother.[145]

Intimate relationships between servants in commoner houses were naturally common. In the Numano household, the maids were sometimes discovered "misbehaving" with the shopclerks (no doubt the latter shared responsibility for at least some of the six recorded pregnancies), and were then summarily dismissed. On the twenty-fifth day of the second month of Kaei 7 (1854), for example: "The said Kayo seen misbehaving with Genpei; dismissed, Chūgen, Year of the Hare." And an entry for the very next day: "The said Sawa has, in addition to great improprieties, become intimate with Heimon of the shop, and was therefore dismissed on the morning of the twenty-first day, seventh month, Year of the Elder Brother of Water." One would like to know what happened to Genpei and Heimon.[146]

Certainly the avoidance of affairs between servants was a matter of great concern to employers. This is indicated by a "Memorandum on Family Traditions Transmitted to Manservants" (*meshitsukai no otoko*) which the wealthy Takada-han peasant, already mentioned, issued to his servants in 1755. While such rural households may have been more conservative than their urban counterparts, the consciousness revealed in this document probably existed to some degree in the cities as well.

Eight of the fifteen articles deal with manservants' relations with maidservants. (Only three, in contrast, deal with fire, suggesting, perhaps, that this problem was less pressing?) They carefully regulate all possibility of social interaction between the sexes. Manservants are not to ask the maids to remove thorns or pins from their skin, or specks from their eyes. They are not, for their own part, to assist the women with their clogs or Mino straw raincoats. They are not to join the women around the bonfire, and when the female cook, at dinnertime, approaches with the rice kettle, they must not talk to her as she ladles them their rice. "No one," the document warns, "should use the women for his own purposes."[147]

It is not clear whether this intolerance for affairs among the servants stemmed from fundamental moral convictions or from an anxiety (which Japanese employers still reflect) concerning the destabilizing effect of romance among employees in the same environment. Probably the latter was a greater concern; in the case of male employees, an occasional visit to the pleasure quarter seems to have been viewed with tolerance, and servants of both sexes seem to have been allowed to form relationships outside the household.

In samurai households, however, maidservants if not manservants were expected to be chaste, and affairs between servants might be severely punished. In Kanazawa in 1663, for example, a rear vassal and maidservant received the death sentence after their illicit relationship was discovered.[148] In a famous scandal in 1714, a senior lady-in-waiting (*rōjō*) of the shogun's seraglio was punished after holding an unrestrained party with a kabuki actor with whom, investigators learned, she had been intimate for nine years. Eleven other women in the party were also disciplined.[149]

Given the lack of privacy enjoyed by live-in servants, how could relationships develop among them? In early-modern England, live-in servants enjoyed few opportunities for sexual indulgence, but such seasonal events as hiring fairs invariably involved "the debauching of Servants, Apprentices and other unwary people" and resulted in a conspicuous increase in bastard births to maidservants nine months later.[150] In Japan, no such fairs were held, but shrines might provide the scene for bacchanalia such as the yearly *zakone* ("group sleep") at Ohara Shrine near Kyoto, where manservants might even approach their masters' wives.[151] Carnivalesque activities, including free love, might also accompany the regular pilgrimages to Ise (*Ise-mairi*), which became a craze during the Tokugawa period.[152]

One institution catering to servants, and incidently facilitating servant sex, was the hito-yado. Its employment agency functions have already been described, but it also lent out rooms for daytime trysts (forming, in short, the prototype of the modern Japanese "love hotel"). Saikaku depicts both commoner and samurai-household servants taking advantage of rented rooms in such establishments, and notes as an exception that wet nurses are not allowed there even for brief outings.[153]

At times masters themselves sought to arrange marriages between those in their employ. (The mistress Osan, at the beginning of Chikamatsu's *Koi hakke hashiragoyomi*, seems particularly eager to pair her maidservant Otama with the shopclerk Mohei.)[154] The Numano wage book records that the twenty-six-year old Toyo was married off (*kashitsuku*) to one Jinbei (probably a shopclerk) in 1847: "Both [employer and employee] happy to have her leave in happy circumstances." This marriage, if not arranged, certainly met with the approval of the master, who furnished the couple with an oblong chest, raw silk thread, and furoshiki as congratulations.[155]

Problems could emerge, though, if the servant had independent ideas. Both Chikamatsu and his contemporary Ki no Kaion wrote puppet plays concerning an incident that occurred in Osaka in 1710. A clerk, Jirōbei, and a housemaid, Okisa, are employed by the same Osaka shop. Having fallen in love, they even make excuses in order to win a few days' leave to be together. The master, however, has decided to marry Okisa to a branch manager, Yachibei, to whom he feels obligations. Although the master's wife and mother are both sympathetic to the lovers, the latter realize the hopelessness of the situation and commit their love-suicide in the grounds of Imamiya Ebisu Shrine.[156]

This situation represents an extreme, however. In general servants probably married as they, or their parents, wished, but then had to leave service. As noted, most shops would not allow their men to marry until late in life, and although there are some examples of married maidservants (including some with spouses in the employ of the same household), most maidservants would be set on their way. This was the case with all six married maids recorded in the Numano notebook.

Sexual relationships between masters and manservants were also common and widely accepted. The whole topic of homosexuality in Tokugawa society has not yet received the attention it deserves, but it seems clear that certain forms of bisexual behavior, and perhaps even exclusive homosexuality, were very common.[157] Homosexual relationships between men of comparable ages and status were rare, however; there prevailed what Foucault called the "principle of isomorphism between sexual relations and social relations." Sexual relations "were seen as being of the same type as the relationship between a superior and a subordinate, an individual who dominates and one who is dominated, one who commands and one who complies."[158] Foucault's work dealt with ancient Greece and Rome, but in early-modern Europe as well, the typical homosexual partner of a free adult was a social inferior: a student, hired male prostitute, boy actor, or manservant. Homosexual relationships between masters and servants were indeed "a widespread institution."[159]

In Tokugawa Japan, too, references to homosexual activity almost always involve male prostitutes, kabuki actors, or servants—including some hired specifically for the purpose. Homosexuality seems to have been particularly common in samurai mansions.[160] Many of Saikaku's samurai tales involve youths who find employ as pages or sandal-bearers in daimyo households, soon acquiring the status of *yoru no tomo* ("nightmate") or *chōdō* ("beloved boy"). Pederasty was the preferred relationship, with boys between ten and fifteen—foreheads yet unshaven—admired most. But ideally, Yamamoto's *Hagakure* suggests,[161] affairs should last a lifetime, a view also expressed in a 1706 poem:

Itsumademo	Forever and ever
kōsho mo gomotsu	the page still the cherished one
dono mo dono	lover and beloved[162]

Unfortunately such relationships, however idealized, were obviously highly exploitative and often associated with brutal violence. The ban on sale of humans notwithstanding, unscrupulous employment agents often kidnapped attractive boys in order to meet the demands of samurai mansions. *Kiyū shoran*, a cyclopedia of manners edited by Kitamura Nobuyo in 1830, reports in its section on homosexuality (*nanchō*) that parents of handsome boys in the seventeenth century scarcely allowed them out of the house for fear of such predators.[163] Many bloody episodes involving homosexual love triangles among samurai manservants are on record.[164]

Homosexuality as such was never banned by the shoguns, a number of whom, in fact, carried on open sexual relationships with their pages.[165] But various laws, interesting in their specificity, addressed the problem of master-manservant sex. A law (*hatto*) of 1650, for example, prohibited samurai employed in constructing the West Tower of Edo Castle from meeting in private residences for homosexual (*nanshoku*) trysts.[166] Another, issued four years later, forbids the shogun's bannermen from retaining youths as footboys for sexual purposes.[167]

In the *Collected Edicts* (*Ofuregaki*), meanwhile, one finds at least twenty ordinances, issued in Edo between 1648 and 1709, forbidding overnight visits of kabuki actors (who typically doubled as catamites) to private homes.[168] Here, too, the regime sought to reduce the instances of violence involving homosexual infatuations. Yamamoto describes one such incident that occurred in Saga in the late seventeenth century. One of the daimyo's pages (koshō) became so enamoured of a famous actor that, in order to procure the latter's sexual favors, he pawned all his goods and finally resorted to stealing from other servants. He and the actor both were sentenced to death.[169]

Among servants in commoner households, however, homosexual behavior does not appear to have been widespread. Certainly samurai had no monopoly on homosexuality; it is quite clear that commoners frequented the homosexual brothels as well.[170] But contemporary literature offers only scattered references to master-servant homosexual relationships in such households. In the famous Edo arson incident involving the maidservant Oshichi, the girl's boyfriend Kichisaburō was a temple acolyte sexually involved with an "older brother" on Mt. Koya. In Saikaku's treatment, he is sexually harassed by Oshichi's manservant Kyūshichi.[171] Genroku-period fiction refers to mistress-maidservant lesbian relationships as well.[172]

Master-servant relations, then, could take many forms, ranging from genuine affection and intimacy to bitter enmity. But most of these relationships probably were not characterized by love—of the sort lifelong, familial ties are apt to produce—or by the hatred born of involuntary servitude. Rather, the relationships were generally cool and indifferent; even voluntary sexual involvements between masters and servants typically seem to have lacked true warmth or mutuality. Tokugawa servants, unlike the fudai or hikan of earlier eras, were not lifetime retainers but free proletarians, principally out for themselves. The legal records concerning servants' crimes, the household records citing servants' misbehavior and sloth, suggest that in ongoing, subdued and individual ways servants struggled with masters over the conditions of their employment. They were also willing and able, when entering into new positions, to bargain over the terms at which they exchanged their labor power.

FORMS OF COMPENSATION

But how were they compensated for that labor power? We know that masters in Tokugawa Japan, like masters in other preindustrial societies, often provided servants with lodging, meals, livery, education and training. When boys, for example, were taken in as shophands, their parents would be paid small sums, but the real return for their labor power was training, room and board.[173] The youngest servant in the Numano household, a thirteen-year-old nursemaid named Kiku (who, the mistress writes, "cannot do anything") is the only maid listed as receiving "no wage," but clearly she is housed and fed and the notebook entry states "Plan to give livery."

Servants were also given such cash payments as tips (*kokorozuke*) to reward specific acts, and bonuses to mark special holidays. The greater part of servant compensation, however, took the form of money wages.[174] Authorities often tried to fix wage levels, but even then masters and servants bargained over pay, formalizing their agreements in written contracts.[175] Ishii Ryōsuke has found a number of such contracts, written in Kyoto and dated Genroku 6 (1693), all following a similar format:

> Item: This woman named _____ is contracted to work at a wage [*kyūbun*] of _____ per year, and will receive this rate for five years while serving as a wet nurse. This woman was born in _____ village in _____ province, the daughter of _____, and is not a Christian (whose faith is) forbidden by law.
>
> Item: She will conscientiously care for the child day and night. It should be understood from the outset that she will receive gifts [*goshugi*] of haircuts or pleated skirts.
>
> Item: During the term (of service) she should not make unreasonable requests for time off, and if she becomes ill, or her milk becomes insufficient, she will be replaced.[176]

The specified wages could be paid at the beginning of an employment term, but advance wages (*maegane*) were less common in the towns and cities than in peasant villages.[177] Among the Numano maidservants, only one—a nursemaid named Kimaki—seems to have been of this type. A payment in silver to her father, one Kishimatsu, is recorded next to her name in the notebook. She was probably very young.[178]

In most cases, wages were probably fixed at the point of hire but paid at irregular intervals, usually at the employee's request, rather than on a weekly or monthly basis. The balance would then be paid at the end of the term. If the employer extended the servant's tenure, he or she would take into account past performance in setting the wage for the next term. Merchant households, in particular, gave much thought to such decisions: the Shingaku savant Ishida Baigan (1685–1744) stressed the ability to evaluate employees' performance and reward them appropriately as one of the skills most crucial to a master. Not only must a master know how to calculate and use an abacus;

> when he employs servants [he must make] the distinction between the clerk [who receives a wage of] ten [and one who receives] five *mai*, and the man-servant [who receives] 100 monme, and he [who gets] 50 monme. Observing these fellows at work, [the master] should increase the wages of those with [greater] merit.[179]

Wages, Baigan believed, should be paid strictly according to work and experience, not contingent upon a worker's personal vices or virtues. The wage schedule of the Shirokiya dry goods store in Tomizawa-chō, Edo, seems to reflect this attitude. In 1769 annual wages (*kyūkin*) varied from four gold ryō for beginning employees to ten ryō for branch managers.[180] These wages would not be paid out on a fixed day each year, and employees' purchases from the shop would be deducted from the agreed-upon wage.

Hayashi Reiko, who has studied the Shirokiya documents, suggests that these shops were little concerned with accurate wage payments.[181] But employers clearly attached specific value to labor power in terms of time. The Kōnoike shops of Osaka also compensated labor on a yearly basis, if by a roundabout means. In Kyōhō 4 (1719) the three shops established a new method for remunerating employees who, having reached nineteen years of age and undergone the *genpuku* (coming of age) ceremony, were considered likely to remain with the business for many years. A Kōnoike document contains the following:

> When it is decided that clerks will continue on indefinitely, from that time 80 kanme silver, referred to as *moyai-kin*, will be invested individually, and every year [the shop] should tally up for each [clerk] the interest money on the said [principal]. . . . [The moyai-kin] is provided for [the clerk] to continue making a living successfully in the distant future after having worked

very diligently. Since this is to provide for [the clerk's] own living when, in due course, he has his separate household, he will work all the more attentively for such results, honorably and to the great mutual happiness [of employee and employer].[182]

The document goes on to specify that the 80 kanme (80,000 monme) will be invested at 10 percent monthly interest, and in the eleventh month of each year a payment of two hundred monme will be earmarked for each of the clerks and recorded in a book alongside the clerk's name. These sums were not exactly wages, however; the rule book specifies that even in cases of need these funds were not to be touched while the clerk was still employed. The funds were not set aside for apprentices, but only to clerks who, in the Kōnoike case, were usually nineteen or older. (A similar fund for chambermaids, however, was set up in Kyōhō 10.)

The sums were payable at the point the employee left to set up an independent business or branch shop, and even then "those not suiting the company's convenience" might be denied these funds upon departure. (In 1730, at least seven out of forty main shop clerks listed were dismissed without receiving this pay.)[183] Even so, the system itself suggests that the shops were attaching a specific, yearly value to the labor power they employed, and that they recognized the value of monetary incentives in producing a more motivated staff. Quite possibly the company was confronted with considerable competition for labor from employers prepared to pay yearly wages. The yearly two-hundred-monme installments into the fund approximate the wages of a high-class manservant during this period, and represented a rather high income. The price of one koku of rice was around seventy monme in 1719. Methods of compensating domestic servants were more direct. The Numano wage notebook begins with a series of simple calculations such as the following:

Item: 90 me [me = monme]
    1 day 2 bu 5 ri
Item: 80 me
    1 day 2 bu 2 rin 2 mō 222
Item: 70 me
    1 day 1 bu 9 rin 444[184]

Obviously the mistress has simply divided yearly wages by 360 to obtain figures for daily wages. When dismissing workers, she consulted her tables and, calculating their service tenures, paid them to the day. On the eighteenth day of the second month in Kōka 2 (March 25, 1845), for example, she dismissed one Yasu, a thirty-three-year-old chambermaid from Minabe. Yasu had been with the household since the twenty-sixth day of the first month (March 4), or 22 days. Her yearly wage had been set at 110 monme, so the appropriate wage was 6 monme 7 bu 2 rin. "She's nothing but a bungler," her mistress wrote, but perhaps since, as the record notes, she was "in ill health," she received a few bu over the sum: "Gave 7 monme in paper money."

The year before Tsune, another chambermaid from Sekido, was dismissed after twenty-five days. Her wage, too, was set at 110 monme, so we would expect her to receive 7 monme 6 bu 4 rin. The actual figure recorded is 7 monme 6 bu. Such figures are closely calculated enough to demonstrate that, at least in the Numano case, the employer sought, rather conscientiously, to compensate fixed quantities of labor time with fixed monetary sums. One must imagine, too, that some employees were numerate enough to check the calculations as well.

Other forms of monetary compensation were insignificant compared with the wage itself, as the averaged figures in Table 3.6 illustrate. True, some might handily supplement their wage with gifts; a chambermaid named Yoshi, hired at age eighteen in 1841, stayed only a year before leaving "because of a nervous disorder." In the meantime, however, she had garnered numerous tips over her 110-monme wage: "Gave 3 monme. The above given as a tip [*kokorozuke*] due to her scrupulous attention to the summer washing. . . . For putting forth her best effort at this and that, gave five bills paper money. . . . For clever and diligent work, receives from the master another 800 mon."[185]

Altogether Yoshi's tips apparently constituted 24 percent of her monetary income. But in the vast majority of cases, servants received little more than a few extra monme during chūgen, the holiday celebrated during the seventh lunar month, if that. Table 3.6 shows the Numano maidservants' nonwage compensation as a percentage of their total compensation. The slight difference in the two columns is mostly attributable to recorded gifts such as collars, bolts of cloth, *furoshiki* (wrapping cloths) and perfume, often given to the servant at her departure from the household. Very often livery items, if noted, are not valued, so the figures in Table 3.6 understate the total value of nonmonetary gifts received. (It is also possi-

TABLE 3.6
Bonuses, Tips, and Valued Gifts as Percentage of Numano Maidservants' Compensation

	Bonuses and Tips	Valued Gifts and Bonuses
chambermaids	3.77	3.97
parlormaids	.86	.86
scullery maids	2.42	2.42
nursemaids	1.81	3.72

Source: See Table 2.19.

ble that some livery items were retained by the household on the servant's departure. In some commercial houses, the livery would have the character of a peculiar uniform, and the employee would have little use for it, having severed connections with the household or business.) One is struck, in any case, by the relatively small value of these nonwage grants.

Some household budgets that have survived allow us to compare employers' expenses on gifts for servants with the servants' fixed wages. The budget of the household of Nagasawa Motochika, a hatamoto with an income of 1960 koku, spent about 160 ryō on wages in 1711. This would have represented about one-third of his rice income converted to cash. The value of the gifts he bestowed on his employees that year was comparatively miniscule: 1.56 ryō.[186]

"Free" room and board, of course, were also very important forms of compensation. Furushima Toshio, in a discussion of Kinai villages, cites the household record of an employer of agricultural day laborers who, in addition to paying their wages, provided at least one hundred monme worth of meals, rice wine, and clothing to his workers.[187] Assuming that the Numano family spent somewhere around this figure in providing room, board and clothing for their maids, the women would receive about half their compensation in nonmonetary form.

This fact might be interpreted as an indication that the commodification of labor power had not progressed very far. On the other hand, if the monetary compensation actually represented a living wage, the other forms of compensation would appear, not as indispensable supplements to the wage, but rather as fringe benefits. And indeed, the purchasing power of the maidservants' wages was not negligible. At this time it was a rule of thumb that an income of 1.8 koku of rice would cover an adult male's minimum yearly expenses.[188] A woman would require from 1.1 to 1.4 koku. The Numano chambermaids on average could have exchanged their wages for 1.3 koku of high quality white rice on the Osaka retail market, while the lowest-paid servants, the nursemaids and scullery maids, could have exchanged their wages for 1.1 koku. These are unenviable wages, but they were indeed living wages, capable of sustaining life, rather than mere tips or bonuses provided within an essentially nonmonetary system of remuneration.

In some cases, holidays were paid, and thus can be viewed as a form of compensation. The Numano mistress apparently paid her year-term servants the full yearly wage, even though she probably allowed vacations of one to three days at Oshōgatsu (the sixteenth day of the first month, plus, perhaps the two or three following days) and Obon (from the sixteenth day of the seventh month). Indeed, she records several brief vacations (*yabuiri, yado-ori, yado-iri*) of this type. The Numano household also may have allowed servants the first, fifteenth, and twenty-eighth days of each month off; merchant households commonly observed these as holidays. Such leaves seem paltry when compared to the Sabbaths and numerous saint's days of contemporary Europe, or for that matter, to the forty to fifty-five obligatory holidays (*yūjitsu* or "play days") observed in some han,[189] but an understanding master might grant an employee additional time off for family business, for religious devotions, or recuperation from illness.[190] Employers must have felt some hesitation in granting leaves, since they could provide opportunities to abscond. The Numano servant Suma, allowed to return to her parents' home "because of her mother's illness" on the twenty-fifth day of the sixth month of 1844, was back by the eighth day of the following month. On another occasion, however, the parlormaid Tane, after asking for one day off to return home, got married and disappeared, to the mistress's evident irritation. One Kiyo, after asking for "a little time off," had not returned after twenty-one days. "I checked her clothes and personal effects," notes the mistress. "Most had been removed."[191]

Servants did not, however, hesitate to request time off, and apparently it was often granted. A document labeled *Genin kashitsukekata oboechō* (*Notebook on cash advances to servants*), left by the Nagakura household of Fukushima, includes numerous memos concerning money advanced to servants as well as leaves they were granted. Sketchier even than the Numano notebook, it dates from the same period (1835) and, like the other document, indicates that total pay was closely linked to the number of days actually worked. According to the record, one manservant was granted, during a four and a half month interval, twenty-four days off, several of which were spent attending plays (*shibai*).[192]

If we can credit the somewhat tongue-in-cheek testimony of Saikaku, servants did not hesitate to request time off even when applying for jobs. The guarantor of one young woman in *Saikaku Oritome* tells a hito-yado clerk:

> If [my client] is to have a relationship with an employer, it must be established that she will have free time during six evenings per month and, if you please, she must also receive time off on two afternoons. On top of that, she needs six days each year for her Kōshin visit, and the early evenings on the eighth and twelfth each month for prayers to Yakushi. Then, too, she makes monthly temple visits to worship the spirit of Tenjin-sama. And she needs free time from dusk to the first night watch.[193]

We are not told whether she expects full pay for her reduced work schedule. Admittedly this is a humorous sketch (the reader is supposed to guess that, while requesting time off for religious observances, the maidservant part-times as a prostitute), but we may safely assume that servants could bargain with prospective employers for regular days off when contracts were being drawn up.

Chapter Four

SERVANTS IN SOCIETY

Trouble never arises if servants know their places.
—Honzō in *Chūshingura*

FROM POPULAR and scholarly literature, along with iconographic evidence, we can garner some idea of servants' popular image. It is a mixed one. Much literature, including *bunraku* and *kabuki* plays, depicts servants in a highly favorable light, as paragons of honesty and loyalty.[1] But often as not, like the Step-'n-Fetch-It Black of old American films, the servant is cruelly burlesqued. Partly this is due to longstanding—and perhaps universal—theatrical convention; "Comedy," Aristotle observed, "is the imitation of the worst sort of people." If the "archetypal servant in seventeenth-century French comedy was *balourd*, a bumbling fool whose stupidity and physical clumsiness outweighed his occasional display of ingenuity in pulling his master out of a tight situation,"[2] the servant in medieval *kyōgen* comedy (still popular and widely performed during the Tokugawa period) represents a not dissimilar type. Attendants, invariably named Tarō, provoked the mirth of the audience by their outrageously clever solutions to their lords' dilemmas, but their failings prompt the latter to constantly berate them as imbeciles and scoundrels.[3] In kabuki, meanwhile, the *tedai-gataki*, a clerk who is always causing mischief in the household, is a standard role.[4]

In bunraku, the puppet employed to depict manservants is itself an unflattering caricature. He sports "a rather distorted face, a flat nose, the mouth open or twisted, and a stupidly licentious expression."[5] Other genres convey the same image. *Kobanashi* (humorous anecdotes) afford many laughs at servants' expense, and *senryū* (short comical verse) "has no good to say of maidservants. They are always pig-nosed, stupid, vain, envious and greedy."[6] In a more serious vein, scholars attacked samurai-household servants for their idleness and shallow loyalty. And while the latter were, at least in Edo and other cities directly administered by the shogunate, commonly viewed as arrogant, violent parasites, commoner servants were, at worse, not perceived as threatening, but simply lazy, gossip-prone, gluttonous, drunken, and lewd.

Samurai and commoner servants were thus viewed somewhat differently. The shogunate, for its own reasons, had encouraged the samurai to surround themselves with large retinues of servants, but samurai and commoner scholars alike minced few words in attacking these liveried members of samurai households. They particularly deplored the money wasted on maintaining useless attendants, and the violence to which these idlers were prone.

Ogyū Sorai (1666–1728), an early critic, expressed his indignation about the practice of samurai going about "accompanied by multitudous retinues of boisterous, useless day-laborers (*hikoyōmono*) who jam [the streets]."[7] Several generations later, social critic Gamō Kunpei (1768–1813) lashed out at samurai mansions which, he charged, were filled with male and female servants, "all of whom performed almost no real services."[8] When Andō Shōeki (1703?-62), the iconoclastic physician-philosopher of Akita, denounced the whole samurai caste as "parasites" with "haughty" attitudes, utterly incapable of performing a useful day's labor, we may imagine he was venting part of his spleen on their conspicuously otiose attendants.[9] The great Mito scholar Aizawa Seishihai also accused samurai servants of "luxurious living" in his famous work *Shinron* (1825). Samurai, Aizawa implied, had been corrupted by their own attendants:

> The original purpose in providing the samurai a stipend is so that he might employ attendants. . . . [Nevertheless] when the samurai leave the land . . . they get by with the services of unemployed city dwellers, setting them to a wide variety of tasks. Such idlers fill the castle towns, but would be of no use if it ever came to war.[10]

Idle hands, of course, do the devil's work, and samurai-household manservants were famous for disorderly conduct. What samurai in Edo "most detest," wrote Ogyū, is the occurrence of quarrelsome incidents among their underlings (*shimojimo*)."[11] The image of these manservants was not enhanced by the fact that they were wont to join in the *yakko* gangs that troubled major cities through much of the seventeenth century. Originally organized by alienated bannermen, members of these groups, like their twentieth-century counterparts in the American inner city, sported bizarre costumes and hairstyles which set them off from society. Vowing absolute loyalty to one another, they constituted a criminal underworld whose lifestyle simultaneously attracted and repelled the townsmen. *Machi-yakko* consisting of commoners formed to resist encroachments by the *hatamoto-yakko*. However the latter, while finally suppressed in 1686, during the reign of the Shogun Tsunayoshi, have been immortalized in numerous dramas of the characteristically bourgeois kabuki theater. Figures such as Mizuno Jurōzaemon, a page of the shogun Iemitsu who had later become an important yakko chief, were glorified as *otokodate* (braves) in plays that Sansom likened to *The Beggar's Opera*.[12]

There was a political quality to some of this violence involving samurai-household manservants. In the Keian Incident of 1652, one of the three official valet-chiefs (*chūgen-gashira*) of the shogunate, Ōoka Genzaemon, was exiled to Sado Island after conspiring with unemployed samurai (*rōnin*) to blow up part of Edo Castle as a protest against samurai impoverishment.[13] Episodes like this ensured that samurai-household manservants in Edo were widely despised and feared:

Iki wa Fukugawa	For life, Fukugawa
Isami wa Kanda	For cheer, Kanda
Hito no warui wa Idachō[14]	For scoundrels, Idachō

Ida was a ward where chūgen in shogunate employ lived.

In some domains, samurai-household valets and pages enjoyed more respect and a better press, but in Osaka, where samurai, huddled around the castle in the neighborhood of Nakanoshima, were very few, and in Kyoto, with its proud, ancient traditions, a similarly negative view prevailed. Thus in Jippensha Ikku's *Hizakurige*, when the Edo ne'er-do-well Kitahachi is mistaken for a samurai's valet (*mōrosuke* or *orisuke*) in a Kyoto theater, the surrounding crowd does not hesitate to laugh him to scorn because of his curious speech.[15]

Servants in general were accused of frequent drunkenness, but the vice was particularly associated with servants of the samurai. The *Hagakure* offers many examples of drunken pages accosting commoners or otherwise getting into mischief.[16] When a samurai in one of Saikaku's tales offers his jacket to a servant, the latter is disappointed that the gift is not a keg of wine.[17] Commoners' servants, meanwhile, were accused of all the vices, except arrogance and violence, associated with their samurai-household counterparts. Their greatest sin, of course, was laziness. Like Kakusuke in Chikamatsu's *Yari no Gonza kasane katabira*, they tended to sleep until noon.[18] The scene recurs time and again in senryū:

Me wo samashi	The maidservant wakes
gejo ashi wo kaki	scratches her leg
mata ibiki	and snores again[19]

In a Saikaku tale about an Osaka merchant house the maidservant, annoyed upon being awakened by her mistress and told to heat water and set up the dining trays, "makes an irritable face," while the houseboy Kyūshichi refuses to draw New Year's ritual water. That, he indignantly observes, is not *his* task. The clerk, meanwhile, refuses to be roused: "Don't wake me until I'm good and ready to wake up (*hitori me no aku made ware o okosu na*)!" he grumbles in language innocent of honorifics. Saikaku concludes, superfluously, "There is no profit in employing many servants."[20]

"All servants are chatterboxes (*kuchimame*)," says the narrator in Chikamatsu's *Horikawa nami no tsuzumi*,[21] and Kaibara's reference to the destructive consequences of maids' gossip has already been cited. Not only women are faulted with this vice; Ishida Baigan warns that shop-boys and manservants will discuss a rakish master's adventures even if paid to keep silent.[22]

Servants eat too much, and tend to obesity. "The gejo in senryū is a stock figure," noted R. H. Blyth, "with large red hands, a snub nose, and extremely bulky in the rear."[23] Shikitei's fat maidservant slips on the bathhouse floor, nearly producing an earthquake; when she gets back on her feet, the pomegranate she has been munching is still in her mouth.[24] The Shingaku cleric uses the lazy servant Chōkichi as an exam-ple of a wayward soul: awakened by his master and ordered to clean up after a banquet, he becomes wide awake at the sight of leftover squid and hastily pockets a number of them before the master catches him in the act.[25]

Servants from certain areas, such as the *Oshina* or Shinano migrant workers, had reputations for especially voracious appetites.[26] Saikaku has a Kyoto resident from Sendai write home to his brother that, "What one maidservant back there consumes in a day will easily suffice for five women here in the Capital. . . . Back home, you spend one *zeni* to buy fourteen or fifteen raw sardines, and the maidservant (*gesu*) alone con-sumes ten, including the heads." In Kyoto, in contrast, one *zeni* buys six-teen or seventeen little dried sardines, and each household member re-ceives just three. "Not even maidservants eat the heads!"[27]

Commoner servants are associated with drunkenness, too. Ornery Oman, maidservant in Chikamatsu's *Meido no hikyaku*, combines a number of servant vices. Her master, Chūbei, returns home from the plea-sure quarter and finds her on the way to the sake shop. Hoping to pry some information from her concerning the day's business in the shop, he realizes that, given her disagreeable nature, he won't acquire the informa-tion for nothing. Thus he pretends to be in love with her, and although her initial response is rude, she agrees readily enough to meet him in bed later that evening.[28]

Kobanashi convey the same image of servant lustiness. One such joke told during the period runs as follows. A certain maidservant often passed gas in her master's presence. Angered, he would thrash her with a whip, but excited by the sight of her white thighs, he would always wind up mounting the maid. One day when he was in his study, there was a knock on the door. "Who's there?" he asked, and the maidservant entered. "What's your business?" he demanded. "I just farted."[29]

Shibata Kyūō told the following anecdote in a sermon dealing with the evils of another servant vice, vanity:

The scullery maid (*meshitaki*) Osan is scrubbing pots at the sink. Chokichi the shopboy (*detchi*) draws over to her side.

"Osan-don," he informs her, "There's a coal-smudge on your nose. Didn't you realize that?"

"Oh really? Where?" Wrapping her fingertip in a towel, she squints down ludicrously to scrutinize her nose. Twiddling about with her fingers there, she reminds one of [the famed swordsmith] Goto carving an ornamental sword-hilt.

"Chokichi-don, is it off yet?"

"On the contrary, you've smeared it all over your cheeks."

"No! Where?" Thus, her face reflected in the sink water, she cleans up.

Thereafter Osan thinks to herself, "That Chokichi's such a sweet boy!" and with each helping of vegetables she serves him at dinner, she reflects, "Shouldn't I thank him?" and she happily expresses her gratitude without reserve.

But had this Chokichi said, "Osan-don, you've got the sourest temper! Would you mind looking a little less sulky?" what would Osan have replied? Think about it.

She'd probably have turned into a devil—only minus the horns—and hissed: "You arrogant little shopboy! If my heart really *were* so perverse, so three-cornered, would I be doing these chores for you? Well then, I'll forget about you completely. Even if you wet your bedclothes, I won't wash them for you!"[30]

Servants, finally, are ignorant and uncultured. In one kobanashi a kindly master, pleased with his manservant's performance, takes him to a temple to view the cherry blossoms. How was it? asks the mistress upon their return, and the servant, unimpressed, displays his complete ignorance of Japanese aesthetics by regretting that the blossoms were all *falling*.[31] In another story, told around 1740, a page or footboy is out walking with his master. Since it's a crowded area, the servant remarks, they had best look out for pickpockets. "Sharp of you to observe that," the master replies. "Be careful with that bundle you're holding for me." "Alas," says the servant, "That was just stolen."[32] According to another anecdote, a master is pursuaded that his manservant's stupidity must be due to possession by a fox-spirit. The spirit is duly exorcized but the servant remains foolish as ever. As the master berates the poor lout, a fox pokes his head in the door, declaring, "He was that way to begin with!"[33]

Many servants would of course have been illiterate or semi-illiterate, and writers often poked fun at this disability. In Saikaku's *Kōshoku gonin onna*, the maidservant Rin is unable to write her own love letters, and the manservant she dictates them to can only manage a childish scrawl.[34] In Book II of the *Yanagidaru* (late eighteenth century) we find the same problem:

Gejo no fumi   The maidservant's letter:
bonji wo hineru   she writes as if twirling
yo ni kaki   Sanskrit letters[35]

(She writes, that is, with great difficulty.) She cannot, moreover, read what she receives:

Misemosezu   Not showing it to anyone
muhitsu wa fumi   the illiterate does not know
wo moteamashi   what to do with the letter[36]

On the other hand, Ronald Dore has shown how literacy rates in general improved, and how the educational level of the masses rose during the Tokugawa centuries. Various literary works designed at least partly for servant consumption were available in the latter half of the period. If the world of the in-servant was not completely forgotten in the chapbook literature of England in Pepys' day,[37] the maidservant in Tokugawa Japan might have such works as *Shujū nichiyō jōmoku* at hand for reference. This guidebook to "Rules for Masters and Servants in Daily Life," penned by the ukiyo-e artist Ikeda (Keisai) Eisen (1790–1848), provided homely counsel and warnings against gossiping too much about sexual matters with colleagues and taking too many holidays from work. A Western visitor to Edo in 1869 noted that "the Japanese are a reading people"; he "often found the servants, when not on duty, engaged in reading . . . sensational novels" with lavish illustrations. Such works, he regretted, were "not more free from grossness and immorality" than those of "civilized nations."[38]

The speech of many servants, along with their lack of learning, became the butt of jokes. Their outrageous dialects, their misuse (or overuse) of honorifics, their awkwardness in greeting customers with the appropriate remarks, are celebrated in many kobanashi.[39] Such lampooning was, however, good-natured enough, and servants would usually have been treated with a reasonable degree of civility by other members of society. A house code might, for example, specify that employees were "not to be discourteous to maidservants or even children."[40]

Another passage from Shikitei Sanba's *Ukiyoburo* sums up a number of stereotypes concerning servants, while suggesting the complexity of masters' feelings towards them. First one matron compliments her friend's servant:

"Your parlormaid's a real hard worker, isn't she? When the water's cut off [due to repairs] she carries water in buckets. Such a good-natured girl, don't you think? Our San and the rest are all good-for-nothings. They give us nothing but trouble. The other day [San] said she'd caught a cold, so she's in bed."

"How inconvenient for you! That's the worst—when parlormaids or houseboys [*kozō*] get sick."

"Well, it can't be helped, anyway. If you don't want to take medicine, and it's an illness that really lays you low, all you can do is eat and sleep. [Sickness] is unpredictable. It could happen to any servant."

" 'A servant's nature,' as they say, is to eat. But does she have trouble sleeping? Anybody—even the sturdiest—gets weak by missing meals. All the more reason to take good care of yourself when you're sick. We don't, after all, notice all the dangers."

"I've tried employing any number of people, you know, but they don't work for me. *I* work for *them*."

"Really? That Osan-dono with you until last year seemed such an amiable type."

"Yes, I had her a long time, but she found a proper husband so I sent her off."

"How nice!"

"The one we've got now has such horrible manners, I don't know what we'll do with her. If I scold her she throws a fit—even breaks things!—and if I keep quiet that just encourages her. The worst part is that she sulks, making that sullen face, even in her sleep."

"Just like that damn Rin [*Rin-me*] of ours! Always poking her nose in. When people hear her voice, they just leave her to herself. After breakfast she cleans up, heads upstairs, and spends half the day putting her hair up. Then until I order her to fix dinner, she's out at the clothesline gossiping away. She's always making such an issue about trifles, laughing and crying while shirking her chores. 'I'll fetch some water,' she says, but when she leaves for the well it takes her an hour to get back with her pail full. I guess it's not surprising—she throws herself, like a fool, at every young guy in the tenement, and then when she takes time out from that, she's slandering our personal lives in front of other parlormaids! The other day I wondered what she was talking about, so I listened from the shadows of the outhouse. She was singing the praises of her former master!

" 'The world is full of whitewashed walls' [i.e., there are many masters and job openings, she was saying.] 'When the third month comes, [I'll say] "So long!" [They'll] grasp my hands and say, "Won't you please stay in this poor household?" Rather than pay all those employment hostel expenses, worrying as they pile up, I'll stay on here [just for the time being].' Running off at the mouth like that!"[41]

SITES OF SOCIAL INTERACTION

Burdened though they may have been by such stereotyped images, servants shared the pleasures and vices of society, rubbing shoulders with members of all classes at the barber-shop, *sumo* wrestling matches, fireworks displays, festivals, and visits to temples and shrines.[42] Their life-styles were indeed not terribly dissimilar from those of their employers; the typical servant, in both samurai and commoner households, was an in-servant who worked, ate and slept in close proximity to master and family members. Those serving employers at the bottom of the social scale, sharing their tiny rented lodgings in backstreet tenements (nagaya), often would have lacked the comfort of a personal room, but so would some members of the master's family. Even the homes of householders, typically sporting a frontage of twenty-four to thirty feet, and in the case of wealthy merchants, sometimes measuring up to six thousand square feet,[43] would not necessarily have offered their inhabitants much privacy.

Conditions in Tokugawa Japan thus resembled those of seventeenth-century Europe, where masters bathed, dressed, deloused, and made love oblivious to the presence of their servants, rather than the conditions of the late eighteenth and nineteenth centuries, when new notions of domes-tic intimacy caused masters to physically and mentally distance them-selves from their employees.[44] In Tokugawa cities, there was no counter-part to the "upstairs, downstairs" dichotomy of Victorian England; there does not seem to have been any particular principle according to which servants were assigned rooms.

A servant might have a room to herself, like Oman in Chikamatsu's Meido no hikyaku who arranges to meet her master there for a secret tryst,[45] or Rin in Shikitei Sanba's Ukiyoburo who heads upstairs every morning after breakfast to spend hours doing her hair.[46] Or servants might have to share quarters. The head clerk in one of Saikaku's stories shares both his room and pillow with a houseboy; they "wake up with legs intertwined." Apparently such arrangements aroused little concern.[47]

Architectural plans of samurai-mansions show a wide variety of ser-vant rooming patterns. Servants' quarters (chūgenbeya, koshōbeya, etc.), along with storerooms and stables, were often located adjacent to the large gates that led into samurai-household compounds. Examples of such quarters survive in historical parks like Edo-mura outside Ka-nazawa. But there might also be chūgenbeya near the entrance of the mansion or in the interior.[48] Within castle precincts, servants' rooms seem to have been randomly distributed. Charts at the Matsumoto castle grounds suggest this, as do the observations of Edo Castle by Englebert Kaempfer in the 1690s.[49]

So numerous were the servants in the employ of a ranking lord that often the castle or mansion itself could not lodge them all. In Kanazawa an entire ward, Okobitomachi, was peopled by pages whom the samurai households were unable to house.[50] Where space permitted, however, liv-ing arrangements encouraged a degree of master-servant intimacy. Meals might be taken together, at least in commoners' households, although men would commonly dine apart from the women.[51] Saikaku describes one Osaka merchant household where "master and servant sitting all together, without distinction" partake of the Kaga rice, soup, sprats, and vegetables, the employees expressing their appreciation by raising their chopstick-boxes and intoning, "Thanks to the master" before digging in.[52] Merchant codes and family constitutions, like that of the Mogi family (of Kikkoman soy sauce fame) stressed the health benefits of simple fare and counseled employers to share their servants' diet.[53] Charles Dunn has observed that a diet of rice or rice mixed with wheat, containing husk and germ, along with miso and vegetables, would have been available to even the lowest employee. Vitamin deficiency, he adds, was not a major problem.[54]

If the household was wealthy enough to afford a bath (often housed in a building separate from the living quarters), the servants would be entitled to use it, carefully observing the order of hierarchy.[55] The American scholar William Elliot Griffis, in Japan during the 1870s and fitted with a Japanese staff, recorded that after his own ablutions, his valet would use the tub, followed by the valet's wife, an eleven-year-old maid, and finally Gonji, his worthless little page.[56]

Sharing the same food, bathwater, and often enough the same futon bedding, masters and servants inhabited the same cultural world. Principles of deference and hierarchy were naturally respected. Terms of address were of course based on rank, and priorities of access to conveniences were observed, but there was not a separate servant subculture in society.

Servants would meet and socialize with other commoners every day as they went about their chores. Many hours might be spent at the neighborhood well, often the only spot for doing laundry, washing rice and procuring drinking water. In the Edo ward of Nezumonchō during the Bunsei era (1818–29), there was only one well serving twenty-seven households.[57] Surely it was a center for the dissemination of news and gossip as well.

Servants naturally handled much of the shopping. Act Two of Chikamatsu's *Amijima Shinjū* opens with the paper-shop mistress Osan wondering why her maidservant Tama is still not back from Ichinokawa, the vegetable market near Tenjin Bridge in Osaka.[58] Loath as the samurai were to handle money, their servants, too, counted shopping among their domestic duties. Woodblock prints often feature such scenes as valets buying vegetables or fish.[59] A samurai woman, reminiscing about her childhood in Bakumatsu Mito, recalled that "even shopping was left to the retainers," adding, however, that "this was a period when there was generally little to buy, so that wasn't too inconvenient."[60] Samurai seem to have struggled to maintain servants in part to avoid the indignity of shopping themselves. Fukuzawa Yukichi, referring to his hometown of Nakatsu, noted that "since all the samurai of small means kept no servants, they were obliged to go out and do their own shopping." The profound shame of this chore, however, obliged them to hide their faces in towels, and to perform their errands only at night.[61] How preferable it would have been to send a page!

The bathhouse was another frequent site where members of nearly all classes met, as the opening passage of Shikitei Sanba's *Ukiyoburo* so ebulliently notes:

> When you really think about it, there's no finer shortcut to insight than the public bath (*sentō*). This is because wise and foolish, honest and false, wealthy and poor, high and low alike are all naked when they bathe. In the natural Way of Heaven and Earth, both Buddha and Confucius, both maidservant (*osan*) and manservant (*gonsuke*) enter the tub just as they were born. . . . The naked forms of master and footman (*orisuke*) are indistinguishable. . . . [Lice] pass from the bath-accessories of the hillbilly maidservant to the young wife's finest clothes.[62]

William Elliot Griffis also observed the democratic atmosphere of the public baths late in the period:

> The Japanese are a clean people; every one bathes every day. The mechanic, day-laborers—all, male and female, old and young,—bathe every day after their labor is completed. There are many public bath-houses in Shimoda. The charge is six sen, or the eighth part of one cent. The wealthy people have their baths in their own houses, but the working classes, all of both sexes, old and young, enter the same bath-room, and there perform their ablutions.[63]

The uninhibited atmosphere of the baths, as Shikitei's humorous sketches reveal, provided servants with the ideal forum to air their gripes about their masters.[64]

Servants also frequently visited the crowded theaters in such entertainment centers as Edo's Kobiki-chō, Sakai-chō, and Fukiya-chō; Kyoto's Shijō-gawara, and Osaka's Dōtonbori and Horie districts. Alone, or in the company of master or family members, they make up a sizeable section of the audiences depicted in *ukiyo-e* prints. Employers seem to have tolerated their servants' interest in the performances. When Osome, in Chikamatsu Hanji's puppet-play *Shinpan Utazaimon* (1780), meets her boyfriend for a tryst, she sends her maid Oden off to the theater.[65] The mistress of the Sakai-suji shop in Osaka, in *Saikaku oritome*, recalls that before her husband died, when the business was being run efficiently, servants sent on errands near the theater would be dispatched before breakfast to ensure that hunger would hurry them home.[66] Theater-going, in moderation, was not itself considered objectionable; even daimyo sent their maidservants to the performances to learn new dances.[67]

Popular theater, however, has suffered criticism in many societies, partly on grounds of the dramas' allegedly immoral content, and partly because of the threat audiences themselves might pose to social order.[68] Some Confucian savants, and officials of the Tokugawa shogunate held a similarly low opinion of kabuki and puppet theater (although the aristocratic nō was seldom criticized). Hayashi Razan (1583–1657) complained of the "base songs," "vulgar dances," and "lewd voices" of kabuki.[69]

The musical accompaniment itself met with opposition. "The sound of a shamisen," objected an eighteenth-century Kyūshū scholar, "is enough to put lewd thoughts into the mind of a saintly priest with years of Zen meditation behind him."[70] Scenes explicitly depicting the pleasure quarters, treatments of the love-suicide topic, story lines involving current scandals, were all seen as corrupting public morals and were repeatedly—unsuccessfully—banned by the regime.[71] Scholars debated whether the issuance of laws, or a policy of censorship, might better regulate the production of popular theatrical works, but concern with the theater's "lewdness" was widespread.

The shogunate was equally concerned, however, with the nature and behavior of the theater audience itself. The large gatherings that formed, practically every day, to enjoy the most popular entertainment a pre-cinema, pretelevision society might offer, clearly required policing. This was all the more so, given the contemptible social level of many fans. Just as an English critic of the Augustan period objected to "such Rubbish as *Butlers*, *Chambermaids*, quacking *Apothecaries*, and *Apprentices*, . . . Ladies Waiting-Women, *Lawyers Clerks*, and *Valets de Chambre*" among London theater audiences,[72] so Japanese opponents of the popular stage disparaged the composition of theater audiences and the disorders they were apt to produce.

Quarrels and sword fights broke out over unintentional jostling, heckling of actors, and rivalries over the attentions of kabuki performers.[73] In many such incidents, servants were involved. In Kanazawa, for example, early in the seventeenth century, samurai-household servants (*wakatō* and *okachi*) attempted to gain free entry into the theater by impersonating sumo wrestlers and low-ranking samurai traditionally accorded this privilege. Their ruse discovered, they resorted to violence, causing the temporary closure of the playhouses.[74] But whereas similar incidents in eighteenth-century England led to a ban on servants in the theaters, in Japan this group was not singled out for special treatment.[75]

Not a few servants, meanwhile, came to grief by dissipating their incomes on the purchase of actors' favors.[76] For such reasons, no doubt, an edict in Edo in 1668 specified that servants (*hōkōnin*) were not to meet with actors after their performances.[77] Pleasure quarters also invited their share of servant customers. The mistress in the Saikaku story cited earlier reminisced that, "When [we had a servant] go near the Pleasure Quarters, we'd tell him without notice, and send him from the yard without time to change his obi or grab his tissue-paper purse."[78] Kobanashi also suggest that manservants often repaired to the red light district when given time off.[79] Their masters do not seem to have been unduly concerned about such behavior. Takizawa Bakin, touring Osaka in the 1790s, credited much of the prosperity of the city's brothels to servant patronage.

> Even the shopboys [komono] of the commercial houses have their own work and can profit from their business. During the daytime they conduct their operations diligently, without taking the shortest break. After the fifth hour [about 7 P.M.], the commercial houses' employers and employees alike take their leisure. To forget the day's toil, they head to the brothels [girō] to drink and enjoy themselves.
>
> Even the servants of commercial houses [come to the brothels], spending the money [they make at] their work-places, but so long as they do not embezzle their masters' funds, the masters do not stand in their way. Obviously this is why the brothels are so prosperous.[80]

Other servant pastimes were apt to place them on the wrong side of the law. Gambling was a common, though dangerously criminal, amusement of commoner servants as well as buke hōkōnin.[81] Gaming with dice and cards was "an everyday occurrence, especially among palanquin-bearers and valets" in the servant quarters of daimyo and bannermen. It was not unusual for outsiders to participate in such games, despite the fact that gambling was a capital offense from Ieyasu's day. Another center was the employment agency (hito-yado) itself.[82] In the second act of Chūshingura, the manservant Bekusuke declares that if he had lots of money he would open his own gambling joint.[83]

Commoners' servants were also much taken with this vice.

> Mugoi yatsu ni mon yon mon de ni fun yusuri
> hyaku makete koko ni aware wo gejo todome[84]

> From her two or four mon
> the cruel fellow yields two fun
> then the sorrow of losing one hundred—
> the finishing blow to the maidservant!

Hayashi Reiko's study of the Shirokiya dry-goods shops of Edo provides the following incident. Kitamura Shōroku, a hōkōnin in the Nihonbashi shop during the Kaei period (1848–53), repeatedly visited brothels, running up a bill of three gold ryō, then amassed gambling debts exceeding fifteen ryō. His savings of thirteen ryō, combined with some sly profits shaved from the kitchen budget and shared with a kitchen servant, could not cover this large liability. To pay the debt he enticed one of the shop-boys (*komono*), and then a clerk, into stealing for him before he was finally apprehended and punished.[85]

The Kikuyachō documents also include a lengthy legal brief, dated 1810, entitled "The Case of the Gambling of Kinzō, Servant of the Iyo Shop." Poor Kinzō died while in custody.[86] Illegal gambling took place even in areas of top security; in 1794 a clerk of the Esatori shop was found gambling with a caterer within the Edo Shogunal Palace itself. The culprits were exiled.[87]

Full participants in the pleasures and vices of society, did servants join in the urban riots and uprisings that grew more common in the course of the period? There is little evidence of their involvement. In the seventeenth century, as we have shown, valets and other samurai manservants often became involved in murderous conspiracies and even in rebellion, but they were as apt to vent their fury against one another, or social inferiors, as against the higher authorities. Commoner servants, meanwhile, manifested little consciousness of themselves as a class with special interests. When they did participate in collective action, they took no leading role; in the large-scale Osaka *uchikowashi* of Meiwa 4 (1767), twelve of the seventy-five rioters arrested (16%) were listed as hōkōnin, but as about one-fifth of the population of the Senba area, the center of the uprising, were servants, this number is not large.[88] In the Matsushiro Rising early in the Meiji period (1870), only one of sixteen rioters arrested in the castle-town of Matsushiro, and two of forty-two arrested in Zenkōji (Nagano), were servants.[89] Ann Walthall finds some evidence of clerks participating in urban rice riots, but those employed by targeted merchant houses were more likely to be on the receiving end of these disturbances.[90] Small merchants and day laborers, who had to purchase their rice with money wages, were more prone to participate in these collective actions than servants whose meals were provided by their employers.[91]

SOCIAL MOBILITY OF SERVANTS

Since servants appear to have been well-integrated into society, we might assume they enjoyed wide opportunities for upward social mobility. The hyōshō records suggest that they did, in fact, often move on to better things. Of the 183 Edo tenants recorded as having received these awards from 1726 to 1843, biographical data is available for 121. Of these, 37 (31%) had hōkōnin backgrounds. Their occupations at the time of receiving the awards are shown in Table 4.1.[92]

In most cases, those listed as artisans or merchants would have become independent tradesman, earning incomes substantially greater than they

TABLE 4.1
Occupations of Edo Tenant Hyōshō Grantees with Service Backgrounds

service occupations
 1 palanquin bearer
 1 cook
 1 fire watchman
 1 barber
 1 laundress (F)
 1 dockhand
 2 masseur (1 F)

artisans
 1 blacksmith
 1 tatami mat-maker
 1 umbrella maker
 1 broom maker
 1 knife handle-maker
 1 dyer
 2 carpenters

merchants or peddlers
 1 miso merchant
 1 fishmonger
 1 pawnbroker
 1 used tool merchant
 1 dry-goods auctioneer
 1 seasonal goods (*toki no mono*)
   merchant

wage laborers (temadōri)
 1 employee of wicker basket-maker
 2 employees of dyer
 1 employee of confectioner

other (priest, ward officials)
 3

(F indicates female. In eight cases, trade is unknown or only family trade is given.)

Source: Ikegami Akihito, "Kōki Edo kasō chōnin no seikatsu," in Nishiyama Matsuno-suke, ed., *Edo chōnin no kenkyū*, vol. 2 (Tokyo: Yoshikawa kobunkan, 1974), 176f.

had during their years of service. Some former servants even attained fame for their learning; Kusama Naokata (1753–1831) and Yamagata Bantō (1748–1821) both great Osaka merchant scholars, had originally served as detchi kozō before being adopted by their employers.[93]

For samurai-household servants, the very association with a samurai master could represent a rise in social status. The short-term servants (*karuki hōkōnin*), usually drawn from the the commoners' ranks, enjoyed quasi-samurai status. Upon leaving service, they could sometimes turn their acquired skills to their advantage. Even women who had served so long in samurai mansions that they had ruined their prospects for marriage might become schoolteachers at the temple schools (*terakoya*) which catered to commoners' children.[94]

Manservants might rise from humble, menial jobs to positions of great authority. Iwasaki Yotarō, the son of a Tosa peasant, became a samurai's attendant (*jūsha*) in 1854 at age twenty. Soon he was handling much of the domain's Nagasaki trade and, after the Restoration, established the Mitsubishi Trading Company.[95] In Satsuma, such key figures in pre-Restoration domain politics as Saigō Takamori and Ōkubo Toshimichi had both been pages, and Zusho Shōzaemon rose from tea-server to chancellor (*karō*).[96]

The education acquired in service was a primary factor in social advancement. Since footsoldiers (*ashigaru*) were commonly excluded from the han-sponsored schools, valets and pages of similarly low status would also have been denied admittance.[97] However, higher-ranked samurai enrolled at such establishments would typically come attended by footboys or other servants to hold their umbrellas and extra footwear. Possibly these menials would have been able to overhear lessons as they waited outside the lecture hall.[98]

Servants might be appointed as study companions to sons of the master's household. This was the case with both Matsuo Bashō (1644–94), greatest haiku poet of the age, and with Yamamoto Tsunetomo. Bashō, the youngest of seven children in a samurai family, entered the service of the eleven-year-old son of Tōdō Takatora, the daimyo of Ueno in Iga province, at age nine. Both boys studied poetry composition in Kyoto under Kitamura Kigin, publishing their first works in the same collection which appeared in 1664.[99]

Tsunetomo, employed as a page by Saga daimyo Nabeshima Mitsushige at age nine, was allowed to study letters with the daimyo's son Tsunashige under Mitsushige's own tutor Kuranaga Rihei. The latter, indeed, would have liked to appoint Tsunetomo as his own successor, but Tsunetomo was apparently not interested.[100]

Chikamatsu is another whose education was acquired at least in part while in service, though in the households of Kyoto nobility rather than buke yashiki. In his death-bed message (*jisei*) he declared, "I was born of a warrior's family, but severing my connections with the soldier class, I served more than one noble house."[101] Indeed, his early interest in jōruri has been attributed to contacts made as a servant in Kyoto during his teens.[102] Takizawa Bakin, also born a samurai, served in various military households before becoming a writer at age 24.[103]

SERVICE: A BRIDGING OCCUPATION?

Servants (at least domestic servants) have sometimes been treated as a class that bridged "the world of the dominant classes and the popular classes."[104] L. Broom and J. H. Smith, for example, argued in a seminal article that domestic service is particularly "strong on bridging attributes." It resocializes, exposing the servant to new habits, dress, and manners of speech; it allows a considerable degree of independence, since the servant need not observe a long-term commitment to his employer; it gives the servant better than average prospects of remaining healthy; it facilitates access to persons in a position to offer one assistance in advancing socially; and it allows the servant to accumulate savings.[105]

The cited examples of mobility illustrate some of these features. Servants experienced horizontal mobility (becoming peddlers or dockhands, for example) as well as mobility up and down the social scale. In their employment careers, they bridged town and village, and (as buke hōkōnin) commoner and samurai classes. Many in the ruling class were uneasy about such movements, regarding them as a threat to the social order. Thus Ogyū Sorai and Dazai Shundai, among others, suggested a return to the old system of lifetime military household servants, and the strict enforcement of the ban on dekasegi migration.

But few samurai in positions of authority would have favored such radical proposals. Shogunate leaders probably felt it was inevitable that servants in urban households would bridge samurai and commoner, and urban and rural, worlds. What troubled them was egregious violations of that primary rule of Tokugawa society: "*Mi no hodo o shire*" (Know your place). And in such a society, where outward appearances counted far more than they do today, the clothing, accessories, hairstyles, and public habits of the servant drew much comment.

Kiseki pointed out one of the main principles of social bridging: "Inferiors learn from their betters by imitating them." Therefore,

> It is natural . . . that all the maids—chambermaids, parlormaids, even scullery maids whose right hands bear the mark of the ladle—should whet the fish-slicer, shave their eyebrows, cut the short hairs in the hollow of the neck, put rice-bran in an old tea-bag, and, after soaking for hours in a hot tub (each heedless of the others), scrub themselves furiously.[106]

But if maids learn vanity from their mistresses, the latter, for their part, take cues from the maidservants of higher-status households. Commoner mistresses imitate samurai parlormaids: "Lately, too, ladies wearing oiled-paper raincoats, in the fashion of parlormaids from samurai households (*buke no jochū*), have been seen in the capital."[107] Worse yet, he notes, the city folk learn from country bumpkins: a Kyoto mistress at dusk "gleefully hitches up her skirt like a peasant girl going to weed a rice field, and her conduct becomes so loose that you can hardly tell the mistress from a scullery maid."

Ishida Baigan, lacking Kiseki's humor, found this blurring of class distinctions distressing:

> Ostentatious people of the present world not only wear fine clothes themselves but dress their maids in clothing made of thin damask and figured satin with embroidery and applique. Someone from the country seeing them would take them for court nobles or feudal dignitaries, but would wonder why they are not being attended by samurai followers.[108]

In futile efforts to eliminate this confusion, the shogunate incessantly reissued sartorial laws. They were an important item in every major reform effort.

In early-modern Europe, social critics voiced similar concern with the mingling of classes. Daniel Defoe, a contemporary of Baigan's, complained that "our servant wenches are so puff'd up with pride now a days that they never think they go fine enough: it is a hard matter to know the mistress from the maid by their dress."[109] P. J. Grosely, referring to London maidservants in 1765, remarked that the maids "attend their ladies in the streets and in the public walks, in such a manner that, if the mistress be not known, it is no easy matter to distinguish her from her maid."[110]

In Japan, the endless promulgation of sartorial laws proves they were ineffective; in England, such laws were allowed to lapse from the early eighteenth century. But if servants' wardrobes could not be regulated effectively, how could such pleasures as tea drinking, tobacco smoking, theater going, shamisen playing, tea ceremony and card playing—all of which became popular among the masses during this period—have been denied them? The lowest brothel servant in kabuki plays lights up her *kiseru* pipe as she reflects over her romantic dilemma; the humblest menial chants *jōruri* (librettos of puppet plays) as he marches to work. Surely the majority of hōkōnin, who passed through their service tenures before returning to their villages, switching to day labor or other work, or entering business for themselves, brought with them customs and ideas that helped to advance the cultural and material levels of society.

Chapter Five

CASUAL LABORERS

LIKE SERVANTS, casual laborers constituted a broad and varied category. The general term for them was *hiyatoi* (literally "day-hires"), but many other terms also referred to wage-earning, unskilled manual workers. Even some workers considered for legal purposes artisans (*shokunin*), for example, those treated as such in the "Artisan" sections of the *Ofuregaki* (*Collected Edicts*), were in fact little more than day-laborers. Some groups, such as the less skilled carpenters, occupied an ambiguous position. In the Edicts, carpenters are treated in the "Day-Laborer" section, but they were commonly regarded as artisans of the "outdoors" variety. (Artisans were divided into indoor [*ijoku*] and outdoor [*deshoku*] types.) Certainly there would have been a range of carpenter types, from highly trained professionals to mere hired coolies.

Such terms as *hiyatoi, hiyō, hiyōtori, hiyatoi-kasegi, hikaseginin,* and *tematori* were sometimes stretched to cover peddlers as well, but usually they referred to unskilled construction workers such as sawyers, plasterers, masons, thatchers, tilers, ditch-diggers, and earth-movers, or transport workers such as porters, palanquin-bearers, and packhorsemen. These workers were employed on a daily, ten-day, twenty-day, or monthly basis. Casual laborer types, and the English equivalents I will use, are given in Table 5.1.

CASUAL LABOR POPULATIONS

Few urban aggregate figures on these workers during the period are available, and there are no good data for the great cities, but early Meiji period data is suggestive. Statistics for the whole city of Edo (newly rechristened Tokyo) in 1873 show 41 percent of her residents classified as *zatsugyōsha* ("people of miscellaneous occupations"). According to Saitō Osamu, these were mainly hawkers and day laborers.[1]

The data surviving from the Tokugawa period shows great variation in the the proportion of day laborers from city to city and town to town. In the mid-seventeenth century they accounted for about 60 percent of the households in Tondabayashi, the sake-brewing center east of Osaka (population 1,669 in 1686).[2] In the castle-town of Okayama, numbering about 28,000 at this time, 28 percent of all households were headed by day laborers.[3] The record for Kasama, a much smaller castle-town, shows

TABLE 5.1
Casual Laborer Types

Laborer Type	English Equivalents
hiyatoi	day laborer
hiyō	
hiyōtori	
hiyatoi-kaseginin	
hikaseginin	
tematori	
zatsugyōsha	person of miscellaneous occupations
seoi	porter
karuko	porter, palanquin bearer
karuko-mochi	
mochikomi hiyatoi	deliveryman day laborer
nimotsu-mochi	baggage carrier
nikachi-mochi	
ninsoku	coolie
rokushaku	coolie; porter; palanquin bearer
nagamochi-ninsoku	trunk porter
shariki	carter
kago-kaki	palanquin bearer
kago-nobori	
rikishaku	
kumosuke	
umakata	packhorseman
mago	
nakashi	dockworker; stevedore
ko-age	
okinakashi	
chōroku	
hyōbetsu-nakashi	bag-separating dockworker
kura-nakashi	warehouse worker
tonya-naksashi	wholesaler's laborer
dashimono nakashi	deliveryman
ni-bu kiri nakashi	menial laborer
shita-nakashi	
anko-nakashi	
orai-nakashi	street laborer

that in 1705 workers listed as *hiyatoitōri* formed the second largest occupational group—thirty-two out of 483 households. If we add to this figure a few of the less skilled carpenter, thatcher, and sawyer households, the actual actual number of households engaged in casual labor comes to well over 10 percent of Kasama's population.[4] In Hirado, a castle-town in

TABLE 5.2
Occupational Structure of Household Heads in Ikeda-mura

Year	A	B	C	D	E	Total
1697	230	84	794	284	43	1,435
1780	359	130	117	1,219	346	2,171

A—merchants   D—casual laborers, peddlers
B—artisans   (zatsugyōsha)
C—peasants   E—other

Source: Chihōshi kenkyū kyōgikai, eds., Nihon no toshi to machi: sono rekishi to genjō (Tokyo: Yūzankaku, 1982), 189.

the Kyushu domain of Hizen, day laborers seem to have been the second largest among seventy occupational groups, outnumbered only by peddlers in 1703.[5]

Certain population centers bearing the name "village" (mura) but in fact constituting towns, also had large worker populations. In charcoal-producing Ikeda-mura, north of Osaka, 284 of 1,435 household heads (20%) were described as zatsugyōsha in 1697. At this point, peasants (hyakushō) formed the majority of residents (55%). By 1780, however, 1,219 of 2,171 households (56%) were headed by zatsugyōsha, while a mere 5 percent were engaged primarily in agriculture (Table 5.2). Some of these "people of miscellaneous occupations" were probably not day laborers, but on the other hand, the "artisan" (shokunin) category may have been included hired, unskilled workers along with trained craftsmen. And in eight "villages" within the limits of Settsu's Itami-ōmachi, held in fief by Grand Chamberlain Yanagisawa Yoshiyasu from 1692 to 1704, 182 out of 454 households (40%) were headed by day laborers.[6]

Data for individual urban wards, meanwhile, show that in some wards casual laborers predominated. In Ue-no-chō in Mukōmachi (Yamashiro province), day laborers headed 113 of 197 households (57%) in 1616.[7] In some Kanazawa wards, too, day laborers formed a sizeable part of the community; in 1818 they headed 14 of 55 households (25%) in Ushiroka-nayachō. Here they lived side by side with low-ranking samurai, whose households made up 23 percent of the ward total. In Kanazawa's Daiju-me-kawaramachi, meanwhile, they headed 12 of 59 households (20%).[8] In Osaka's Kita Horie 6 chōme, day laborers and those listed as migrant workers (dekaseginin) comprised over 19 percent of the ward total in 1871.[9] Day laborers headed 15 of 143 households (10%) in Edo's Kōjimachi 12 chōme in 1865, and in the same year, 14 of 96 household heads (15%) in Shitani Denmachō Shin Itchōme were day laborers or carpenters.[10]

Contemporary descriptions of city life often allude to large numbers of day laborers. Engelbert Kaempfer observed that the port of Nagasaki circa 1690 was thinly inhabited by merchants and wealthy people. "The greatest part of its Inhabitants is made up by workmen, labourers, and ordinary people, who must get their livelihood by their daily labour."[11] A century and a half later, Westerners in Japan's treaty ports note the ubiquitous presence of porters, servants, dock workers, drivers of *jinrikisha* ("rickshaws") and those whom they simply referred to as "coolies."[12]

Ogyū Sorai observed that in Edo, early in the eighteenth century,

> There has been a daily increase in the number of peasants, who, after coming to Edo to find temporary work as servants, decide to settle down permanently here either as day labourers or as hawkers, with the result that the city has expanded to the extent of five *ri* [12.5 miles] with a great density of houses.[13]

Saikaku, writing half a century earlier, had often enumerated the various types of casual laborers in detail. "There are various ways to earn a living (*yo ni mi sugi wa samazama nari*)," he had declared; one need only take a long walk around the Kyoto, beginning at the West Gate of Kiyomizu Temple, to observe the employment prospects at first hand:

> Someone with a carpenter's plane will shave down a chopping-board [*mana-ita*], big or small, for three mon each. . . . To clear out a large gutter, men work for one mon per one ken [of waste removed], supplying their own cleaning-rakes, bamboo brooms, and bins. For five fun someone will prune your tree, and will graft on branches for one fun per branch. Part-time carpenters charge six fun [per hour]. . . . An ordinary person who doesn't idle should be able to make a living in this world—if he simply stirs his hands and feet. [*Tatai naku teashi ugokaseba hito-nami ni yo wa watarubeshi.*][14]

Elsewhere the observant novelist describes ways to make a living in Fushimi: one can replaster furnaces, polish pots and pans for five mon per large pot or two mon for smaller ones, wash rice for four mon per bushel, or wall-paper people's homes.[15]

It was not uncommon even for impoverished members of the samurai class to make their livings as day laborers. Ogyū specifically denied that there was anything dishonorable in a samurai doing such work,[16] and by the nineteenth century even a warrior receiving an average stipend was obliged to seek wage work. "The Edo samurai," Fujimori Taiga wrote in 1855, "cannot make a living on their regular income. From their youthful days, they are accustomed to supplementing their income by outside work."[17] Such observations seem to justify Takizawa Matsuyo's view that "wage-laborers . . . constituted the masses of city population. . . . They were usually unskilled, they wandered about the city and took any job that would keep them and their families alive."[18]

Workers in Transport

The two largest categories of casual workers were connected with transport (of people and goods), or with construction and such menial tasks as ditch-digging and earth removal. The former can be divided into four main types: porters who carry goods on their backs or over their shoulders, carters who pull their own vehicles, palanquin-bearers who taxi people about with their muscle-power, and packhorsemen and draymen whose animals, led along by their masters, bear people or goods upon their backs. There were also dockers and stevedores hired to transport rice and other goods from the docks to wholesalers' warehouses.

Laborers of the first type were known by many names: *seoi* (porter), *mochikomi hiyatoi* (deliveryman–day laborer), *nimotsu-mochi* or *nika-chi-mochi* (baggage-bearer), *ninsoku* (coolie) or *rokushaku*. The latter term sometimes referred to palanquin bearers employed as servants in samurai (and sometimes merchant) households, but more commonly it referred to porters organized under foremen and in some cities supervised by an official labor-registry. They could be hired to cheaply transport personal belongings, or to help stock fish and vegetable markets. Fresh fish, brought to the Osaka market from Sakai and Amagasaki, were relayed by the cool of night on to Kyoto by runners known as *uoni*.[19]

Sporting short cloaks (*kanban*) tied with a cloth sash over a loincloth, their bodies often displaying the tattoos workmen were disposed to flaunt, porters carried their burdens in several ways. Most typically, they shouldered a bamboo pole which supported two pieces of cargo (often buckets) suspended by rope; or they might carry two poles supporting two buckets, one across each shoulder. This arrangement would even allow them to proceed at a dogtrot.[20] Some, called *nagamochi-ninsoku*, worked in teams of six, bearing large trunks (*nagamochi*), fitted with shoulder-poles.[21] An individual porter could be expected to carry baggage of up to twenty kilograms; this was the officially fixed limit on the great highways.[22]

Shariki or carters pulled carts called *niguruma* (lit., "baggage vehicle") or larger vehicles called *daihachi-guruma*. (The latter term—"great eight vehicle"—refers to the fact that the cart can carry as great a load as eight porters would normally bear.)[23] Vehicles of both types were awkward, two-wheeled affairs, and not much used except for heavy hauling; one laborer could pull a cart of the first type, but two or three would be needed to move a daihachi-guruma.

Palanquins (*kago* or *norimono*),[24] born by coolies called *kago-nobori*, *kagokaki*, *rokushaku* or *rikishaku* (or sometimes by the derogatory term *kumosuke*), were the preferred means of travel. (The terms *karuko* and *karuko-mochi* originally referred to "light palanquin bearers" but could also simply mean "porters.") The origin of these vehicles—boxes attached to a pole supported by the shoulders of several men—is unclear, but the term *norimono* appears in a Japanese-Portuguese dictionary published in Manila in 1630.[25]

Initially restricted to the use by a privileged few, including ranking samurai and physicians, palanquins soon transported commoner passengers as well.[26] Nothwithstanding the ban on commoner patronage, private palanquins (*shikago*, also known as *tsuji-kago* or street-corner palanquins; *machi-kago* or town palanquins; or vulgarly, in the Edo pleasure quarters as *"hoi"-kago*) soon appeared. Beginning in 1677, such palanquins were licensed, and although four years later their use was restricted by law to those over fifty years of age, such rules, along with much other sumptuary legislation, were widely ignored. In 1700, commoner women and children, as well as the sick and the aged, were legally permitted to hire this service, at least within certain wards of Edo.[27] Literary evidence shows that able-bodied, adult male commoners employed palanquins as well, and there were periodic efforts to discourage this violation of the laws. In 1720, for example, Edo authorities ordered that the blinds concealing passengers in private palanquins be removed—the better to aid in the law's enforcement.[28]

Status distinctions, however, had to be observed—in transport as well as in clothing and housing. Palanquins varied greatly in quality, the finer sometimes being called norimono. Kaempfer, who with the Dutch mission traveled much of the way from Nagasaki to Edo in such a vehicle, describes the types in detail in his *History of Japan*:

> Besides going on horseback, there is another more stately and expensive way of travelling in this country, and that is to be carried in Norimons [*norimono*] and Cangos [*kago*], or particular sorts of chairs, or litters. The same is usual likewise in the cities. People of quality are carried about in this manner for state, others for ease and convenience. There is a wide difference between the litters men of quality go in, and those of ordinary people. The former are sumptuous and magnificent, according to one's rank and riches. The latter are plain and simple. The former are commonly call'd Norimons, the latter Cangos. The vulgar (in all nations masters of the language) have call'd them by two different names, tho' in fact they are but one thing. Norimon signifies, properly speaking, a thing to sit in, Cangos, a basket, or dosser. Both sorts rise thro' such a variety of degrees, from the lowest to the highest, from the plainest to the most curious, that a fine Cangos is scarce to be distinguished from a plain and simple Norimon, but for its pole. The pole of a Cangos is plain, massy, all of one piece, and smaller than that of a Norimon, which is large, curiously adorn'd, and hollow. The pole of a Norimon is made up of four thin boards, neatly join'd together in the form of a

wide arch, and much lighter than it appears to be. The bigness and length of these poles hath been determined by the political laws of the Empire, proportionable to every one's quality. . . .

The Norimon itself is a small room, of an oblong square figure, big enough for one person conveniently to sit or lie in, curiously twisted of fine thin split Bambous, sometimes japan'd (lacquered) and finely painted, with a small folding-door on each side, sometimes a small window before and behind. Sometimes it is fitted up for the conveniency of sleeping in it. It ends in a small roof, which in rainy weather is cover'd with a covering of varnished paper. It is carried by two, four, eight or more men, according to the quality of the person in it, who, if he be a Prince, or Lord of a Province, they carry the pole on the palms of their hands, otherwise they lay it on their shoulders. All these Norimon-men are clad in the same livery, with the coat of arms, or mark of their masters. They are every now and then reliev'd by others, who in the mean time walk by the Norimons side. The Cangos are not near so fine, nor so well attended. They are much of the same figure, but smaller, with a square, solid, sometimes with a round pole, which is either fasten'd to the upper part of the roof, or put thro' it underneath. The Cangos commonly made use of for travelling, chiefly carrying people over mountains, are very poor and plain, and withal so small, that one cannot sit in them without very great inconveniency, bowing his head downward, and laying the legs across; for they are not unlike a basket with a round bottom, and flat roof, which one reaches with his head. In such Cangos we are carried over the rocks and mountains, which are not easily to be pass'd on horseback. Three men are appointed for every Cango, who indeed, for the heaviness of the burden, have enough to do.[29]

It was sweated labor, and the men dressed appropriately. Kaempfer remarks elsewhere how "it appears ridiculous to an European, to see all the Pike bearers and Norimon-men, with their cloaths tuck'd up above their waste, exposing their naked backs to the spectator's view, having only their privities cover'd with a piece of cloath."[30]

A fourth type of transport worker, the packhorseman (*umakata*, *mumakata* or *mago*), delivered passengers or merchandise on horseback, and constituted much of the traffic on the great highways linking the principal cities. Many of these drivers (and a good many porters as well) worked for the post stations (*shukuba*) that had been established by the shogunate along these major arteries. The post stations employed full-time professional drivers to service shogunate officers, daimyos' cavalcades making their regular sankin-kōtai journeys to and from Edo, and the large number of commoners who traveled on these highways.

They also conscripted corvee laborers from the villages in the vicinity. The Five Highways[31] were directly administered by the shogunate, and the villages within a radius of ten to eighteen kilometers were obliged to provide porters and packhorsemen to the stations, regardless of the political status of the local barony. It is not clear when the shogunate first imposed the conscription system, but by 1637 it seems likely that at least some of the porters and drivers were corvee laborers rather than independent professionals, and after 1694 a corvee system (called *sukego* or "assisting villages") was certainly in place.[32]

Professional packhorsemen and conscripted drivers alike were obliged to observe three types of rates for their services. Shogunate officials were serviced free. Daimyo paid fixed prices, but when they required over half the personnel available at one station they were obliged to negotiate rates, just like commoners, and usually wound up paying roughly twice the officially fixed fee.[33]

During the course of the eighteenth century, the conscription system began to give way to a system of free, voluntary, contracted labor. Many villages requested that their post station labor-tax be commuted to a cash payment, or as an alternative, they chose to hire packhorsemen and porters to perform the required labor-service. As Constantine Vaporis notes, transport workers then formed labor pools at each post station.[34]

In reading through Tokugawa period fiction, or perusing ukiyo-e prints, one frequently meets with these packhorsemen, lingering at the post stations as they purchase refreshment, receive a rubdown, and solicit customers who had boarded overnight in the inns. Those in Chikamatsu's celebrated puppet play *Tanba Yosaku* (1708) are clearly professional, rather than conscripted, workers,[35] as are most of those we encounter in Jippensha Ikkū's *Hizakurige*. Kaempfer seems to refer to free professionals in the following passage:

> In some places, both within and without cities and villages, one meets sometimes empty Cangos and Palanquins, or empty and saddled, tho' otherwise but meanlooking horses, and the men to attend them, who offer themselves and their horses to carry weary foot-travellers to the next post-house, or where they please, for a small matter. Commonly they have been already employ'd, and would be obliged to return empty to the place, from whence they set out, if they did not pick up some body by the way, that will, or hath occasion to make use of them.[36]

Transportation workers in general, and packhorsemen in particular, had a poor reputation. "Ships' captains, packhorsemen, wetnurses—they're all the same," went the proverb:[37] in the popular mind they ranked with these others as ill-tempered wretches. They are masters of verbal abuse. Packhorsemen in Jippensha's comic work accost one another on the road with such greetings as "Hello, beast! (*hē chikushōme*),"

"Eat shit (*kuso kurae*)!" "Suck my asshole (*ketsu demo shabure*)!" The
exchanges are good-natured enough, however, and they are, the writer,
observes, the only salutations they seem to know.[38] Palanquin-bearers
show no more refinement. One resting against the wall of a teahouse calls
to a passing comrade: "Hey there, Hachibei! Better hurry on home, you
animal, and keep an eye on that wife of yours! Her lover's sneaking in!"
"Fool!" comes the reply. "Don't you know your father's just hung himself? Go take a shit!"[39]

Naturally packhorsemen and palanquin-bearers treated their customers with somewhat greater courtesy, but their reputation as smart alecks
was probably well deserved. One young packhorseman in *Hizakurige*
boldly entreats a samurai for a larger tip while indulging in vulgar jokes
at his customer's expense.[40] A regulation issued by an Edo magistrate in
1711 warns that there "must be no impertinence" towards officials hiring
the laborers' services.[41] (However corvee laborers, as opposed to the professionals, may have been more deferential to their patrons. I find only
one agreeable packhorseman in *Hizakurige*, and of him the author explains, "He was a peasant called up to do corvee labor service, so he was
polite." He is also depicted as hopelessly ignorant, inquiring of his rider,
"Where's Edo?"[42])

Foul mouths were not the only unsavory feature of these workers.
Many, like the porters and palanquin bearers licensed to carry travelers
across the Ōi River near Kyoto on the Tōkaidō, were notorious for ex-
torting tips to supplement the official wage. The term used for "tip,"
sakate, approximates the French *pourboire*.[43] Some were accused of even
graver offenses. In his memoirs (ca. 1720) Arai Hakuseki reported that
porters on the Tōkaidō highway often abandoned their customers along
the way. They were difficult to discipline because innkeepers and other
post-station personnel were often intimidated by the workers and their
gangs, and would not cooperate in official investigations:

> Both in Edo and in Kyoto and Osaka, there are so-called casual laborers who
> are hired as temporary attendants by travelers passing from one capital to
> the other. One example of the lawlessness of these bearers is that they say
> they are tired and demand horses and palanquins and then ride themselves
> while they make the regular bearers carry what they themselves should
> carry. Telling the regular bearers that if they want to return home quickly
> they will let them go, they exact money and then let them go. Also, if they
> have a grudge against anyone at the post-stations, they tell their fellows, and
> in the end, they take revenge on him in some way, so that innkeepers at the
> post-stations will give no information.[44]

Yet workers of this type do present an appealing aspect: their habit of
easing their monotonous labor by singing work-songs, many of which

survive, their content ranging from nonsense to romantic love to the beauty of the wild iris.[45] The play *Tanba Yosaku* gives the impression that daimyo tended to take vocal skills, as well as personal appearances, into consideration when hiring a packhorseman.[46] Porters' and packhorse-mens' songs color such travel tales as Asai Ryōi's *Tōkaidō Meishoki* (Famous Sites along the Tōkaidō, 1659) and *Hizakurige*. The second volume of the latter work begins on a gentle note: "The porters' song about the 'eight *ri* to Hakone' quiets the heart of their boss (*sairyō*), and the pack-horsemen's song about the sparrows in the bamboo warms the strong rice-wine."[47] Perhaps Jippensha was thinking of such verses as these, common to many packhorsemen's songs:

Nagai dōchū de	On your long journey,
ame furu naraba	when it rains,
washi no namida	to please, remember
omoute kure	my tears!
Ao yo naku na you	Blacky! don't cry, horse!
ora uchi'a chikai	We're almost home.
mori no naka kara	You can see the lights
hi ga mieru	from inside the woods.
Kokoro-sabishiya	Ah, how lonely it is!
bakuro no yomichi	a wretched packhorse-driver's night road,
naru wa kutsuwa no	the jangling of the bit
oto bakari	the only sound.[48]

But while some of these songs are touching, others, such as the one that asks "What happened to Hachibei? What? Devoured by the horse? Dokoi! Dokoi!" are clearly just for fun.[49]

From the early seventeenth century an official express postal system also made use of the highways and their post-stations, and employed large numbers of official postmen. Messengers on horseback called "fly-ing feet" (*hikyaku*) were provided with horses maintained for official purposes. By horse, news could reach Osaka from Edo in ninety-six hours, or Kyoto from Edo in eighty-two. Later, this form of postal ser-vice was called "fast horse" (*haya-uma*), to distinguish it from a slower system of express runners now referred to as hikyaku. Two runners (*goyōbako-ninsoku*; "official mailbox carriers") would work as a team, the first carrying a paper lantern inscribed with the characters "official business" (*goyō*). The lantern, and the bearer's cry "*Ei-sassa, ei-sassa!*" signaled pedestrians to make way for the runner carrying the letter-box (*goyōbako* or "official business box").[50] Pedestrians who ignored the warning, like Yaji in *Hizakurige*, risked a blow on the head from the passing box.[51]

TABLE 5.3
Number of Licensed Postal Express Firms

	Osaka	Kyoto	Edo
1663	4	3	7
1751	12	16	9
1773	9	13	9

Source: Neil Skene Smith, ed., "Materials on Japanese Social and Economic History: Tokugawa Japan," Transactions of the Asiatic Society of Japan, 2d ser., XIV (1937).

In Osaka in 1663, merchants formed postal express firms for the use of ordinary people, employing carriers who left on the second, twelfth, and twenty-second days of each month. Licensed by urban authorities, they were allowed the use of three horses maintained at the post-stations. In Osaka and Kyoto, each firm employed fifteen carriers, whose efficiency was examined each month by a senior employee.[52] Such postal services seem to have boomed into the mid-nineteenth century, when Western visitors remarked upon their efficiency. (Philipp Franz von Siebold, in Japan from 1823 to 1829, found them "wonderfully expeditious," and three decades later Sir Rutherford Alcock praised their swiftness, punctuality and trustworthiness.)[53] Their numbers probably declined in the Kansai cities because of population stagnation from the mid-eighteenth century (Table 5.3). Edo may have benefited from this decline, since the names of the city's postal express firms (Osaka-ya, Yamada-ya, Yamashiro-ya, Fushimi-ya, Izumi-ya), clearly suggest Western origins.

An 1806 regulation indicates that on the average a letter mailed through one of these private Edo postal firms, on the second, fifth, or eighth days of the month took twenty-five to twenty-six days to reach Osaka, while the fastest ones took ten days. But the efficiency and speed praised by Siebold and Alcock had a high price: the charge for sixty-one kan (8.25 pounds) would cost fifty monme to send.[54] This equalled perhaps one-half a maidservant's annual earnings.

One final group of workers engaged in the delivery of goods deserves mention. Stevedores (nakashi or nakashū in Osaka, ko-age in Edo) and other dock workers unloaded cargoes at the wharves of coastal cities (such as those of Kitahama in Osaka), often transporting them on to waiting warehouses (kurashiki). Such sites would present a picture of frenzied activity as menial laborers of a dozen types went about their tasks, and fortunately detailed descriptions have survived. A guide to Osaka's Dojima Rice Exchange, authored by one Tōhaku in 1748 and entitled Beikoku baibai shusse guruma,[55] and Saikaku's Nippon eitaigura (1693) are particularly useful.

Once the small rice-boats arrive at Kitahama, writes Tōhaku, they are

unloaded by warehouse employees called *nakashū*. (The term is an abbre-
viation of *nakama-shū* or "group of comrades" which had come to mean
"dockworker." *Nakashi* was also used.) Under the supervision of a foreman (*kashira*), the same workers examine the bales of rice to ensure they
are of proper weight and have suffered no water-damage.[56] (Saikaku describes how they ascertained the condition of the grain. Employing sharp-
ened bamboo shafts called *kome-sashi* ("rice-stabbers"), workers would
pierce the bales, extracting a measure of rice in the hollow of the shafts.
"The powerful youths, violently [piercing the rice-bales] with the tips of
their *kura-sashi*, remind one of tigers crouching in a bamboo forest."[57])

These are called *hyōbetsu* (bale-separating laborers). Then on to the
warehouse: well-muscled dock workers called *kura-nakashi* (warehouse
laborers) load bales of rice weighing 50 to 90 liters "as though the bales
were made of paper-mache" onto the backs of waiting packhorses or carrying poles of coolies. "Truly the best acrobatics show in Japan!" Tōhaku
declares.[58]

Saikaku mentions that other workers sweep the fallen rice from the
docks. They are not included in Tōhaku's work, but his list nevertheless
seems quite comprehensive:

> Those who distribute the rice to the wholesalers are known as *tonya-nakashi*
> [wholesalers' laborers] or *dashimono-nakashi* [laborers who deliver goods].
> The foreman [*gashira*] of the *tonya-nakashi* is also responsible for various
> minor laborers who are colloquially known as *ni bu kiri nakashi* ["half-inch
> laborers"], *shitanakashi* ["under-laborers"], *orai-nakashi* [street laborers],
> *miso-nakashi* ["bean-paste laborers"] or *anko-nakashi* [bean-jam laborers]
> and so on.[59]

We are not told the significance of these curious appellations. Perhaps
they refer to the goods that various laborers unloaded, but they seem to
reflect someone's sense of humor.[60]

WORKERS IN CONSTRUCTION AND OTHER FIELDS

Workers in construction and civil engineering included unskilled carpenters, masons, earth removers, stone haulers, ditch diggers, and miscellaneous coolies referred to by such terms as *ninsoku* (written with the
characters for "person" and "foot"). During the latter half of the period,
all such workers came to be called *shigotoshi* (lit. "worker"). *Daiku*
and *takumi*, general terms for carpenters, included such laborers along
with skilled artisans. Menial workers might also be numbered among
masons (*sakon*), or specialists in castle construction (*anou*). Two specific
categories, *tobi no mono* and *teko no mono*, seem to have been especially
numerous.

Workers of both types were so named after the tools they carried. Tobi no mono ("tobi-men", also called *tobiguchi, tobi-ninpu, tobi-shaku,* or simply *tobi*) wielded axes called *tobi-guchi* ("kite's beaks"). Fitted with iron hooks thought to resemble the beak of a kite, tobi-guchi were all-purpose tools. Raftsmen used them in steering; firemen, in tearing down buildings in the path of a blaze. I will refer to those who use these as "hookmen." Teko no mono ("teko-men," or *teko no shū, teko no mae*) carried *teko* or levers, used in moving large rocks or trees to construction sites; some worked with "wood-levers" (*ki no teko*), others with "metal-levers" (*kin no teko*). Chikamatsu makes a reference to a *"teko no shū* working the bellows of a blacksmith's shop;"[61] clearly the term was often synonymous with "workman." I render it as "leverman." Originally hookmen seem to have been official workers (*jō tobi*) conscripted from the commoner population. In Edo, each ward was to provide one worker, invariably a tenant or servant, to aid in official construction projects and to serve as firemen. Some of these these served under ward police officers. All official hookmen were forbidden to hire themselves out to private employers, but soon they were soon joined by free, independent workers referred to as *kaketsuke-tobi* or *kakae-tobi* ("hired hookmen"). By the Tenmei period (1781–88), workers of the latter sort were more numerous; in the seventh year of that era a City Commissioner's report stresses that while wards must fulfill their obligation to provide official hookmen, they might also employ independent workers.[62]

It may seem curious that both hookmen and levermen served as fire-fighters in addition to their duties as manual laborers. It was however common, in preindustrial societies, to hire common workmen for this least appealing of chores. (London residents were by law required to take precautions against fire and to keep water-jugs and ladders on hand, but as late as the Great Fire of 1666 the city had no official fire brigade.[63]) In Japan, hookmen and levermen were best suited for the task, wielding their equipment to level buildings, creating fire-breaks in the path of the blaze.

Edo had possessed a substantial fire-fighting force as early as 1629, but the original firemen (*hikeshi*) were low-ranking samurai furnished by the daimyo (*daimyō hikeshi*). These were soon supplemented by firemen conscripted from the commoner classes (*sadame-hikeshi*) who served under samurai leaders. In 1718 units of commoner firemen (*machi hikeshi*), drawn from the ranks of hookmen and other menials, were organized under their own cap tains. Due to friction between the samurai and commoner groups, they generally confined their attentions to predominantly samurai wards, and mainly commoner wards respectively.[64] (In Osaka, fire-fighters were drawn almost entirely from commoner hookmen and levermen.[65])

Kaempfer caught a glimpse of a group of firemen while visiting Edo in 1691:

> Among other people we met a company of fire-men on foot, being about one hundred in number, walking in much the same military order as ours do in Europe: they were clad in brown leather-coats to defend them against the fire, and some carried long pikes, others fire-hooks upon their shoulders: their Captain rode in the middle.[66]

Here "fire-hooks" presumably means tobi.

Carpenters also included many unskilled, casual laborers. The great construction boom of the early Tokugawa period had accelerated the process, underway from the middle of the Muromachi period, whereby teams of carpenters became independent from temple or political patrons.[67] Meanwhile, technological advances, and the increasing standardization of techniques, allowed skilled carpenters to employ and supervise a larger number of unskilled workers.[68]

Some scholars of the period (Ogyū, Dazai, and Miura Baien, for example) deplored these changes, and attributed a supposed decline in building quality to the transition to a wage labor system. Given the increasingly complex division of labor in the construction industry, they said, shogunate contractors know nothing of carpentry, and carpenters know nothing of the timber industry. Moreover, Ogyū complains,

> Formerly each family of carpenters had a scroll which was handed down from generation to generation and whose provisions were rigidly adhered to, but now carpenters are driven by the necessity of making a livelihood to undertake as much work as they can. As a result, their work has become increasingly inferior in quality and the houses they build soon fall into disrepair.[69]

Nevertheless, the work of Tokugawa carpenters seems to have been of high quality by world standards. While foreigners had few words of praise for Japanese architecture of commoners' homes, they consistently gave the Japanese carpenter high marks. Rodrigues declared that

> all the houses in the land are built of wood and the architectural art involved in this is as skillful as you will find in any other part of the world. Indeed, in the view of responsible people who have seen various parts of Europe, Japanese construction in wood does not appear to be surpassed or even equalled elsewhere.[70]

Two and a half centuries later, on the eve of the Restoration, Sir Rutherford Alcock opined that the Japanese "are, perhaps, the neatest carpenters and cabinet-makers, and the best coopers in the world."[71]

We glean some sense of the appearance of these workers from Saikaku, who describes teams of thatchers and carpenters crossing Edo's Nihon-bashi bridge at sunset, returning home from work at various daimyos' mansions:

> They were in their groups, 200–300 at a time, and were chattering in high discordant tones. Their side-locks stood out from their cheeks, and their hair was in disorder. Their jackets were dirty at the collar, and they wore their belts over their jackets, which were torn at the cuffs. Some used their rulers as walking-sticks, more hunched their shoulders, with their hands thrust into the front of their kimono, and from their back view as they walked along there was no need of a sign to show what trade they were. Behind them came their apprentices, who were carrying the shavings and cut-off ends, but no one cared if some precious cypress end-bits fell and were left behind.[72]

In the story, a sharp entrepreneur begins to acquire a fortune collecting and selling these fallen wood-shavings.

Rice polishers (*kometsuki*) were another large component of the labor force. Employed by "polished rice shops" (*tsukigomeya*), they would hull the grain, using a type of mortar (*kara-usu*) with a foot-operated pestle. In some shops, large numbers of workers would be employed full-time, working in an unfloored room of the building furnished with numerous mortars.[73] These operations actually resemble manufacturing.

During the Tokugawa period, peddlers (*botefuri*) were often regarded as a type of day laborer. In fact, those who hawked their wares as agents of a shop, and who were obliged to divide their profits with an employer, were comparable to day laborers, but I consider most of them petty merchants. Most did not sell their labor power in return for a wage; rather, they bought goods cheap, and sold them as dear as the market would allow. Tokugawa literature is filled with examples of hawkers who, shrewdly assessing market conditions and the profits to be made from other people's waste, gradually accumulate fortunes.

However, casual workers of the type I have described often supplemented their wage work with peddling. Of the thirty-three day laborers listed in the Edo hyōshō records, ten also worked as peddlers on the side, selling vegetables, sweets, incense sticks, straw sandals, flowering plants, bean curd, or soy sauce.[74]

A word remains to be said about female casual workers. Like their sisters in early-modern England,[75] Japanese women of the Tokugawa period were not confined to the household, limited to the role of wife and mother. They were full participants in the workforce. It was considered ideal for wives to work alongside their husbands. "When husband and wife put their efforts together," wrote Saikaku, "they can make a liv-

TABLE 5.4
Female Casual Hired Workers in Edo Hyōshō

Year of Award	Name	Occupation(s)	Current Age
1793	Sayo	hired seamstress, peddler of incense sticks	38
1801	Mina	laundress, peddler of straw sandals	?
1805	Hisa	wage labor [*chin-shigoto*], peddler of flowering plants, bean curd and soy sauce	33
1805	Chiyo	wage-earning laundress [*chin sentaku*]	?
1805	Seki	wage-earning laundress	?

Source: See Table 2.23.

ing."[76] Unlike women of northern China, who took little part in agriculture, Japanese women worked in the fields with their husbands, fathers and brothers.[77] In some occupations, such as pearl diving, they held a monopoly; in others, such as mining, they were alloted special tasks. Blind women traditionally became masseuses or shamisen players.

In Tokugawa cities, women appear as tailors, laundresses, dyers, textile workshop hands, rice sweepers (on the docks), and many other roles besides prostitutes and servants. Saikaku describes female carpenters, for example, employed by the Imperial Palace in Kyoto:

> In the toolbox, there are drills, planes, an inking device, and a carpenter's square. Take a closer look at [the carpenter's] face, and [you'll see] it's a *woman*. Her nose is flat, and her limbs are brawny. Skillful at carpentry, she does this for a living, residing in Ichijo Modoribashi. "But why," you ask, "when the capital is so big, and there are so many *male* carpenters and cabinet makers, would anyone hire a woman carpenter?"
>
> [They are hired] to fashion the protective spikes over the walls, and the bamboo window lattices, of the women's quarters in the Imperial Palaces. It's simple work, but it's such trouble to investigate the background of male carpenters. It saves time to just hire women for the job.[78]

This is of course a special case; male workers might pose a threat to the virtue of the ladies in the seraglio. But it was not uncommon for women to work as manual laborers. In the large mining town of Aikawa,[79] on the island of Sado, women worked in the gold and silver mines, hauling ore or crushing it with long hammers. Some, infant at breast, operated a panning device called a *nekonagashi*, while experienced, elderly women directed the whole operation.[80]

In 1705, in the castle-town of Kasama, six of the total thirty-two persons registered as day laborers were women. All were widows.[81] The hyōshō records of Edo, which also include a sample of thirty-two casual laborers, include the names of five women. One Hisa is working to support an ill husband. Sayo is apparently widowed; she lives with her mother-in-law and daughter. Seki lives with her seventy-three-year-old mother, a son, and adopted daughter.[82] Four of the women supplement their earnings by hawking incense sticks, straw sandals, flowering plants, bean curd, or soy sauce. (See Table 5.4).

AGES OF CASUAL WORKERS

Work careers often began in childhood. While preteens in a merchant house would be sent off to a household of similar status to serve as apprentices or domestics, children of less affluent backgrounds found jobs as manual workers. Many packhorsemen (like Sankichi in *Tanba Yosaku*) were mere boys.

The Edo hyōshō provide several examples of day laborers who began work at age sixteen (i.e., fourteen or fifteen by our reckoning). However, the average age of the twenty-seven men is suprisingly high: 36.8 years (Table 5.5). Ages for two of the five women are recorded. Both are in their thirties.[83] The Kasama data provide quite a contrast. In 1705, the average age of the thirty-two day laborers in the town was fifty-two; there is no difference between the figures for males and females. The youngest was a mere child of eleven, but all except two were over forty (see Table 5.6). Twenty-one of the total (66%) were migrants into the castle-town, and of these the average age was fifty-five.

The average age of natives was a still rather venerable forty-seven years.[84] These older workers probably had experienced the tragic life cyle of the beggars who, as Ogyū Sorai described them, "came to Edo as hired servants and who, after having gone from one place of employment to another, are now unable in their old age to return to their birthplaces."[85] Day labor was one of the few job options left them.

The older Kasama day laborers, in fact, had few family members to support them. Their households were very small—a mere 1.9 persons, precisely half the town average of 3.8. Only twelve of the thirty-two were married, and all six women were widows. But circumstances in the Hitachi castle-town may have been exceptional. The lack of young laborers might reflect the fact that Edo—a mere 100 kilometers away, eighteen stops down the Tōkaidō highway—had drawn away many of the castle-town's youth. Certainly literary sources do not suggest that casual laborers were generally older people. Saikaku refers to day laborers with "four

TABLE 5.5
Ages of Male Hyōshō Recipients in Edo

Year of Award	Name	Occupation(s)	Age Began Occupation	Current Age
1787	Kichigorō	day laborer, vegetable peddler	15	30
1791	Sadagorō	porter (of earth and sand)	?	41
1791	Inosuke	ward hookman	?	49
1791	Kyūjirō	ward coolie	?	37
1792	Shōzaburō	day laborer	?	36
1796	Chōjirō	day laborer (employed by low-ranking samurai)	?	36
1796	Heizō	day laborer (employed by basket maker)	23	25
1796	Shitarō	palanquin bearer	28?	39
1797	Yohei	day laborer (employed by official mat-maker)	39	42
1797	Yosuke	carter	?	39
1798	Tomosuke	day laborer	?	29
1798	Kichigorō	day laborer	?	24
1799	Kihei	day laborer	?	?
1799	Heigorō	day laborer	?	?
1802	Seizaburō	vegetable peddler, public palanquin bearer	16	25
1802	Chōkichi	carter (of earth)	?	?
1808	Kizaburō	day laborer (employed by dyer)	?	?
1814	Yasugorō	hookman	?	41
1815	Kōkichi	day laborer (employed by tiler)	35	49
1816	Jihei	official coolie	?	?
1816	Yagorō	day laborer, sailor	16	16
1821	Sadagorō	day laborer	?	46
1826	Ginjirō	day laborer (employed by dyer)	?	?
1841	Denzō	day laborer, night peddler	34?	35
1841	Sanjirō	day laborer (employed by confectioner)	20	30
1842	Shūzaburō	day laborer	?	?
1842	Sōkichi	letter carrier, day laborer (employed by metallurgist)	?	?

Source: See Table 2.23.

or five mouths to feed" in Osaka circa 1690,[86] and one hundred years later Ueda Akinari observed numerous children in Osaka's working-class ward of Nagamachi.[87] William Elliot Griffis also noted the many children of "coolies or burden-bearers" in Tokyo in 1871: "In Japan the quiver of poverty is full, while the man of wealth mourns for an heir."[88]

TABLE 5.6
Ages of Kasama Day Laborers, 1705

10–19	1
20–29	1
30–39	—
40–49	9
50–59	13
60–69	7
70–79	1

Source: See Table 1.3.

ORGANIZATION AND CONDITIONS OF LABOR

Urban artisans as well as merchants had from medieval times been organized into closed, privileged groups, usually associated with the imperial court, temples or feudal magnates. Originally called za, they underwent a long evolution before being dismantled by the regimes of Oda Nobunaga (1568–85) and Toyotomi Hideyoshi (1585–98). Soon after the establishment of the Tokugawa administration, however, exclusive trade organizations called nakama resurfaced. Those referred to as kabu-nakama were licensed by the shogunate or daimyo, permitted a fixed number of transferable membership rights (kabu), and subject to taxation.[89]

Some draw a clear distinction between the za and the kabu-nakama, but in fact it is difficult to pin down the differences between these institutions, and indeed many kabu-nakama of the Tokugawa period retained the term "za" in their names. Both were closed, privileged, chartered organizations which featured an apprenticeship system, controlled quality of goods produced or sold, and bound members together by common rituals and religious practices. I think it reasonable to follow the example of Japanese scholars and to translate both these terms into English as "guild."[90]

Skilled workers and artisans were organized into guilds by the late medieval period, and a Kyoto shokunin-za ("artisans' guild") mentioned in a 1633 document had apparently existed for some time.[91] By 1699 there were in Edo officially recognized organizations of carpenters, sawyers, roofers, plasterers, tilers, coopers, and other artisans whose headmen (ki-moiri) were appointed by the shogunate. Later, these artisan groups were superseded by organizations called kumiai or "unions." (The term could also, however, mean a merchant association.) Artisans' kumiai elected their officials, known as gyōji, who represented them in their relations with the shogunate.[92]

Casual workers, however, were probably not included in these institutions. A master craftsman might hire menial laborers to assist with a project, but they did not have any long-term commitment to him and would be clearly distinguished from his small circle of apprentices. Outside the guild system, casual workers formed their own groups (*kumi*) under leaders called *oyakata*, and *oyabun* (both these terms suggesting "parent"), *kashira* ("head" or "chief"), *sōryō* (lit. "elder brother") or *sairyō* (superintendent). Although political authorities sometimes imposed additional layers of organization upon some types of workers, such unchartered, voluntary associations were the principle units of casual labor organization.

These associations, established for mutual security, were bound together by an *esprit de corps* bolstered by ties of "ritual kinship."[93] Members were "brothers" (*kyōdaibun*), observing distinctions of status among themselves (*anikibun* or "older brothers" held more authority than *ototobun* or "younger brothers") and at times bound together by a spirit of antisocial rebelliousness. Groups of construction workers, for example, particularly during the seventeenth century, doubled as urban gangs of the *machi-yakko* variety described in chapter 4. The most famous machi-yakko leader was Banzuiin Chōbei, a labor foreman (oyakata) who supplied workers for shogunate construction projects. Murdered by a *hata-moto-yakko* leader in 1650, Chōbei is celebrated in many semifictional accounts.[94] Gang activity tapered off as the result of police repression late in the seventeenth century, but the organizations never disappeared entirely. In the waning years of the Tokugawa regime, the head of the Edo otokodate, Shinmon Tatsugorō, provided the coolies who accompanied Shogun Iemochi on his journey to the Kyoto court.[95]

The hookmen and levermen in fire brigades seem to have been a particularly disorderly group. Major battles between rival work-teams erupted in Edo in 1718, 1782, 1805, and 1824.[96] A relatively minor brawl between two teams of Edo fire-fighters in 1798 was satirized by Shikitei Sanba in his *Kyan taiheiki mukō hachimaki* the following year.[97] Deeply offended by the lampoon, the members of one of the brigades then attacked houses of Sanba and his publisher. The gang members were imprisoned for their offense (but Sanba was also punished by a prison sentence of fifty days, and the publisher was fined).[98]

The oyakata who headed one of these unruly work-groups was something like the *rôleur* of seventeenth-century France:[99] he organized his workers, contracted jobs on their behalf, assigned tasks, doled out wages, and received a share of the profits. He was usually a man of exceptional physical prowess and natural leadership ability, attracting his workers by these qualities and perhaps by personal charm. The fictional character

Chūroku, a construction foreman (*fushin no hiyō-gashira*) in one of Sai-kaku's works, is "always making jokes" and, with his fine singing voice, is regarded as "the town entertainer."[100]

The relationship between the oyakata and his workers, like the tie between master-artisan and apprentice, or samurai and retainer, was also one of ritual kinship. It has survived well into the twentieth century, when modern sociologists have termed it the "*oyabun-kobun relationship*." (*Oya* means parent, *ko* means child, and the suffix *-bun* or *-kata* indicates the fictive nature of the tie.) Particularly common among miners, stevedores, and construction workers prior to World War II, the ritual kinship system sometimes included not only symbolic parent-child ties but ritual grandfather-grandson relationships as well.[101]

An oyabun-kobun relationship was established by a ceremony which (like the marriage ceremony or rite cementing feudal retainership) involved the ritual drinking of rice wine. An induction of workers into a Fukushima construction company, observed by a Japanese anthropologist in the early 1950s, probably differed little from Tokugawa practice. The inductees join the oyakata at a table laden with wine cups, two flasks of ceremonial rice wine, two cooked fish (laid stomach-to-stomach), and a dish of salt. The wine was poured into the cups, along with a pinch of salt and a piece of the fish. The drink, representing blood, was then imbibed in turn by the oyakata and the new workers in three distinct motions.

The three sips of wine mimic the Shinto marriage ceremony; the fish represent birth. Following this ritual, the oyakata presented the new workers with new names and new working jackets (*happi*)—symbolic "baby clothes." As fictive father, the oyakata must henceforth provide the workers with training, loans when necessary, medical care, and paternal advice. The workers, in turn, meet their obligations to the oyakata, even including payment for his funeral expenses.[102]

Unfortunately this idyllic account conveys only part of the picture. Early twentieth-century oyakata in the building trades, often identifying with the Tokugawa otokodate, were known to brutalize striking workers; they also provided much of the membership in such protofascist societies as the *Dai Nippon Kokusuikai*.[103] Occupation authorities, who estimated that three million Japanese workers (90 percent of all construction workers) were employed under the oyabun-kobun system immediately after World War II, stressed the evils of the system and attempted to destroy it. Workers, a 1949 *Monthly Labor Review* article by a SCAP official noted, were not free to quit their jobs or seek new employment without the oyakata's permission. They were unable to organize to demand higher wages. They were denied a large proportion of their earnings (as much as 30%) withheld by the oyakata. Their wages and working conditions were "far below the standards of the poorest class of *free worker* in Japan [emphasis added]."[104] Significantly perhaps, the oyakata system is today most closely associated with the brutal underworld of *yakuza* gangsters.[105]

Of course the oyakata system must have undergone a long evolution. The modern oyakata attacked by Occupation authorities was a highly exploitive capitalist, but what of his Tokugawa precursor? Even in the early Tokugawa period some oyakata became highly successful entrepreneurs; the famous businessman Kawamura Zuiken (1616–99) may have originally amassed a fortune as a labor contractor of this type.[106] The great folklorist Yanagida Kunio suggested that the nature of the oyakata underwent a transition, beginning in the Tokugawa period, from a "foreman" who actually directed work to "a boss pure and simple."[107] Even in the late nineteeth and early twentieth century, however, the ties between workers and oyakata were so close that modern industrial operations had to procure their labor force through the latter—rather than through direct recruitment. Companies such as the Shibaura Engineering Works also relied upon oyakata to lodge, feed, train and supervise workers on the job. Graduates of technical institutes were not suited for direct management, since they "had little practical understanding of the work process and a strong sense of social distance from the uneducated workers."[108] The first industrial labor unions in Japan *included* oyakata, although by the 1930s many were drawn into the managerial hierarchy of major companies.[109]

Thus the Tokugawa-period oyakata must have had an ambiguous nature. Profiting directly from the labor power of his team, he resembles a modern capitalist. His link to his workers, however, was no mere "cash-nexus" but a profound mutual obligation to provide support.

Among carpenters, the oyakata was called *sōryō* or *sōbeya*. An early seventeenth-century work compares his duties to those of a military commander who is intimately aware of his troops' strengths and weaknesses:

> The Way of a foreman carpenter [*daiku no sōryō*] is the same as the Way of the commander of a warrior house. . . . The foreman carpenter allots his men work according to their ability. Floor layers, makers of sliding doors, thresholds and lintels, ceilings and so on. Those of poor ability lay the floor joists, and those of lesser ability carve wedges and do such miscellaneous work. If the foreman knows and deploys his men well the finished work will be good.[110]

The oyakata is himself drawn from the ranks of the carpenters: "When the carpenter becomes skilled and understands measures he himself can become a foreman."

TABLE 5.7
Organization of Labor among Tōkaidō Packhorsemen

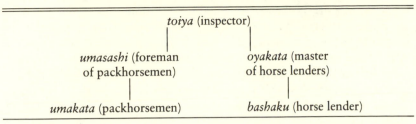

	toiya (inspector)	
umasashi (foreman of packhorsemen)		*oyakata* (master of horse lenders)
umakata (packhorsemen)		*bashaku* (horse lender)

Kōda Rohan's novelette *The Five-Storied Pagoda*, written only twenty-four years after the Meiji Restoration and set in the Tokugawa period, provides some insight into relations among carpenters in preindustrial Japan. The story's hero Jūbei has worked under an oyakata named Genta for about a year. The latter, a renowned craftsman with a staff of many workmen, hopes to win a contract to build a great pagoda for a local temple. Violating all the social norms, his subordinate competes for, and wins, the assignment, thus becoming a foreman (sōryō) in his own right. Receiving only hostility from his former workmates, Jūbei employs his own workers, including unskilled day laborers, to complete the project. The story illustrates the elements of paternalism in the oyakata-worker relationship; Genta frequently wines and dines his men, and his wife helps to clothe them and their families. Jūbei's bid for the construction contract is regarded by his mates as a betrayal of Genta's kindness. The story also suggests, however, that outside a circle of highly trained carpenters who enjoyed a close bond with the oyakata, there were many more unskilled workers, hired for specific jobs on a temporary basis, who worked alongside the master carpenter's work team.[111]

Packhorsemen were subject to the hierarchy of authority shown in Table 5.7. The inspector was ultimately responsible for transportation of goods and the conduct of the workers. He usually doubled as an innkeeper servicing highway travelers. Under him, a foreman called an *umasashi* directed the duties of the packhorseman, while another, referred to as an *oyakata*, supervised not workers but horse lenders who lent out their animals to packhorsemen with none of their own. The individual packhorseman's job depended upon all of these. "How can a public packhorseman (*kōyō umakata*) make a living if he's been denounced to the packhorsemen's foremen and inspectors?" asks a character in *Tanba Yosaku*.[112] "They keep the highways under strict control. Once you're reported to the horse-lenders and inspectors (*bashaku toiya*), nobody'll employ you!"

Workers found jobs through these oyakata, who controlled the labor market in their respective trades. Persons seeking the services of casual laborers generally seem to have worked through them. I find little evidence of employment agencies catering to casual laborers,[113] and although transport workers collected at post-stations and solicited customers, most workers did not approach prospective employers individually. I have found few references to central gathering places where day laborers might converge each morning in the hope of finding temporary work,[114] but there were often wards specializing in employment agencies. Some held seasonal employment fairs. In Kanazawa's Tono-machi, for example, there was an annual "women's market" (*onna no ichiba*) by the fence of a warehouse of a lord's mansion. Here "spirited girls" dressed in their finest were lined up waiting for employment from about seven a.m. to three p.m. on the dekawari day in the third month.[115] But such agencies and fairs arranged employment only for domestic servants.

Most casual laborers were set to work by their foremen before dawn. A packhorseman in Osaka would, according to Saikaku, set out at the seventh hour in the morning, or about an hour before sunrise.[116] Some workers continued after sunset:

Ōishi no	Wedging boulders
katamuku tsuki ni	in the moonlight—
teko no mono[117]	a leverman

So runs a haiku in the *Osaka doku gin shū* (1675).

Nevertheless working hours were apparently rather short by pre-industrial European standards. An edict (*ofure*) issued in Osaka in 1794 specifies the working hours for carpenters, and also probably reflects the conditions of thatchers, stone cutters, sawyers and other manual workers.

> The workers must arrive between the sixth hour and a half [i.e., sunrise] to the fifth hour, and after waiting a bit until all have been assembled, they should begin work before the fifth hour.
>
> At the fourth hour, the earlier short break.
> At mid-day, a lunch break.
> At the eighth hour, the later short break.
> At the sixth hour, return home.
>
> Concerning the above: the lunch break is to be no more than four-tenths of an hour, and each of the short breaks is to be no more than three-tenths of an hour; no more than one hour of breaks per day, and four hours total of work.[118]

"The fifth hour," when work began, would correspond, depending upon the time of year, to anywhere from about six-thirty to around eight o'clock A.M. The daytime "hours" (*toki*) referred to here were units of time representing one-sixth the total daylight time; depending on the time of year, an hour would correspond to from 98 to 145 Western minutes.[119] The "four hours (toki)" of work specified by law thus varied between about six and a half Western hours in the dead of winter and over nine and a half hours in late May, June and early July. Averaging the length of the four-toki workday over the whole year, it appears that carpenters worked only about eight hours per day.

It must be noted, on the other hand, that the peak employment season corresponded to the months from May to July, with their longer working hours. Since daily wages were typically fixed, according to law, without regard to the variable length of the day, it was to the employer's advantage to contract work during these months. Thus the worker was more likely than not to be hired for a workday of nine hours or more. During this peak employment season, however, he would enjoy a longer midday break. The shogunate was sensitive to the debilitating effects of the summer humidity on manual workers, and the edict cited allows for "one hour and six-tenths" breaktime during the period from the eighth day of the fourth lunar month to the first day of the eighth lunar month. In 1794, this period would have corresponded to the interval May 7 to August 25 in the Western calendar, and the length of one toki would have varied from around 130 to 140 Western minutes. Thus the total length of the carpenters' three breaks must have ranged from roughly three and a half hours to three hours and forty-five minutes. To compensate for lost time, the workers toiled longer in the evening cool.

Compare these working hours with those specified in the Statute of Artificers issued in England in 1562. That statute provides that wage- and day laborers must, between March and September, be at work from 5:00 in the morning to 7:30 in the evening. No more than two and a half hours were to be spent at "breakfaste Dinner or Drincking" during these eleven and a half hours.[120] The Common Council of London, meanwhile, established regulations in 1538 which obliged carpenters, masons, joiners, and other day laborers to work between 6:00 and 10:00 A.M., pausing for a fifteen-minute breakfast before "immediately" returning to work. At noon they were allowed an hour-long break, then a fifteen-minute rest for "drinking" at 4:00. Work would then continue until 6:00 with "none other houres or vacant tyme in the hold day other than as aforsayd." This schedule allows one and a half hours of leisure during a twelve-hour workday.

Parisian workers, meanwhile, commonly worked fourteen to sixteen hours per day during the eighteenth century.[121] The eight-hour or shorter workday, which Osaka carpenters enjoyed during most of the year, thus seems comparatively light.[122] Surely the scarcity of such workers in Japan, apparent throughout the Tokugawa period,[123] placed them in a better position than their Western counterparts in bargaining for jobs and setting job conditions.[124]

Workers' Living Conditions

In Tokugawa cities property, as well as occupation, defined one's status. A sake brewer enjoyed higher status than the porter who delivered his rice, not only because of the former's calling, but because he typically owned his own home, and was therefore a full member of the ward community (*machi-gumi*), responsible for paying property taxes (based on shop or house frontage), and eligible to assume ward leadership positions such as "elder" (*toshiyori*).[125] The worker was obliged to rent lodgings—usually a small apartment in a tenement building (*nagaya*) owned by a well-to-do merchant. The bourgeoisie thus exerted control over casual workers, not only as employers but as landlords.

In most urban wards, house-owners (*ienushi*) or caretakers (*yamori*) in their employ constituted 10 to 30 percent of all registered households. Their shops and attached living quarters would face the main avenues of the ward, while the tenements would commonly be located on the back streets. (Tenants here would be called *ura-danagari* or "back-renters," while those enjoying quarters on a main street were called *omote-danagari* or "front-renters.")[126] Residents in the tenements included a wide variety of the working poor: Takizawa lists "low-class servants of the warriors such as kobito and wakatō, low-class artisans, low-income laborers hired by merchants, peddlers of fish and vegetables in the markets, day laborers, palanquin-bearers, porters, ox-drivers, night-stall operators, scrap-paper dealers, and other low wage-earners."[127]

Thus any given ward might include a great variety of residents. Even in wards bearing the name of an occupation (Carpenters', Blacksmiths', Dyers' and Barrel-makers' wards being especially numerous),[128] the residential population was in fact quite diverse. Income, as much as occupation, decided residential patterns; the latter cut across class lines. In Kanazawa's Ushiro Kanaya-chō in 1811, for example, fourteen of the fifty-five households belonged to day laborers, but thirteen belonged to samurai.[129] It was not uncommon for low-ranking or unemployed samurai and laborers to reside next door to one another.

In Edo, casual workers seem to have been most numerous in Kanda, Asakusa and Shitaya; ten of the thirty-three recorded casual laborer recipients of hyōshō lived in these districts.[130] But merchants and artisans lived here as well. There were also, however, wards in which casual laborers predominated—what might even be termed "working-class neighborhoods." In the late seventeenth century Saikaku described "places with many low-class households" in the great cities of Edo, Kyoto, and Osaka. Here the immensely crowded quarters[131] present a picture of frenzied activity as tenants "are busy with quarreling, the laundry, and mending walls."[132]

With his eye for irony, Saikaku points out that, however difficult these tenants' lives may be, they are at least mercifully free of harassment by bill collectors. Those of higher incomes will have to face their creditors, and settle their debts, according to custom before the New Year; but the very poverty of these households allows them a measure of security:

> Since they all [own] items they can pawn, they don't seem at all troubled. In their way of life, they have to pay rent on the last day of each month, but otherwise, since no one will extend them credit, they pay for all their living expenses—rice, bean-paste, firewood, vinegar, soy-sauce, salt, oil—on the day they buy. So when the day to collect accounts comes around, no bill collecter will arrive at their home unexpectedly, nor is there anyone to whom they must appeal [to reschedule their debts]."[133]

Typically such neighborhoods were on the outskirts of town, as the *Seji kenmonroku* (ca. 1816) suggests.

> The families who rent backstreet lodgings [*uradanagari*] and live in the wards on the outskirts of town are people who hawk vegetables and fish in the city, day laborers, palanquin bearers, porters, *saku-tsuna*, night salesmen, scrap-paper buyers, day laborers in various trades [*shoshoku temadori*], all energetically making their livings through back-breaking work.[134]

A good example of a working-class neighborhood was a series of adjoining wards on the southern edge of Osaka: Nagamachi Six, Seven, Eight and Nine-chōme. A seventeenth-century source explains that these wards are

> licensed as cheap lodging house [wards]. One does not see independent travellers [rooming in the lodging houses] there, but homeless beggars who have fallen into bankruptcy, or day laborers who leave the city daily, or porters [*nimotsu-mochi*] and laborers who work in rice-polishing mills, sake breweries, and oil-squeezing shops.[135]

In a work published in 1791, Ueda Akinari observes that on the south side of Nagamachi, "squalid houses are packed in so close there is no room to build inns (*shukuya*)."[136] There are many children about. Saikaku also mentions large families in tenement slums on the outskirts of the three great cities:

> The husbands are day laborers [*hiyōtori*], or well-bucket rope-makers, or makers of pinwheel toys for soothing children. The mothers never know whether the profit of the day's work will be thirty-seven mon, forty-five mon, or as much as fifty mon; it is their task to feed four or five, and to protect them from the cold.[137]

It is a grim picture, but Saikaku also stresses the surprisingly comfortable lifestyle of some of these slum dwellers, who are able, he contends, to supply their three or five children with fashionable padded kimono every New Year's holiday.

Ogyū Sorai (a witness biased, to be sure, by a reactionary concern with reinforcing traditional status distinctions) also suggests that lower-class living conditions were not entirely desperate. Even Edo street-peddlers, he claimed, were eating *miso* soup, drinking fine rice wine, and purchasing such luxurious accoutrements as sliding-doors and *tatami* mats.[138] A century and a half later, the Dutch doctor Pompe van Meerdervoort painted an equally cheerful picture:

> The laborer . . . lives quite cheaply. He has in his room no furnishings other than his bed, a little chest of unfinished wood, the strictly necessary pieces of clothing, and some kitchen utensils. Of course he has no servants, and he lives with his wife and two or three children quite well, on an income of twelve to fourteen *itsebus* [*ichibu*] a month, including the house rent.[139]

The physician refers to conditions in the booming treaty ports (Nagasaki, Yokohama, Hakodate), acknowledging, however, that workers' living standards have declined elsewhere in the country. Even the most impoverished urban neighborhoods seem to have enjoyed a standard of cleanliness unknown in the poorer neighborhoods of European cities.[140]

WORKERS IN SOCIETY

Often living in the most crowded, squalid parts of town, spending their hours at sweated labor, casual laborers were regarded as among the meanest of the town dwellers, only a cut above beggars and outcasts. Even servants in merchant households considered themselves superior to these workers. Yet members of the more privileged urban classes generally conceded a common bond with this stratum, and at least upheld the dignity of physical labor. The great swordsman Miyamoto Musashi, in his celebrated *Gorin no sho* (Book of Five Rings; 1645), compared the Way of the Carpenter to the Way of the Samurai, and urged warriors to study the arts of different craftsmen.[141] His contemporary, the popular Buddhist cleric Suzuki Shōsan (1579–1655), declared that "every profession is a Buddhist exercise," and smiths, carpenters and other workmen are as important to society as samurai, peasants and merchants.[142] The "peasant sage" Ninomiya Sontaku (1787–1856) declared that the meagerest earnings of a common wage laborer were "not alms, but a reward for honest labor, which is the foundation for the rise and prosperity of a state."[143]

In a dialogue in Ishida Baigan's *Tohi Mondō* (early eighteenth century), a merchant's apprentice speaks disparagingly of day laborers, inviting Ishida to retort, "How do we differ from day laborers? It is narrow-minded to regard day laborers as lowly."[144] In fact, the public image of hired workers closely resembled that of servants. They dissipate their earnings in the pleasure quarters.[145] They drink heavily, and recklessly gamble. Carpenters in Kōda Rohan's *Five-Storied Pagoda* miss work as a result of hangovers, and even indulge at the oyakata's house or at his expense.[146] Ninomiya Sontaku warned that a workman's honest earnings could easily be frittered away by immoderate drinking,[147] and Osaka workers, as a Meiji-era newspaper reporter noted, were "a hard-drinking, fighting, gambling type with no care for savings or for the future.[148]

Like servants, casual workers squandered their earnings by gambling. In *Tanba Yosaku* the packhorseman Yosaku not only loses his own savings but gambles away his oyakata's horse.[149] And when overwhelmed with frustration, they turned, like servants, to the most destructive of antisocial crimes: arson. In the years 1722–23, 101 laborers and vagrants were arrested on charges of incendiarism.[150]

In contrast to servants, however, casual laborers were quite likely to engage in collective action. Unlike servants, they were accustomed to working together in large groups; the nature of their labor itself tended to produce the otokodate-style *esprit de corps*.[151] More importantly, because they were often dependent upon daily earnings to purchase life's necessities, they were far more sensitive to the fluctuations in the prices of such basic commodities as rice, oil, bean curd, soy sauce and rice wine. A diarist in Takaoka-machi, a town in the Kaga domain, depicts the suffering caused by the rise in grain prices in 1857–58. Etchūya Yoshiemon, a day laborer (*hikaseginin*) supporting his aged father and mother and eight children, has been out of work for several months. But it makes little difference. "No matter how hard I work," the writer quotes him as complaining, "I can't keep up with the price of rice."[152]

Laborers were therefore a key element in the characteristic type of urban disorder of the Tokugawa period, the *uchikowashi* or "smashing." Directed against the homes and warehouses of rice merchants, these riots expressed popular disapproval of high grain prices. Smashings constituted about 20 percent of all the uprisings of the period,[153] increasing in frequency and intensity particularly from the time of the Tenmei Famine. During the Tenmei era (1781–89), sixty such riots erupted in cities and towns throughout the country, and following crop failures in the Tenpō (1830–44) era, forty-five smashings took place.[154]

One of the largest incidents occurred in Edo in 1787 and involved about five thousand rioters, mainly artisans, laborers, and peddlers.[155] A major rice riot in Hiroshima the same year was touched off by stevedores and fishermen, who were joined by day laborers.[156] Sometimes underclass urban dwellers teamed up with peasants, or even outcasts (*hinin*); when impoverished peasants and *hinin* launched an attack on Tsuyama in 1866, destroying the homes of town rice merchants, local day laborers cheerfully joined in.[157] Officials tended to lump laborers together with criminal and lumpen-proletarian elements. During the Matsushiro Uprising (1870), forty-two residents of the town of Zenkōji were arrested. Most were artisans or peddlers, but they included a fireman, carpenter, packhorse driver, several homeless persons, and eleven "gamblers" who were probably laborers of some type.[158]

A second type of urban disturbance, the *yonaoshi* (lit., "world-rectification") became common in the mid-nineteenth century. Anne Walthall distinguishes these uprisings from earlier rice riots in that they involved even greater participation of day laborers and other marginal strata such as vagrants and drifters. Their rebellions had a consciously democratic content, and were waged, as they put it, "on behalf of the masses" (*banmin no tame*).[159]

Such "world-rectification" movements reached their peak in the closing days of the shogunate, when the rise in prices and the air of political uncertainty nurtured a curious movement known by its slogan, *Ee ja nai ka*? The expression, which has been variously rendered into English as "Isn't it good?" "Who cares what happens?" and "Everything's alright!" reflects the widespread contemporary sense that revolutionary change was in the offing. The gods, it was believed, were signaling a new era by dropping shrine talismans (*fuda*) from the heavens. These were (it was claimed) being found everywhere, their discovery accompanied by much wild dancing, promiscuity and merry-making. Celebrants would dance into the homes of the wealthy, refusing to remove their shoes, and demanding alms.[160]

The urban poor, including laborers, were prominent in these strange festivities.[161] A shogunate official arriving in Nishinomiya in November 1867 reported that "it was impossible to hire even one porter" because they were all singing and dancing in the streets. Another reports his palanquin-bearers' reaction to the discovery of a sacred talisman: "Now is the age of the gods and we can live in idleness; this is truly pleasant."[162]

A more specifically working-class form of collective action was the strike. This was a rare occurrence in the pre-industrial period, but not altogether unheard of. Osaka iron-workers, for example, staged a work stoppage in the 1780s to protest the high cost of iron, a shogunate monopoly. Here the object of attack was the brokers acting on behalf of the official Iron Guild (*Tetsuza*), rather than the workers' employers or oyakata; indeed, iron merchants led the action.[163]

Strikes by carpenters employed by the mines on Sado island involved the more conventional problem of wages. In confrontations in 1727 and 1738, the workers demanded a pay hike. In 1740, striking carpenters marched from the mines to the city of Aikawa, eventually forcing the city commissioner to negotiate an increase in their wages. These workers were also active in Aikawa smashings.[164]

SOCIAL MOBILITY OF CASUAL WORKERS

The phrase *unagi nobori* ("riding an eel") referred to a sudden rise in life. A Hokusai print shows day laborers climbing an eel, implying that upward social mobility was possible for a worker, and Tokugawa-period writings are filled with fictional and factual examples of "those who, before you know it, go from employee to employer."[165] Asakawa Zen'in, writing of Edo in the late eighteenth century, declared that, "A man who was a day laborer last year becomes a doctor this year. Yesterday's fishmonger turns up today in the guise of a teacher of reading and writing."[166] Earlier Ogyū Sorai had complained that valets in samurai households were being recruited from town coolies.[167]

It is not difficult to find specific examples. Hokusai's fellow artist Andō Hiroshige had once been a fire-fighter. Gotō Shinzaburō, whom Ieyasu placed in charge of the national mint, had once been a mere metal worker.[168] Sons of laborers bore no particular stigma and might advance in the world; the philosopher Yamagata Daini (1725–67) began life as the son of a Kōfu day laborer before entering the service of the shogun Ieshige's chamberlain, Ōoka Tadamitsu. Later he advised the daimyo of Kobata.[169] Pompe van Meerdervoort, who lived in Japan from 1857 to 1863, wrote that he knew of many Nagasaki laborers who had become rich merchants.[170]

In fiction, too, such success stories appear. In Chikamatsu's play *Nebiki no kadomatsu* the hero Yohei ("a day laborer making just enough to pass through each day") accepts a gift of gold coins from an Osaka prostitute. With this capital and "back-breaking labor" he amasses a fortune in Edo.[171] The rakish son of a shopkeeper in Kiseki's *Seken musuko katagi*, having been disowned and reduced to carving folding-fans for a living, happens to impress a daimyo with his horsemanship and is able to enter the lord's service.[172] In Ueda Akinari's "Suteishi Maru" (one of the stories in *Harusame monogatari*), the hero starts out as manservant of a wealthy peasant, but absconds and becomes a day laborer. Thereafter he becomes a professional wrestler, then a daimyo's jester before renouncing the world to perform acts of religious piety.[173]

The worker was, however, at least as likely to experience downward mobility. Many, already partly dependent on street peddling, were forced to devote full-time to this occupation. In his *Seidan*, Ogyū Sorai includes porters (*nimotsu-kasugi*) among those reduced to this trade and ultimately to begging.[174] Peddling itself, which many workers pursued as a sideline, was a profession particularly unlikely to lead to a better life.

To be sure, Tokugawa literature adduces many examples of peddlers who rise to riches. But as L. Broom and J. H. Smith pointed out in their article on "bridging occupations," legends concerning such successful salesmen "blur an understanding of the significant attributes that bridge from one kind of enterprise to another." Peddling is unlikely to act as a bridging occupation since it develops few skills, fails to increase independence, has negative effects on health, and seldom furthers access to persons in a position to aid one's caree .[175]

Once reduced to this trade, the worker, particularly if aged and feeble, was unlikely to experience any improvement in his lot. This was not, Ogyū declared, solely the fault of the individual, but rather the symptom of a general social crisis.

> Although it may be said that these men [peddlers and beggars] have fallen into this state because of their lack of industry and the improvidence due to their own foolishness, these things are a result of the condition of society [*seken no fūzoku*], and it is because of the impoverishment and difficulty of obtaining a livelihood [*yowatari seken sugi*] in recent years that such a class of people has appeared. Since the manners and customs of the country have deteriorated as a result of poor administration and since these evils are caused by poverty, the blame in the matter rests ultimately with the authorities.[176]

The individual tragedies of the working poor were due, Ogyū felt, to the sankin-kōtai and warrior-peasant separation policies. By encouraging the formation of large cities through these policies, the shogunate had also fostered a class of rootless urban poor. By favoring the replacement of corvee workers and hereditary servants with free, mobile proletarians, the shogunate had brought a host of new problems upon itself. How was this new class to be controlled?

Chapter Six

STRATEGIES FOR THE CONTROL OF
CASUAL LABORERS

THE APPEARANCE of short-term servants and casual laborers owed much to the fiat of the shogun and daimyo, principally the warrior-peasant separation and alternate attendance policies described in Chapter One. But the ruling class had not forseen all the necessary repercussions of these measures. Many may have imagined that the traditional corvee labor system could suffice to build castle-towns, or that hereditary, lifetime servants could adequately satisfy wealthy households' demand for domestic labor. Instead, as I have shown, the regime came to accept the emergence of free, hired laborers and indeed to favor their employment over the use of conscripted agriculturalists.

If the existence of a free labor market constituted an obvious challenge to the laws against abscondence, contained in the codes of every domain, the regime was obliged to accept the contradiction in order to implement its broader policy goals: vast quantities of labor were needed to construct and service the cities in which the samurai class was to reside. Yet many in the ruling class were frightened by this new working class, and by the lumpen-proletarian elements closely associated with it, including beggars, vagrants, petty thieves, gamblers, and streetwalkers. Already in the early eighteenth century, Ogyū Sorai and Dazai Shundai counseled a return to the older employment relations. Ruling-class fears grew during the latter half of the period, particularly with the increase in urban smashings (uchikowashi).

This fear of the proletariat, particularly of casual laborers, combined with the age-old ruling class view of the poor as fundamentally indolent by nature, led the authorities to impose a range of control mechanisms on the urban underclass. Workers were to be organized under recognized labor chiefs, registered, issued licenses, hedged in by elaborate guarantor systems that involved relatives, landlords and ward officials. The unemployed—those regarded as beggars and vagrants—were also to be licensed and organized, and in some instances, forced to work under state supervision.

These Tokugawa policies had much in common with policies implemented by early modern European regimes. But there is at least one crucial difference between the Japanese and Western experience. In most

Western European cities (if not in society as a whole), there was a labor surplus throughout the sixteenth and seventeenth centuries.[1] Due to complex demographic and institutional changes, the early appearance of a wage-earning proletariat was accompanied by an unemployment (vagrancy) problem of unprecedented proportions. "The sixteenth century," wrote Tawney, "lived in fear of the tramp."[2]

Such conditions helped produce a new emphasis upon the duty of all Christian believers to *work*. Begging had been widely tolerated in medieval society. The mendicant practices of religious orders had lent it a certain sanctity, and the giving of alms to the poor had salved the consciences of pious Catholics eager to acquire religious merit.[3] Beginning in the late fifteenth century, however, Western European cities began taking measures to outlaw, or sternly regulate, begging, while harshly dealing with "masterless men" and vagabonds. The vicious repression of these groups was designed not only to maintain public order, but to remake the individual into a productive human being.

Few blamed social conditions for the problem of poverty, or sought the solution in economic restructuring. The poor themselves were blamed for their lot; it was assumed that they were deliberately shirking their divinely appointed duty to toil.[4] The task, as the Tudors saw it, was "setting the poor awork." But this was no simple project. As Karl Marx suggested, the "'free' proletariat could not possibly be absorbed by the nascent manufactures as fast as it was thrown upon the world," and the early modern proletariat had not yet developed into "a working-class, which by education, tradition, [and] habit, looks upon the condition of that mode of production as self-evident laws of Nature."[5]

Capitalist wage labor is, after all, anything but "natural": "Men, suddenly dragged from their wonted mode of life, could not . . . suddenly adapt themselves to the discipline of their new condition."[6] Indeed, the very idea of working a fixed schedule under the eye of an employer seemed terrifying. Christopher Hill alludes to Dante's image of Hell in describing the peasant's apprehensions: " 'Abandon hope all ye who enter here,' was written over the portals of wage-labour."[7] The new work ethic had to be *foisted* upon the proletarian:

> The problem set by vagabondage and vagrancy was to force men who had been deprived of their independent means of livelihood to enter into "free" contracts to work for a capitalist employer, and to accustom them to the habit of steady work throughout the year. A new pattern of social discipline had to be imposed.[8]

The process by which this discipline is inculcated is, as Alexander Gerschenkron has pointed out, "a most difficult and protracted process."[9] Until it is completed, "poor law" and laws regulating labor are closely related. Vagrants and casual laborers are, indeed, scarcely distinguished from one another, and are alike viewed with apprehension and contempt by the privileged classes. Martin Luther sermonized that "the whole world is full of useless, cheating, wicked scoundrels, day-labourers, lazy artisans, farm-servants, and the idle, vagabond beggar-folk who prowl about everywhere unpunished with their tricks and impudence."[10] They are all one evil dangerous lot.

In Tokugawa Japan, too, poor law and labor law were intimately related. The devices used to control beggars were quite similar to those used to manage casual laborers. In Japan, however, urban demand for labor tended to exceed the supply, particularly during the growth period of the seventeenth century. Here, too, the peasant adjusted to the regimen of hired labor only with difficulty, as masters' complaints about servants' laziness and authorities' charges of laborers' indiscipline, yakko-style violence and unruliness suggest. But the pill was sweetened by high demand for labor, which allowed workers a fairly high level of wages and degree of mobility. If poor people in Tudor England turned to vagabondage partly from necessity, in Japanese cities with a high demand for labor fewer were inclined to voluntarily opt for a vagrant lifestyle. If in England, on the other hand, the poor became beggars partly from antipathy towards wage labor, in Japanese cities the relatively favorable conditions of labor ensured that relatively more of the poor would actively seek urban employment.

These, at least, were the conditions during the first century of Tokugawa rule, while the urban construction boom was still underway and before the process of proletarianization in the villages had progressed to a critical point. Subsequently vagrancy became a matter of truly urgent concern, occupying the attention of all high-ranking administrators, and urban officials intensified their efforts to cope with the problem.[11] During the period as a whole, policies of three general types were employed to regulate the underclass of urban laborers and vagrants: the policy—never entirely abrogated—of discouraging urban migration; the policy of imposing organizational structures upon groups of beggars and workers; and the policy of setting the unemployed poor to work under official auspices.

THE DISCOURAGEMENT OF URBAN MIGRATION

Every domain had laws against abscondence. Control of peasants' movements had indeed been "the fundamental concern" of daimyo since the Sengoku period.[12] Given their mounting financial difficulties during the Tokugawa period, the domains were constantly preoccupied with maintaining a grain-producing, tax-paying peasant workforce. The Tokugawa regime, moreover, periodically imposed restrictions on the numbers who might migrate out of specific provinces.[13] Yet the phenomenon of *dekasegi* or migration for purposes of temporary employment was extremely common. Along main highways, toll station officials examined travelers' papers and could refuse the undocumented permission to proceed further. However, one could easily avoid these thoroughfares and their checkpoints by taking the backroads.[14] Some have therefore suggested that the anti-abscondence laws were a dead letter, and the policing system largely ineffective. "Once [peasants] entered into a big city," writes Hayami Akira, "they seem never to have been caught."[15] The authorities, Hanley and Yamamura contend, "chose not to, or were unable to, enforce this [anti-abscondence] policy."[16]

In fact, however, it was not so simple a matter to quit the ancestral village for the open road. One first had to receive the permission of parents, five-family group heads, and the village headman. If the village was experiencing a labor shortage, their consent was unlikely. At times the shogunate required migrants from shogunate-administered domains to acquire documents from local intendants (*daikan*) and land stewards (*jito*) as well.[17] Of course one might risk embarking without the community's blessing, and without the proper documents issued by the officials. But however lax the police, it was unwise to venture forth lacking travel papers, and it was no simple decision to defy parental and community authority.

Nor was the surveillance system entirely impotent. Some domains, in fact, possessed efficient police networks, and routinely apprehended and punished would-be migrants. Tosa, for example, maintained eighty-six check stations (*sekisho*) on its borders in the eighteenth century, and had extradition treaties with neighboring domains. "Gradually," according to Marius Jansen, "the problem of deserters was brought under control."[18] Even after the migrant had arrived in a town, he might be apprehended as a vagrant while looking for work. Urban administrators in the domains, and officials in the great cities of Edo, Kyoto, and Osaka, organized patrols to search out such people. In Edo, this responsibility was given to the *Hitsuketōzoku Aratame* (Arson and Theft Inspectors), a police unit serving under the *wakadoshiyori* (Junior Elders).[19] Periodically these inspectors arrested undocumented persons in roundups (*karikomi*), forcing them to repatriate to their villages. The latter policy was called *hito-gaeshi* ("people-returning"), and formed a major element in the three great reform efforts of the period: in the Kyōhō (1716–35), Kansei (1789–99), and the Tenpō (1830–43) eras. The last of these efforts was most successful; none were entirely effective. Even so, these periodic searches limited the security of illegal migrants. The workhouses established in major cities during the latter half of the period probably acted as a further disincentive.

THE IMPOSITION OF ORGANIZATIONAL STRUCTURES

Given the scarcity of labor in Tokugawa cities, Japan did not confront a problem of vagabondage on so severe a scale as did early modern European societies. Nevertheless, the inevitable famines, droughts and other natural disasters periodically sent waves of impoverished peasants into the cities, and beggars were an ever-present part of the urban scene. The shogunate, unlike the Tudors, rarely collected funds from townsmen to assist the down-and-out. Many scholars, such as Uezaki Kuhachirō and Yamagata Bantō, advocated such a policy, but shogunate officials such as Matsudaira Sadanobu argued that a forcible redistribution of wealth would have negative effects.[20] Motoori Norinaga, in his *Hihon tamakushige* (1787) took a moderate position, urging the officials to use their moral influence to stimulate charitable activities, without employing coercion.

> It is desirable that the authorities should take measures to cause the rich to distribute their wealth for the benefit of the poor. Care must be taken, however, to see that rich people cooperate willingly. . . . Donations made by them must be devoted to the relief of the poor.[21]

Even so, during the Kansei Reform (1787–93), Edo authorities collected twenty-two thousand ryō from houseowning townsmen, supplementing this with ten thousand in shogunate funds, in order to establish a poor relief office and granary called the Machikaisho. Up to 410,000 needy townspeople were receiving assistance, in the form of rice and money, by the Tenpō period (1830–44). Yoshida Nobuyuki argues that the relative absence of large-scale riots in Edo during the early Tenpō years is attributable to the success of this operation.[22]

Alongside the victims of famine and flood—the honest working poor—there were an array of underclass communities requiring regulation and control. Outcasts, rōnin, religious mendicants, homeless vagabonds, itinerant performers, unlicensed street-walkers, professional gamblers, gang members, and various criminal elements all threatened the peace of society and invited the regime's close attention. Many members of this lumpen-proletariat pursued their lifestyles by inclination rather than necessity; even if respectable callings were available to them, they resisted the discipline such work would entail.

The shogunate never outlawed begging, regarding it as an inevitable evil.[23] It did, however, limit the amount of alms one might give beggars (*hinin, kojiki, yado-nashi*),[24] and early in the period established a registration system for beggars. During the reign of Hidetada, the second shogun (r. 1605–23), a certain Kuruma Zenshichi was appointed as Beggars' Headman (*hiningashira*); he and his descendants were charged with maintaining a registry of licensed beggars (*hininchō*).[25] Later in the century, officials in Kanazawa appointed Beggars' Headmen and issued tags which all beggars were obliged to wear.[26] The system is quite reminiscent of the badging of authorized beggars in Tudor England. In time these beggars evolved into a fixed caste, closely identified with the untouchable *eta* of ancient lineage, but in Saikaku's work they still included such members as merchants recently fallen on hard times.[27]

Religious mendicants, including many simply parading as initiates of legitimate orders, also posed social problems and required official regulation. Discharged menials from samurai mansions, among others, obtained begging licenses issued by temples of the quasi-Buddhist *yamabushi* sect;[28] along with begging, they collected fees for exorcisms and other mystical services. "The government," wrote Hayashi Razan (1583–1651), "is unable to repress them."[29] Their main temple on Mount Asago was closed down by Kyoto authorities during the reign of Iemitsu (1623–51), but they remained a source of irritation through the period. Saikaku refers to the "fake (*shikake*) yamabushi nowadays."[30] Laws forbidding common people to join the yamabushi were repeatedly issued into the Tenpō period (1830–44).

Groups such as these were apparently viewed as greater threats to the social order than casual laborers, who were not targeted by shogunate legislation until midway through the seventeenth century. Their legal status during this first half-century must have been ambiguous, since during the late sixteenth century day labor and abscondence had been nearly synonymous. But as noted, the massive demand for construction workers forced the shogunate to supplement its corvee labor force with hired workers. When the first laws mentioning day laborers appeared, they aimed at controlling, rather than banning, such labor.[31]

Shogunate policies towards laborers resembled those already imposed upon beggars. The first surviving edict to deal with this class was issued in Edo in 1653.

> As it was formerly commanded, people working as day-laborers must receive a license (*fuda*) from the day-laborers' chiefs (*hiyatoi-gashira*). Anyone employing persons without such a license will be fined. This is a criminal offense.[32]

Apparently day laborers' chiefs had been appointed in the recent past, and had been assigned to distribute these licenses. A similar edict was issued in Osaka four years later.[33]

These day laborers' chiefs were, as Yoshida Nobuyuki points out, probably not "affluent day laborers" but rather "merchant capitalists" who, like the shogunate itself, required a large labor supply to pursue their activities: "One can assume that the shogunate, and the class of lords resident in Edo, and the merchant capitalists in general, had basically the same interests."[34] The day laborers' chiefs, as officially authorized suppliers of casual laborers, were also concerned about the emergence of unauthorized competitors. Thus in the wake of the devastating Meireki Fire, the chiefs petitioned the regime to tighten control over unlicensed day laborers, and to enforce existing wage regulations.[35]

The "licenses" issued to beggars and day laborers were not written documents but wooden tags that could be worn on the person. These were a common form of identification during the period. Officials in the town of Hirosaki issued *hiyatoi-fuda* in 1792,[36] and a regulation issued in the hot-springs resort of Yutanaka-no-mura (Shinano) in 1774 specifies that artisans (*shokunin*) are to be employed only if wearing such licenses at their waists (*koshi-fuda*).[37] In the domain of Satsuma, virtually the entire population was issued licenses indicating name, address and status. These measured roughly fifteen by eight by three centimeters, and featured a hole at the top so that they could be slung on a cord.[38] No doubt Edo laborers wore similar tags; in 1698 they were specifically ordered to hang them at their waists.[39]

Edo authorities sought to further control laborers by fixing their wages. While there is no record of officially set wages before the Meireki Fire in the first month of 1657, the following month a regulation (*sadame*) specified that wages should not exceed one ryō in gold per seventy "day laborer coolies" (*hiyō ninsoku*). The next year the following notice (*oboe*) appeared:

1. Hookmen: one ryō gold per 45 persons.
2. Day laborers with their own tools: one ryō gold per 65 persons.
3. Day laborers without their own tools: one ryō gold per 70 persons.
4. Hookmen should also apply to the Day Laborers' Chief for licenses.
5. If an ordinary person works as a day laborer, he should receive the same wage as a regular day laborer.[40]

Workers had seized the opportunity to demand higher wages than usual. The posted wages were undoubtedly ignored, and were followed by even less realistic fixed wages the following year. Now the officials seemed quite alarmed: "If, from this year while wages are fixed, rascals violate [the rules] even slightly, it will be considered a serious crime."[41]

Significantly, when these edicts established wage levels, they did not specifically state the daily wage per worker, but rather the number of workers to be hired per gold ryō. This probably reflects the fact that employers did not pay workers directly, but relied upon oyakata to recruit a specified number of hands. The indicated compensation would be paid out to the oyakata, who might distribute it to the workers at his discretion—naturally appropriating a tidy profit for himself. Later, responsibility for setting wages was invested in the Day Laborers' Registry.

The Edo Day Laborers' Registry

The workers' licensing system in Edo was further strengthened with the establishment of this Registry (*Hiyatoi-za*) in 1665.[42] Two townsmen—probably prominent ward elders—were placed in charge of the office, to be headquartered in the Gold-Beaters' Ward.

> Yasui Chōzaemon and Tsuji Kaneshirō of Hakuya-machi [the Gold-Beaters' Ward] are hereby appointed [chiefs] of the town Day Laborers' Registry. From the first day of the fourth month, hookmen and rice-polishers, porters, and other day laborers living in the city will report to the above-mentioned office and receive licenses and serve in accordance with the instructions of the Day Laborers' Registry.[43]

Domestic servants on contracts longer than six months, and rice polishers in rice-polishing shops were exempt from registration, but the regulation states than all persons employed on terms shorter than one month must register. Workers received licenses from the office in return for a monthly fee (*fudayakusen*) of twenty-four mon.

The same regulation enlists ward heads (*nanushi*) and houseowners (*iemochi*) in the registry's efforts. They are to "investigate and report" about their tenants' employment, and to hire their own employees only after consulting with the registry about wages and other details. To employ unlicensed laborers, the law concludes, will be considered a criminal offense.

During the following half-century the control mechanisms applied through the Day Laborers' Registry grew more rigorous and complex. Every several years, the location of the office moved; with the appointment of a new day laborers' chief, the registry was relocated at the home of this official. In 1695, the post passed to one Mohei of Toriabura-machi, then to a Chūbei of Kita Saya-machi two years later, and to Sai-chirō of Yokoyama-machi, Itchōme in 1700. These men, at least, are the first-named in the edicts; anywhere from one to five officials were placed in charge.[44]

In 1679 landlords were warned against lodging unlicensed workers, and several new categories of workers were placed under the Registry's authority. Levermen, deliverymen (*mochikomi*), and draymen (*bariki*) joined hookmen, rice polishers, and porters; nine years later, laborers connected with official construction projects were ordered to apply for licenses. The 1688 edict suggests that workers were already finding ways to circumvent the rules. It notes that "some day laborers lodge together in groups of three to five and frequently change jobs, taking one man's license, all working with the [one same] license." Such license-sharing, the edict warns, must stop. Violaters were to be reported to the police offices (*bansho*).[45]

A law of 1696 notes that rice polishers assigned to work in the Official Rice Polishing Shop by the Day Laborers' Registry had been shirking their duties and offering excuses to avoid this work. It calls upon the registry to ensure that this service is provided.[46] Three years later an edict notes that many laborers, having completed work on official construction projects, are without employment or resources to return to their hometowns. Detailed reports on these people are to be compiled, and they are to be handed over to officials from their localities. Who is to file these reports and arrange the relocation of these unemployed workers is unclear, but the responsibility may have devolved upon the day laborers' chiefs.[47]

The registration system was made somewhat more efficient in 1705, when the day laborers' chiefs were ordered to go about the city, collecting detailed lists of day laborers from their landlords.[48] Thus not only employers, but landlords as well, were fully recruited into the control effort. Meanwhile the character of the registry changed. From 1701 the officers are identified as guarantors (*ukeoi* or witnesses (*shōnin*), implying that they bore a measure of responsibility for the laborers placed in positions by the agency. They would have to compensate employers when workers left projects incomplete. Moreover, they were obligated to provide coolies for official construction (*goyō ninpu*) at their own expense.[49]

Since the working population under the registry's authority numbered in the tens of thousands, license fees brought the day laborers' chiefs substantial incomes. Even so, the burden of compensating official construction workers could be crippling. In 1736, a report to Junior Elder (*wakatoshiyori*) Honda Iyo-no-kami from the two City Commissioners (*machi-bugyō*) noted that wages for official coolies (numbering 89,303) exceeded the income of the Day-Laborers' Registry. Yoshida Nobuyuki has calculated that while license fees brought in 1,345 *ryō* in gold, these wages amounted to 1,493 *ryō*. Small wonder, then, that the post changed hands so often, or that the original license fee of 24 mon, after dipping to 22 mon in 1695 and 20 mon in 1707, rose to 30 mon in 1718.[50]

Subsequently responsibility for the collection of license fees was placed in the hands of the city commissioner's office, and in 1747 the fee for porters and other transport workers was raised to 46 mon. Transport workers' wages had been rising rapidly. Hookmen and others continued to pay the 30 mon fee. In 1775, responsibility for fee collection was returned to the Day Laborers' Registry, but continuing problems led to the closing of the registry in 1797.[51]

The immediate problem, Yoshida argues, was the difficulty the registry posed for the day laborer chiefs/guarantors. Workers evaded registration, and the shogunate imposed a financial burden on the chiefs. It became difficult to find anyone willing to take the post. The more fundamental problem, he adds, is that the effort to define day labor as a *status* (*mibun*)—through the issuance of day labor licenses—was doomed to failure in an environment in which the day laborer could fairly easily change occupation. With the registry's dissolution, day labor is reduced to a mere *condition* (*jōtai*).[52] By this time, at any rate, the shogunate was experimenting with "new medicine for the poor"; on the one hand, greater relief efforts aimed at the urban underclass, and on the other, the workhouse.

The Day Laborers' Registry seems notably similar to projects advocated or realized in contemporary Europe. The Parisian Bureau d'Adresse, established by the physician Theophraste Renaudot around 1630, on the Rue Calandre on the Île de la Cité, began as a "noninvolved clearinghouse" for goods and services but quickly evolved into a labor registry.[53] Here individual workers could advertise themselves for a small fee (three *sous*) and meet prospective masters one-on-one, face to face. It was a step towards the evolution of a labor market, posing a big challenge to traditional, closed journeymen's associations.

In 1639, the function of the Bureau changed as the Richelieu administration enlisted its services to combat the rising numbers of unemployed vagrants in the city. Now registration became *mandatory*, and soon all tavern-keepers, cabaret-keepers, and hotelkeepers were ordered to register their clients with the Bureau. The ordinance issued on December 9 reads like a contemporary Edo edict:

> All those who are seeking a master will be expected to register at the Bureau within 24 hours of their arrival in this city, and to take the positions indicated to them at the said Bureau, under penalty of the galleys as vagabonds and vagrants.[54]

In June 1640, cabaret and hotel owners were ordered not to lodge unregistered strangers for more than one night.

The Bureau d'Adresse seems to have disappeared in 1644, after the death of Renaudot's patron Richelieu and the discrediting of his social program. Briefly revived by Renaudot in 1647, it fell victim to the general disorder caused by the Fronde—and accusations of "gross usury"—and never reappeared.[55] In England, social reformers suggested (and sometimes abortively implemented) schemes modeled after the French institution throughout the seventeenth and early eighteenth centuries, but all lacked the element of compulsion found in the Edo and Parisian registries.[56]

The Bureau d'Adresse and the Edo Day Laborers' Registry differed in some important respects. The Bureau performed a much wider set of functions: it handled the placement of servants, as well as laborers, and also served as a free clinic and general advertising agency. It was originally established by an individual, under license from the parliament, and always closely associated with its founder. It was short-lived; as a compulsory registration office, it survived only five years as compared to the Edo registry's 133 years.

At least in its propaganda, the Bureau stressed the lessening of the worker's exploitation as one of its major objectives. Through the auspices of the Bureau, the worker was to receive a fairer wage. The Day Laborers' Registry, in contrast, aimed at controlling wage inflation. The French institution responded to conditions of labor surplus (in the form of vagabondage), while the Edo office attempted to cope with conditions of labor shortage.

But the similarities are striking. In both cases urban authorities attempted to police the workforce, using a city-wide compulsory licensing system. In their efforts to police the laborers, they involved both registry personnel and landlords. Efforts to evade the registration system were punished as serious crimes. These points suggest that, whatever conditions of labor supply and demand pertained in the two societies, the ruling classes equally feared the independence of casual laborers, their putative unruliness and unwillingness to work. Registration systems could not solve such problems, and in both Western Europe and Japan, sterner, more punitive measures were directed at the laboring poor.

Workhouses: Setting the Poor to Work

Beggars and vagrants apprehended by urban authorities during the first half of the Tokugawa period seem, as a rule, to have been deported beyond the city limits. Perhaps they were first beaten, perhaps tatooed; forced labor does not seem to have been widely employed as a punishment. Manual labor as a chastisement for vagrants was, however, not unknown. One of the more famous victims of such punishment during the early period is Miyako no Nishiki (b. 1675). This Osaka writer of popular fiction had arrived in Edo in 1704, at a time when room rents were high and the laws against lodging unemployed, undocumented persons were being enforced quite strictly. Arrested on a charge of vagrancy by a particularly zealous Arson and Theft Inspector, he was sentenced to perform hard labor in a Kagoshima gold mine. He escaped several months later, was recaptured, and sentenced to death for this second offense. The sentence was commuted, and five years later, upon the death of Shogun Tsunayoshi, he was released in a general amnesty.[57]

This seems to have been an exceptional case; usually at this time those arrested for vagrancy were simply turned over to relatives or to persons who could act as their guarantors. Miyako no Nishiki was at a particular disadvantage because he had been disinherited by his parents (after wasting study allowances on prostitutes in his youth) and had no friends in Edo. The type of sentence he received was usually meted out to persons convicted of more serious infractions, and possibly he was guilty of another offense aside from vagrancy. But given the widespread practice of such violations (e.g., gambling), an arrest on the charge of vagrancy might, upon investigation, produce evidence of graver offenses as well.

Authorities in the castle-town of Kanazawa (the largest city outside the directly administered territories of the shogunate) also originally dealt with vagrants by returning them to their villages.[58] They seem to have been the first, however, to develop an alternative solution for this problem: the workhouse. Their system of workhouses (*hinin-goya*), established in 1670, achieved great fame and probably inspired other local workhouse projects later in the period. During the Kyōhō period (1716–36), Edo authorities attempted a similar plan, but nothing seems to have come of it. The shogunate did, however, establish a *mizugae ninsoku yoseba* ("water-changer coolies' workshop") on Sado island in 1778; this housed vagrants arrested in Edo, Nagasaki and other cities controlled by the shogunate. In Edo itself, another workshop (*yōikusho*) for the unemployed was built in 1780, and although this was abandoned in 1786, it was replaced by a far more enduring institution, the *ninsoku yoseba*, in 1790. Analogous institutions appeared in Nagasaki (1814), Osaka (1843), Nagaoka (Echigo) (1851–52), Usubetsu (Hokkaido) (1861), Matsuyama (or Takahashi, in Bitchū) (1867), Yokosuka, and Kai (1868).

This trend of workhouse construction parallels a movement in European poor law beginning with the establishment of England's first "house of correction" in 1575. (Charles David Sheldon, referring to the Edo workhouse built in 1790, was struck by the similar treatment of the poor in Tokugawa Japan and Elizabethan England.)[59] During the period Michel Foucault called "the Great Confinement," the rootless poor were forcibly institutionalized; 1 percent of the Parisian population in the seventeenth century spent some months in the workhouses called *hôpital general*.[60]

The character of these institutions (houses of correction, workhouses, poorhouses, *hôpital generaux*, *atelier*, *Zuchthausern*, *Arbeithauser*, *Tuchthuis*, etc.) was complex. They combined several functions. Some writers have stressed their charitable aspects, including their provision of medical care.[61] They often provided rehabilitation through moral instruction, job training, and basic education. Certainly they featured punitive aspects—punishment of a new type.[62] Foucault contrasts the medieval method of castigation (cruelly and conspicuously inflicted upon the body) with the modern practice of punishment through discipline and behavioral conditioning. The "punitive city" of the early modern age consisted of "hundreds of tiny theatres of punishment" in the form of workshops, public works and mines in which the poor involuntarily toiled.[63]

"Confinement," according to Foucault, became "an abusive amalgam of heterogeneous elements," but the historian must seek the "principle of cohesion" in these elements. Confinement was "an imperative of labor": the idle poor had to be conditioned to the harsh regimen of wage labor necessary to nascent capitalism.[64] "The best way of punishing [beggars]," wrote Brissot in 1781, "is to *employ* them" (emphasis added).[65]

The Tokugawa-period yoseba reflect a similar mentality. The work-houses established in Kanazawa in 1670 attracted wide attention and contributed to the reputation of the Kaga daimyo, Maeda Tsunanori, as an exemplary administrator. "There is not one beggar [hinin] in Kaga," declared Ogyū Sorai half a century later.[66] This was an overstatement; the real point was that thousands who would otherwise be begging on the streets were being housed under official supervision and set to work.

From the daimyo's point of view, the workhouses were an example of "benevolent government" (*jinsei*), but this ideal could assume rather bru-tal forms in practice. Modern historians are at any rate divided in their assessment of the Kaga system. Surely Tsunanori's motives were less than purely altruistic. James McClain, who describes the workhouses (or poor-houses, as he calls them) in detail, suggests that the prime motive of the domainal authorities was *fear*. Throughout the 1660s, the number of beg-gars and vagrants flocking to this castle-town had reached a dangerous level, and flooding during the summer of 1669 had produced more home-less migrants. The regime, apprehensive about an increase in crime and the possibility of violent uprisings, sought to contain the problem by physically confining the uprooted poor. At the same time, it planned to set rehabilitated vagrants to work as peasants in new agricultural villages composed exclusively of former workhouse inmates.[67]

In the sixth month of Kanbun 10 (1670), forty-five workhouses were opened in Kasamaemachi, a ward on the southeastern edge of Kanazawa. Each structure was about 130 square meters in size, and according to a contemporary document, "Tsunanori was adamant that the structure [of the workhouses] be exactly like a stable." (This point should qualify the praise of those who see the workhouses as humanitarian institutions. One scholar suggests "there was the aim of temporarily using [the work-houses] as stables during [military] emergencies"!)[68]

Within a year the number of inmates had risen to over 1,700 (or almost forty per workhouse). During the late 1670s, the number declined, rising in the following two decades and reaching a peak of 4,455 in 1699. In that year 3,685 persons were newly admitted; of these, 27 percent were impoverished castle-town residents, while 36 percent were ruined mer-chant, artisans, and day laborers who hailed from the rural areas in the immediate proximity of the city. By 1717, the number had fallen to about 1,100.[69]

Residents of the workhouses were a mixed lot. Most were innocent poor people, who entered the workhouse voluntarily, applying for admission in person or submitting a petition countersigned by village or ward officials. These petitions affirmed that the applicant was unable to support himself or to find succor from family and community. Sometimes the authorities also interned criminals who had been convicted for light offenses. These individuals were called *satogo* ("foster children"). Abandoned children or persons found starving within the castle-town were also placed in the workhouses. Inmates were divided into three types: the elderly or ill, the poor lacking any means of support, and the satogo. Tasks were allotted accordingly, with the most unpleasant tasks going to the latter.[70]

Whether or not the inmate had voluntarily entered the workhouse, he had to petition for discharge. To receive permission, the applicant had to acquire guarantors and demonstrate an ability to support himself. Some, as noted earlier, were used to populate new villages established under the auspices of the domain. The turnover rate was quite rapid (81 percent in 1699), but it is unclear how many left the workhouse, or died within its walls.[71]

Conditions were not ideal. McClain estimates that 16 percent of all workhouse residents may have died while lodged in the structures.[72] They were, to be sure, supplied with the basics. Half a liter of rice, and an allowance or bean paste (*miso*) each day satisfied minimal caloric requirements. There were also individual allotments of salt, firewood, clothing, and such personal effects as ladles, brooms, and hand buckets.

Able-bodied inmates were obliged to work, for their own edification and to defray the expenses of workhouse construction and management. Most made simple commodities such as scrub brushes, rain gear, and other straw or hemp items for sale in Kanazawa, although later in the period more specialized goods, including swords, were also produced.[73]

Staffed by a City Commissioner (*machi bugyō*), an Accountant Office Commissioner (*sannyō bugyō*), doctors, and samurai officials, the workhouses originally featured a "mixture of protection, control and self-interest."[74] Later in the period, their character softens as the welfare purpose comes to dominate; in the mid-eighteenth century, the institutions are renamed *buikujo* (Care Places), then in the Tenmei to Tenpō periods (1781–1844) *gosuke koya* (Assistance Workhouses).[75]

The workhouses for "water changers" on Sado Island were set up in 1778, on order from the rōjū Matsudaira Ukyōnosuke (in office for a second time from 1761–81). In that year Ukyōnosuke sent an instruction to the Edo City Commissioner which clearly states the purpose of the workshops:

Since there are many vagrants these days, evil deeds are being done. There-fore [I] have decided to send 40 or 50 innocent vagrants who have commit-ted no other particular offense [*muzai no mushuku*] to Sado as water-changers [*mizugae*]. Since there are such people, put them in workhouses [*koya*] and set them to work. If some among them mend their ways, they should [be allowed to] return home. In any case, this is to discipline immoral, dissipated vagrants.[76]

In recognizing that the vagrants were not criminals, yet because of their "immoral" and "dissipated" lifestyles were in need of confinement and discipline, the rōjū sounds much like the great reformer of the Span-ish Netherlands, Juan Luis Vives. His work *De subventione pauperum* (1525) declared that while "no one should die from starvation, those who have ruined themselves in disgraceful and base ways" should be allotted "the more disagreeable tasks . . . and harder fare, so that they may be an example to others."[77] T. R. Malthus, in the early nineteenth century, con-ceded the same grudging support for workhouses. For the most unfortu-nate, he wrote, it might be appropriate to establish such houses, but not as "comfortable asylums"; and while "severe distress" must "find some alleviation," the "fare should be hard."[78]

Destined for such hard fare, thirty-six vagrants, ranging in age from eighteen to forty-nine, were dispatched from Edo to the Japan Sea island. The average age was twenty-nine. Two, including the eldest, died en route. Upon arrival the remaining thirty-four were quartered in a *nagaya*-style building of 136 *tsubo* (538 square yards), initially allowing four times the space per inmate afforded by the Kanazawa workhouses. But the regimen was harsh. There was at the time a severe shortage of water changers; the mine administration had already resorted to conscripting day laborers from the wards of Aikawa. Thus the vagrants were subjected to particularly ruthless exploitation, working twenty-four-hour shifts every other day.[79]

While the first vagrants were sent to Sado at the initiative of authorities in Edo, local officials were soon requesting additional laborers. Edo was happy to comply, and after the Edo ninsoku yoseba had been established in 1790, the most incorrigible inmates of that workhouse were sent to Sado. Thus the island's workhouse population grew to about two hun-dred in 1788. By 1817, however, the numbers had dropped to sixty-nine, mostly as a result of escapes.[80]

Aside from the hazardous conditions in the mines, inmates faced other dangers as well. Fires destroyed the workshop in 1782, 1812, and 1826. Sixty-four inmates from Edo and Nagasaki escaped in the 1812 fire, and others attempted the same in the latter year. Unfortunately they were apprehended and executed. Disease carried off many in 1830.[81]

Even if an inmate escaped, he was unlikely to find refuge on the island. Local people feared and despised these "wild dogs from Edo" (*Edo yama-inu*). The officials originally viewed them as outcasts (*hinin*), lower on the social scale than the criminals regularly sent to Sado as exiles (*ryūjin*).[82] With time, however, the two categories became confused, and the Edo vagrants met with slightly better treatment. In 1807, for example, a paper-making workhouse was established for rehabilitated vagrants.[83]

The Edo ninsoku yoseba (or more properly, the *kayakukata* [temporary extra worker] *ninsoku yoseba*) was by far the most important workhouse experiment of the period. Perhaps the best description of this institution has been left by Matsudaira Sadanobu, the vigorous reformer who served as rōjū from 1787 to 1812. In his autobiography, Matsudaira noted that the traditional punishment for vagrants and thieves (tattooing, deportation) had been ineffective; if authorities could obtain no confession of a crime, the detained person would simply be freed "to go on loitering."[84]

New measures were called for. In 1780 a workhouse (*yōikusho*) was erected in Fukugawa Morin-machi to house some of the poor who were converging on the city in the wake of the Tenmei Famine and being apprehended in regular police round-ups (*karikomi*).[85] This is often seen as a precedent for yoseba, but in 1786 it was abolished.[86] The problem of vagrancy continued to grow, however, causing numerous social problems; in the fifth month of 1787 a great "smashing" occurred in Edo. Three years later an Arson and Theft Inspector, Hasegawa Sadao, proposed that vagrants arrested by police on their rounds be confined in a compound on the small island of Ishikawa near the mouth of the Sumida River.[87] A daimyo's mansion was removed to make room. Sadanobu recalled,

> At that time the Workhouse was established. Homeless vagrants had been committing misdeeds since the Kyōhō era (1716–36), when somebody had proposed that it would be appropriate to confine them in a prison-yard. This, however, was not implemented. Later, perhaps in the An'ei period (1772–81) someone suggested the establishment of a charitable hospital [*yōikushō*], but this was not [permanently] implemented either.
>
> Now (1790) [the shogunate] sought out someone with a plan. One Hasegawa, who had been active in rehabilitating thieves, was in charge. There is an island next to Tsukuda Island, where he built [the Workhouse] and placed the vagrants. . . . The amount of rice and money for one year was calculated and provided at public expense. Because of this [project] vagrants have today become quite rare. Previously they would flock to the wards with bridges, and line up to the right and left of these bridges, [begging]; but now they are gone. There are also fewer thieves and the like.[88]

The compound measured some 3030 *tsubo*, or 11,981 square yards. It accommodated several buildings, including inmates' lodgings, a bath room, a sick room, and various workshops. Designed to house 120 to 130 persons at a time, it was overcrowded from the beginning, generally housing 140 to 150 during its first three decades, then up to six hundred at a time during the Tenpō period (1830–43).[89] As Sadanobu mentions, the establishment was publicly supported, receiving five hundred bags of rice and five hundred ryō of silver for the first year, and three hundred bags and three hundred ryō the following year.[90]

Like the other workhouses I have described, the Edo yoseba housed a range of inmate types. At first only vagrants (innocent of any other offense) were interned; Sadanobu, who always blames the vagrant for his fate, refers to sons disinherited because of their dissipation and merchants whose morals have deteriorated.[91] Kabukimono also seem to have been confined in the workhouse from an early date, and after 1820 those guilty of minor criminal offenses, who would otherwise would have been deported from the city, were added to the mix.[92] Inmates were separated from one another according to the nature of their offense, state of health, age, gender and type of work.[93]

In the *tewaza-jo* or Craft House, inmates arriving with skills were set to carpentry, cabinet making, dyeing, and paper making. The unskilled polished rice, burned oyster shells to produce lime, made charcoal balls, or produced simple items from straw. After the Tenpō period (1830–1843), oil squeezing became the largest enterprise, bringing the workhouse eight hundred gold ryō in profits every year. Inmates guilty of no offense other than vagrancy were sometimes sent outside the workhouse to serve as coolies in construction projects. While severe, work conditions were considered better than those in the Sado workshops. Inmates were paid for their work, but firmly forced to save one-third of their wages.[94] It is unclear how they may have spent the remainder, but perhaps some spent it on authorized excursions outside the compound, or sent it to relatives.

Hasegawa, the Theft and Arson Inspector who had suggested the Edo yoseba, was originally appointed to manage the operation. He mismanaged the project, however, and exploited the inmates for his own profit.[95] In 1792 he was dismissed, and a commissioner (*bugyō*) appointed to oversee the workhouse.[96] Under this official served an elaborate bureaucracy, including a Controller (*motojime-yaku*), Superintendant of Manual Labor (*tewaza-gakari*), Turnkey (*kagi-ban-yaku*), Kiln Officer (*kaki-bai-seisho-gakari*), Fieldwork Officer (*hatake-gakari*), Officer in Charge of Oil Presses (*abura-shime-gata*), and others.[97]

These officials made the rules. Inmates were to serve a basic term of three years, after which, if their behavior had been satisfactory, they were given a small sum of money (and their wage savings) and allowed to leave. Those with satisfactory work records, and guarantors willing to help them in returning to society, could be released at any time. As a rule, peasants were returned to the land; Sadanobu writes that about two hundred each year were settled back in their villages. Edo-born inmates were set up in trades in the castle-town.[98]

All inmates were to wear uniforms. Upon admission, each received a light-brown garment dyed with a pattern of white water-(tear-?) drops. The second year, this was replaced with a garment with fewer drops, and in the third year, the robe was of a solid color. One could tell at a glance how long each inmate had been confined.[99]

The *Yoseba go-shioki tsuki* (Yoseba Official Punishments) issued in 1797 provide some insight into conditions in this example of "benevolent government":

1. Persons who break the Workhouse enclosure and escape will be given the death penalty.
2. Persons who flee work within the Workhouse will be tattooed, flogged, then placed back in the Workhouse as before.
3. Persons who escape [while on] Workhouse errands, [stealing property of] over 10 ryō will receive the death penalty. [Those stealing property of] under 1 ryō will be tattooed and heavily flogged.
4. Persons who escape from errands [assigned by] the Workhouse will be heavily flogged. A person who has been tattooed and heavily flogged once, but repeats the offense again will receive the death penalty.
5. Persons who escape the Workhouse, and [also] commit theft will receive the death penalty.
6. Persons who steal, then attempt to flee, hiding within the grounds will receive the death penalty.
7. Persons in the Workhouse who steal [property of] over 10 ryō will receive the death penalty. [Those stealing property of] under 10 ryō will be tatooed and flogged.
8. Persons who try to escape and hide within the grounds will be heavily flogged.
9. Persons who escape from the Workhouse and return home by themselves will be tattooed and heavily flogged.
10. Persons who conspire to escape, but fearing the consequences, do not [actually attempt to] escape will be placed in manacles for 300 days.
11. Persons leaving the grounds without permission will be placed in manacles for 20 days.
12. Persons who leave [the Workhouse grounds] upon request and return home in the evening will be placed in manacles for 20 days.

13. Persons who gamble in the Workhouse will, for the first offense, be exiled to a distant island. Others will be heavily flogged.

14. Persons who enter the Workhouse concealing the fact that they are *hinin* will be turned over to [Outcast] Headman Danzaemon.

15. Persons shirking work will be placed in manacles for 30, 50 or 100 days.

16. Punishments for persons under 15 years of age will be one degree lighter than those for adults.

17. When it appears [people] have been conspiring about something [*totoga-mashii koto o shita toki*], punishment will be in accordance with the Regulations [*Go-sadame gaki*].

18. When persons afflicted with leprosy or syphilis request to bathe, they will be provided with proper care, and released [to go to medicinal springs?]

19. Informers [*mikkokusha*] will be rewarded.[100]

The list clearly indicates the officials' overriding concern with inmates' escape, and suggest that their administration of the workhouse amounted to a reign of terror. European workhouses, indeed, were designed to inspire dread; as an English commentator declared in 1770, the "ideal workhouse" is a "House of Terror."[101] Matthew Marryott, writing in 1732, found the advantage of the workhouse stems "from the apprehensions the poor have of it. These prompt them to exert and do their utmost to keep themselves off the parish, and render them exceedingly averse to submit to come into the house until extreme necessity compels them."[102]

Precisely such views were echoed by Sadanobu. Acknowledging that there had been complaints about the workhouse (one thousand inmates had died one year), he nevertheless justified the institution on the grounds that it inspired an edifying type of terror.

> There were people who said that conditions [in the Workhouse] were harsh, but I think that bestowing money and grain on lowly people [in itself] constitutes benevolent government. By a harsh experience in the workhouse, the [confined] person as well as his aquaintances will fear. And the fact that the very people who are now becoming vagrants will fear the workhouse is government of unlimited benevolence.[103]

Dread and toil were not, however, the only features of workhouse life. The harsh regimen imposed upon the yoseba inmates was interrupted three times a month by a rehabilitation program of a softer sort. Just as the inmates of European workhouses were commonly subjected to the sermonizing of Christian clergy, yoseba residents were obliged to attend lectures given by scholars of the Shingaku school. The Shingaku movement had been initiated in 1729 by Ishida Baigan, a Kyoto commoner and had quickly become influential among the merchant class. It was essentially a moral doctrine, amalgamating Confucian, Shinto, and Buddhist elements, but differing from other schools in its unabashed affirmation of the dignity of labor and of the merchant's calling. The Way of the Merchant, taught Ishida, is the same as the Way of the Samurai; a merchant's profit does not differ from the samurai's stipend. In these aspects, Shingaku may originally have borne some seeds of social protest, but by Matsudaira Sadanobu's time, it had lost any radical features, its exponents, in Miyamoto Mataji's words, had become "ruling class robots."[104] Sadanobu himself, indeed, was very interested in Shingaku teachings, and clearly felt them useful in remolding the thoughts of apprehended vagrants in a way amenable to ruling class interests.[105]

The first surviving reference to Shingaku sermons at the yoseba is dated 1799, but it is thought they were part of the program from the very beginning. Seven principal scholars, and a number of their assistants, were employed to preach up until the very end of the period. These included some of the most renowned figures in the Shingaku movement, such as Nakazawa Dōni (1725–1803), Wakizawa Gidō (d. 1818), and Ōshima Yūrin. All emphasized the merits of hard work. Wakizawa, who had also preached to the inmates of a prison in Kyoto, exhorted his audience to "Know that blessings are to be found in work and cherish your work of today."[106]

Nagasaki was the next major city to implement a workhouse scheme. In the tenth month of Bunka 11 (1814) the City Commissioner Ōyama Saemon established a *saikujo* within the premises of a prison in Urakami-mura. Criminals convicted of light offenses, vagrants and prodigal youths placed in the workshop at relatives' request were set to work at rope making and other crafts.[107] Those reformed would be provided with goods to start a new livelihood.[108] In Osaka, a similar operation was established during the city's Tenpō-era reforms, when the management of the prison was removed from the barbers' guild.[109] Kawai Keinosuke, a reform-minded official in Nagaoka-han, set up a workhouse in 1851 or 1852.[110] A decade later, much of the Edo workhouse population was removed to a "yoseba" in Usubetsu, near Hakodate, where vagrants, prostitutes, adulterous clergy, and minor offenders were set to work fishing along the coast. The inmate population, numbering between 130 and 230, also included a small number of Ainu.[111]

Thus the shogunate, having experimented with a number of strategies to control the urban underclass, became increasingly interested in the institution of the workhouse. Although never as comprehensive as the Western workhouse movement (knowledge of which may have influenced some of the institutions in the last days of the Tokugawa regime),[112] the shogunate's attempt to "set the poor awork" resembles the efforts of early modern European regimes. In Europe, the workhouse, hemming in large numbers of persons obliged to toil under centralized supervision, co-evolved into (and sometimes functioned as the model for) both the prison and the manufacturing workshop.[113] Adam Smith, indeed, used the term "workhouse" as a synonym for manufactory.[114] In Japan, too, workhouses and manufactures co-evolved, the former perhaps serving as the necessary schoolhouse for a workforce only gradually acquiring the discipline necessary for wage labor.

AFTERWORD

THE EMERGENCE of an urban working class in Tokugawa Japan is striking for several reasons. Not the slow development of commerce, nor the consequent expropriation of producers from the soil, but rather feudal authority served as the midwife in its birth. Ruling-class policies designed to strengthen lords facing challenges from their samurai subordinates, and shoguns facing threats from their baronial vassals, created large cities demanding quantities of labor power which could only have been provided by a free labor market.

The swift pace with which this labor market formed corresponded to the dramatic rapidity of urban growth in the late sixteenth and early seventeenth centuries. Observers in the late seventeenth and early eighteenth centuries were well aware that in recent memory major changes had occurred in the organization of labor, in master-servant ties, and in the role of money in mediating human relationships. Not all agreed that the changes had been positive, and some even held out hopes for their reversal, but the boldest thinkers even came to view the samurai's stipend as a *wage* remunerating services rendered.

Finally, the existence of this working class impresses one in its historical rarity. By 1700 Japan was one of the most "urbanized" societies on the globe, and surely the most urban of non-Western societies. In her towns and cities, one-fifth to one-third of the population typically consisted of hired servants, shophands and manual laborers. Few other societies have embarked upon the road to industrialization with so large and experienced an urban proletariat at hand.

A NOTE ON SOURCES

NINBETSUCHŌ

Much of my data on worker and employer populations, servants' employment tenures, ages, sex ratios, etc. is derived from the population records called ninbetsuchō. Several English-language works have described the nature of such documents,[1] without, however, noting the special features and problems of *urban* ninbetsuchō. Neither Japanese nor Western scholars have made great use of the latter; village ninbetsuchō are far more numerous, more relevant to the issues that have been of interest to historical demographers, and perhaps easier to work with.

Urban censuses had been compiled from ancient times, and records using a format similar to the ninbetsuchō I refer to date from at least the early seventeenth century. There survives, for example, a *ninzu aratame no chō* (population investigation record) drawn up in Hiradomachi, a ward in the port of Nagasaki, in 1633. Keeping such records was officially mandated, however, only in 1638, when the shogunate, pursuing its relentless campaign against Christianity, ordered that all commoner households under its direct jurisdiction (roughly one-quarter of the country) formally register as adherents of a Buddhist sect.[2] (The militant Ikkō sect of Buddhism was, however, coupled with Christianity as an "evil sect" to be renounced.) This registration alone, of course, provided no assurance that a Christian proselyte had indeed apostasized, but it allowed the regime a greater degree of intelligence concerning the "Christian threat" than it had formerly enjoyed. Moreover in some cases, registration was accompanied by a ritual "treading on the image" (*fumie*) rite; it was believed clandestine Christians would be exposed by their hesitation to trample an image of Jesus or Mary.

These records were referred to by various terms: *shūmon ninbetsu aratame chō* (Records of Investigation of Religious Sect and Population), *shūmon aratame fumie machikata no shūmon chō* (Record of Religious Investigation and Image-Trampling), *shakuya iemochi shūshi aratame fumie chō* (Record of the Investigation of Religious Sects of Houseowners and Tenants and their Image-Trampling), *aratame chō* (Record of the Investigation of Townspeople's Religious Sects), etc. Certain similar records, such as the *Kasama machikata kenbetsu aratame chō* (Record of the Investigation of Townspeople's Shop-Frontage) followed a comparable format but included no religious information at all.

In 1665 all domains were ordered to comply with the population registration policy, and in 1671 the shogunate demanded yearly compilations. But various domains seem to have enjoyed special exemptions from the rule, and the conflagrations that so often leveled Japanese cities have destroyed the great bulk of this material. While registers for individual years are scattered through numerous local histories, very few data series extending over decades have survived, and of these, only those for a few urban wards (*machi* or *chō*) date back as far as the seventeenth century.

These include the registers for two Osaka's Kikuyachō (a mixed commercial ward of middling affluence, bordering the Dōtonbori entertainment district) and Dōshōmachi San-chōme (a prosperous ward to the north of the city, close to the Castle, which was well known for its medicine venders). Dating back to 1639 and 1659 respectively, each gives figures for four or five years during the seventeenth century, and virtually year-to-year data for the period from around 1720 to the Restoration. The other half-dozen data series for Osaka wards are less helpful; all date from the last decades of the eighteenth century.

Only one Kyoto ward register yields comparable coverage. Shijō Tateuri Naka no machi's register spans the period from 1697 to 1868; records for other wards date from from the late eighteenth century. For Edo, there is virtually nothing until the last decade of the period. Okeyamachi, the "Barrel-makers' Ward" in Nagasaki, has left a fairly complete record from the 1740s, while several of Takayama's ward registers cover the late eighteenth century through the Restoration. There is little else; data series for cities outside direct shogunate control seem to be nonexistent.[3]

In comparison with village ninbetsuchō, these records reflect a complex social structure. Those whose names are entered in the village records were, of course, overwhelmingly peasants, while the urban registers indicate the residence of people in myriad occupations. Doctors, priests, ward officials, and day laborers would be listed as such, while merchants and artisans are identified by the name of their shop, serving in lieu of a surname. "Kamiya Chōzaburō" would be Chōzaburō the paper-dealer (or perhaps paper-maker). Unfortunately in most cases shops simply bear the names of places: Kawachiya, Harimaya, Kyōya, Ikedaya. "Hiranoya Shichibei," for example, means Shichibei of the Hirano Shop—an identification of only limited value, since it does not tell us whether Shichibei is an artisan, merchant or pawnbroker, or what type of shop he runs. He deals, perhaps, in Hirano goods. Or maybe he is from Hirano. We do not know.

The fact that the registers do not give the specific occupation of the great majority of ward residents is thus one of their major limitations as historical sources. Sometimes, however, there are telltale signs. If, for example, a shop has a "string" radical in the characters for its title, one may suspect it produces or trades in textiles. If it employs half a dozen "maid-servants"—favored as weavers—this explanation seems even more plausible. But one cannot be certain.

Typically ward residents are listed as householders (*iemochi*); caretakers or surrogate householders (*yamori* or *iemori*); or tenants (*shakuya* in the Kansai, *tanagari* in the Kantō). The latter are given as tenants of specific householders. Usually, although not necessarily, all householders and caretakers are recorded first, with the ward Elder (*machi-toshiyori*) heading the list. This official is often one of the wealthiest members of the community, to judge by the size of his service staff.

The format of these documents is as follows. There is a brief preamble explaining the purpose of the register, including an increasingly *pro forma* allusion to the receding threat of Christianity. All those I have seen specify the register's scope: all residents, "down to the manservants and maidservants," are to be listed. This statement is signed by ward officials, and followed by the names of all residents under their temple affiliation. (See the sample register below, from Osaka's Kikuyachō, in English.)

In many cases, all the members of the household, including servants, are registered at the same temple. This should not be interpreted as a valid indication of religious preference, however. The Kikuyachō registers during the early period often show households with several sect affiliations represented, even among family members; with time, however, such cases become rare, and dependents are routinely listed under the temple of the household head. In Kyoto, on other hand, formal religious affiliation may have been taken more seriously. Here servants not of the master's sect are not listed with the master's family members, but indicated with the note, "Other servants listed separately." They are recorded in a catch-all section after other ward residents, along with their temple and the name of their master's household.

The most elaborate ninbetsuchō include the ages of those recorded, although it is not always clear how soon newborn children were included. Explanations of moves, servant hires, dismissals and abscondences may appear. Such notes were written in, or appended on separate strips of paper to bound volumes already compiled. At the end of each subsection (corresponding to a block or row of tenements) one usually finds sub-totals, broken down into economic groups (householders, tenants, servants) and gender groups.

Working with such documents involves several problems. The sub-totals and totals, for example, do not always jibe with the number of persons recorded. This could be due to careless arithmetic, or to the additional of newcomers arriving after the original count had been made. The discrepancies are seldom significant, but they can be irritating. Another problem is the enigmatic symbols that scribes have penned upon these texts: data are crossed out, marked with an "X" or circled. Sometimes these markings seem to explain the discrepancies between names listed and subtotals given, but it is a difficult problem. If one must rely on photocopies for some register data, there is the additional problem of distinguishing the lines produced by worms from those inked by human hands.

Terms also pose various problems, as explained in Chapter 2. The meaning of the term "manservant" (*genin*) is problematic enough; when one finds local, idiosyncratic terminology, interpretation becomes even less certain. Even so, notwithstanding the problems these documents pose, they are among the richest sources for information concerning Tokugawa urban workers.

SAIKAKU AND OTHER POPULAR WRITERS

Most critics of Tokugawa literature agree that a type of "realism" emerged during the period, and that Ihara Saikaku (1642–1693) was a key figure in this movement. Himself an Osaka townsman, Saikaku authored works which, while not devoid of supernatural or burlesque elements, depict Tokugawa society in painstaking detail. This is especially true of his *chōnin-mono* (novels dealing with the townsman class), but in all of his work he treats the reader to rich and accurate descriptions of contemporary life. When Saikaku describes a character's costume, he will often digress on the price of each article of clothing; when he introduces a tale about a parlormaid, he will typically describe the duties of such servants and how their wages have dropped or risen during the past year.

Because of his keen interest in social and economic themes (such as the shortening of service tenures, various ways to make a living, debt collection), Saikaku has been compared to both Daniel Defoe and Henri Balzac. Like them, he is an invaluable and trustworthy source of information about the society in which he lived. I have relied heavily upon his work in treating such topics as master-servant relations.

To a lesser extent, I have made use of kabuki dramas, especially the *sewamono* or domestic play, dealing with townspeople's lives, pioneered by the great dramatist Chikamatsu Monzaemon (1653–1725). Such works often deal with the lives of the lower classes, and in sometimes only thinly veiled fashion, depict contemporary events. A shopclerk commits *shinjū* (love-suicide) with his master's daughter; a maid wages a vendetta in defense of her dead mistress's honor; a debauched monk plummets into a life of thievery; a vagrant, redeemed by love, renounces gambling. These are fairly representative figures in this genre. They are unique to the Tokugawa period. While medieval *kyōgen* (comic *nō* drama) often featured the Tarō or page-boy character, the realistic portrayal of underclass life does not occur before kabuki. I have found such works useful in illustrating some aspects of servants' lives and their public image.

OTHER SOURCES

Senryū (comical short poems), *kobanashi* (humorous anecdotes), and parables taken from popular sermons tend to caricature laborers and servants, but these, too, are useful in exploring the image of these workers in society. They sometimes provide, aside from their color, acute pyschological insights. They decribe how a manservant feels on the day he receives new, unfashionable livery, how a country bumpkin reacts to her first day in a merchant household, how a maidservant despairs on learning that her mistress is pregnant and there will soon be much more work in store.

A SAMPLE NINBETSUCHŌ ENTRY

West Honganji, Lower Kitaborie, Ward 2 (Head Temple, Nishi Shoji)

Caretaker for Nakajima Iyabei. Cosmetics Dealer: Sōbei
Wife: Fusa
Child: Kyūtarō
  [note written above] Second month: child Kichizō born
Child: Tomozō
Mother [of Sōbei]: Tatsu
Servant: Kichibei
Servant: Ichitarō
Servant: Kohei
  [note above] Kohei dismissed in the tenth month
Maidservant: Rin
  [note above] Ninth month: maidservant dismissed and hired
Maidservant: Toyo
  [note above] Third month: maidservant Toyo dismissed, servant
  Jihei hired[4]

This entry describes the household of Sōbei, a cosmetics dealer in Osaka's Kikuyachō, in the tenth lunar month of the first year of Meiwa (1764). He lives with his mother, wife, and two sons when the record is first made; a newborn baby is added in later. Initially, five servants are recorded, and during the course of the year the manservant Kohei and maidservants Rin and Toyo are dismissed, all being quickly replaced with new employees. Note the temple affiliation heading the entry.

MONEY

THE MONETARY system of the Tokugawa period was extremely complex. Gold, silver, and copper coins were all produced on a monopoly basis by shogunate mints; gold coins were used more widely in the Kantō region, while silver prevailed in the Kansai. In general, coins were valued according to the following weight relationships:

1 *kan* (132 oz.) = 1,000 *monme* = 10,000 *bu* = 100,000 *rin*

Coins were not necessarily denominated in these weights, however. There was, for example, no gold coin weighing one *monme* (.132 oz.). Instead, the following gold coins were in circulation in the mid-nineteenth century:

ōban	44.0 *monme* (5.8 oz.)
koban	3.0 *monme*
ichibu	0.75 *monme*
nibu	1.52 *monme*
nishu	0.54 *monme*

The denominational unit by which all these coins were compared was the *ryō*, one of which equaled four *bu* or 16 *shu*. Workers' wages typically would be recorded in terms of these units, rather than in terms of the specific coins used. One *koban* always equalled one *ryō*, despite fluctuations in the coin's weight.

In Wakayama, where silver coins were more commonly used, wages were recorded in terms of *monme, bu, rin,* and *mō,* that is, by weight rather than the specific coins. Various copper coins known as *zeni,* meanwhile, were denominated by *monme* and *kan* units which, while originally referring to the coins' weight, gradually lost this meaning as lighter *zeni* were minted.

As a rule of thumb, one *ryō* of gold equaled 60 *monme* of silver or four *kanmon* of copper (3840 *zeni*) through most of the Tokugawa period.

NOTES

Preface

1. Karl Marx, *Grundrisse: Introduction to the Critique of Political Economy*, trans. Martin Nicolaus (New York: Vintage, 1973), 167.

2. E. L. Jones, *The European Miracle: Environments, Economies, and Geopolitics in the History of Europe and Asia* (Cambridge: Cambridge University Press, 1981), 158–59.

3. "*Only* in Japan," wrote economist Ernest Mandel, "was it possible to repeat, starting in the eighteenth century . . . the evolution of capitalism in Europe, independently of the latter." *Marxist Economic Theory*, vol. 1 (New York: Monthly Review Press, 1962), 124. Ferdinand Braudel agreed: "Capitalism succeeded in Europe, made a beginning in [Tokugawa] Japan, and failed . . . almost everywhere else." Civilization and Capitalism, 15th–18th Century, volume II: The Wheels of Commerce (New York: Harper and Row, 1982), 581–82. See also Paul A. Baran, *The Political Economy of Growth* (Monthly Review Press, 1957), 152–53, and Perry Anderson, *Lineages of the Absolutist State* (London: New Left Books, 1974), 415.

4. Sumiya Mikio and Taira Koji, eds., *An Outline of Japanese Economic History, 1603–1868* (Tokyo: Tokyo University Press, 1979), 130–51.

5. For an English-language summary of the prewar debates over "manufacture" and its periodization, see Germaine A. Hoston, *Marxism and the Crisis of Development in Prewar Japan* (Princeton, N.J.: Princeton University Press, 1986), 95f.

6. Marx 1973, 469.

Introduction

1. Throughout this study, by "cities" I mean population centers of 10,000 persons or more; by "towns," centers of commerce or nonagricultural production that exceed 1,000 persons or whose names include the suffix *-machi*. "Castletowns" (*jokamachi*) are sometimes cities, sometimes towns, but always centers of political authority..

2. While the term *chōnin* ("wardsperson") often is used to refer to townspeople in general, during the Tokugawa period it had the more specific meaning of an urban landowner or householder. The general term for all townspeople was *machikata*. See Maki Hidemasa, *Koyō no rekishi* (Tokyo: 1977), Kōbundō, 42.

3. Matsumoto Shirō, "Bakumatsu Ishinki ni okeru toshi to kaikyū tōsō," *Rekishigaku kenkyū*, supplementary volume (October 1970).

4. Saitō Osamu, "Shōka hōkōnin to zatsugyōsha: Kinsei toshi rōdō shijo ni okeru nijū kōzō no keisei," *Keizai kenkyū* 36, no. 3 (August 1985): 255 chart 3.

5. Yasuoka Shigeaki, "Kyōhō ki ni okeru shoka hōkōnin no seikatsu—Kōnoike no baai," *Ōsaka no kenkyū* (1969), 249.

6. Robert LeRoy Innes, "The Door Ajar: Japan's Foreign Trade in the Seventeenth Century" (Ph.D. diss., University of Michigan, 1980), 492.

7. Gilbert Rozman, *Urban Networks in Ch'ing China and Tokugawa Japan* (Princeton, N.J.: Princeton University Press, 1973), 265.

8. John Whitney Hall, "The Castle Town and Japan's Modern Urbanization," in *Studies in the Institutional History of Early Modern Japan*, edited by John W. Hall and Marius B. Jansen (Princeton, N.J.: Princeton University Press, 1968), 178.

9. Hiroshima Shiyakusho, *Hiroshima-shi shi* (Hiroshima: Hiroshima Shiyakusho, 1922), 633–34.

10. Yazaki Takeo, *Social Change and the City in Japan: From the Earliest Times through the Industrial Revolution* (Tokyo: Japan Publications, 1978), 140.

11. Wakita Haruko with Susan B. Hanley, "Dimensions of Development: Cities in Fifteenth- and Sixteenth-Century Japan," in *Japan Before Tokugawa*, edited by John W. Hall et al. (Princeton, N.J.: Princeton University Press, 1981), 301.

12. Minami Ryōshin, *The Economic Development of Japan* (Tokyo: The Oriental Economist, 1986), 17.

13. T. C. Smith, *The Agrarian Origins of Modern Japan* (Stanford: Stanford University Press, 1959), 212. William B. Hauser, *Economic Institutional Change in Tokugawa Japan: Osaka and the Kinai Cotton Trade* (Cambridge: Cambridge University Press, 1974), 188, writes that "Tokugawa period—by employment and rural trade provided a backlog of cottage industrial and organizational experience which could be translated into skills necessary for a modern industrial labor force and modern economic growth."

14. Sumiya Mikio, *Nihon chinrōdō ron* (Tokyo 1955), 9–15; Sheldon Garon, *The State and Labor in Modern Japan* (Berkeley: University of California Press, 1987), 12.

15. Andrew Gordon, *The Evolution of Labor Relations in Japan: Heavy Industry, 1853–1955* (Cambridge: Harvard University Press, 1985), 19.

Gordon has disputed T. C. Smith's contention that Tokugawa-period experiences prepared the Japanese work force for the discipline of later factory labor; see footnote 78, 449. Smith has however strengthened his case with the article "Peasant Time and Factory Time in Japan," *Past and Present*, 111 (May 1986): 165–97.

16. Gordon 1985, 17–25.

17. Jeffrey Kaplow, *The Names of Kings: The Parisian Laboring Poor in the Eighteenth Century* (New York: Basic Books, 1972), 20–22.

CHAPTER ONE
LABOR AND THE PAX TOKUGAWA

1. For discussions of the application to Japan of the concept "feudalism," see John W. Hall, "Feudalism in Japan—A Reassessment," in Hall and Marius B. Jansen, eds., *Studies in the Institutional History of Early Modern Japan* (Princeton, N.J.: Princeton University Press, 1968); E. O. Reischauer, "Japan," in Rushton Coulborn, ed., *Feudalism in History* (Princeton, N.J.: Princeton University

Press, 1956), and Marc Bloch, *Feudal Society*, vol. 2 (Chicago: University of Chicago Press, 1961), 446f.

2. R. H. Hilton, "Introduction," in Paul Sweezy, Maurice Dobb, et al., *The Transition from Feudalism to Capitalism* (Norfolk: Verso, 1978), 30.

3. David John Lu, *Sources of Japanese History* (New York: McGraw-Hill, 1974), 30–31.

4. Quoted in George B. Sansom, *A History of Japan, 1615–1867* (Stanford: Stanford University Press, 1963), 99.

5. Ōishi Shinzaburō, "The Bakuhan System," in Nakane Chie and Ōishi Shinzaburō, eds., *Tokugawa Japan: The Social and Economic Antecedents of Modern Japan* (Tokyo: Tokyo University Press, 1990), 34.

6. Marius B. Jansen, "Tosa in the Seventeenth Century: The Establishment of Yamauchi Rule," in John W. Hall and Marius B. Jansen, eds., *Studies in the Institutional History of Early Modern Japan* (Princeton, N.J.: Princeton University Press, 1968), 120.

7. Susan Hanley and Kozo Yamamura, *Economic and Demographic Change in Preindustrial Japan, 1600–1868* (Princeton University Press, 1977), 97; Hayami Akira, "Population Changes," in Gilbert Rozman and Marius B. Jansen, *Japan in Transition: From Tokugawa to Meiji* (Princeton, N.J.: Princeton University Press, 1986), 291; Anne Walthall, *Social Protest and Popular Culture in Eighteenth-Century Japan* (Tucson: University of Arizona Press, 1986), 213.

8. R. H. Hilton, "A Crisis of Feudalism," in T. H. Aston and C. H. E. Philpin, eds., *The Brenner Debate: Agrarian Class Structure and Economic Development in Pre-industrial Europe* (Cambridge: Cambridge University Press, 1985), 128–31.

9. Quoted in Maruyama Masao, *Studies in the Intellectual History of Tokugawa Japan* (Princeton, N.J.: Princeton University Press, 1974), 128.

The peasants, for their part, might express this inherent conflict in equally lucid terms. Around 1760 a peasant of Matsushiro *han*, Shinano province, declared that: "Whenever some thing is good for the lord, the peasants suffer hardships, and when we try to do something good for the peasants, it does not benefit the lord. . . . [If our demands] are bad for the lord, that is unavoidable." Quoted in Walthall, 30.

10. Aoki Kōji, *Hyakushō ikki no nenjiteki kenkyū* (Tokyo: Shinseisha, 1966), 36–37.

11. T. C. Smith, "The Land Tax in the Tokugawa Period," in *Native Sources of Japanese Industrialization, 1750–1920* (Berkeley: University of California Press, 1988), 53, 59.

12. James W. White, "State Growth and Popular Protest in Tokugawa Japan," *Journal of Japanese Studies*, 14, 1 (1988): 18.

13. For a general account of Ieyasu's policies, see J. W. Hall, *Japan from Prehistory to Modern Times* (New York: Dell, 1980), 169–73.

14. The standard work on the *sankin-kōtai* system in English is Toshio G. Tsukahira, *Feudal Control in Tokugawa Japan: The Sankin Kōtai System* (Harvard East Asian Monographs, 1966).

15. Roland Mousnier, *Les XVIᵉ et XVIIᵉ siècles* (Paris: Presses Universitaires de France, 1954).

16. John W. Hall, "History of Japan (Edo History)," *Kodansha Encyclopedia of Japan*, 3: 187–88.

17. Bernard Sussler, "The Toyotomi Regime and the Daimyo," in Jeffrey P. Mass and William B. Hauser, eds., *The Bakufu in Japanese History* (Stanford: Stanford University Press, 1985), 142.

18. On peasant resistance, see Walthall 1986, xiv; on urban gangs, see Jinbō Kazuya, "Otokodate," in Nishiyama Matsunosuke, ed., *Edo chōnin no kenkyū* (Tokyo: Yoshikawa Kōbunkan, 1943), 298–300.

19. Edwin Dowdy, *Japanese Bureaucracy: Its Development and Modernization* (Melbourne, Australia: Cheshire, 1973).

20. John Whitney Hall, "The Castle Town and Japan's Modern Urbanization," in Hall and Jansen, eds., 1968, 176. Compare Gilbert Rozman, *Urban Networks in Ch'ing China and Tokugawa Japan* (Princeton, N.J.: Princeton University Press, 1973), 6: "The sudden increase in Japan's urban population in the century and a half prior to the 1700s may well have had no parallel in world history before industrialization."

21. John Whitney Hall, "Kyoto as Historical Background," in John W. Hall and Jeffrey P. Mass, eds., *Medieval Japan: Essays in Institutional History* (New Haven: Yale University Press, 1974).

22. These population figures are taken from a variety of sources, but principally Hall, in Hall and Jansen, eds. 1968; Yazaki Takeo, *Social Change and the City in Japan: From the Earliest Times through the Industrial Revolution* (Tokyo: Japan Publications, 1978); Rozman; and Toyoda Takeshi, *A History of Pre-Meiji Commerce in Japan* (Tokyo: Kokusai Bunka Shinkokai, 1969).

23. Hall, in Hall and Jansen, eds. 1968, 176.

24. Yazaki 1978, 133.

25. James McClain, *Kanazawa: A Seventeenth-Century Japanese Castle Town* (New Haven: Yale University Press, 1982), 1.

26. Thomas C. Smith, *The Agrarian Origins of Modern Japan* (Stanford: Stanford University Press, 1959), 4.

27. Nakamura Satoru, "Bakumatsu-ki Senchū ni okeru nōminsō no bunkai: Nihon shihonshugi seiritsu no kiso katei no kyūmei," *Rekishigaku kenkyū*, nos. 236–37 (December 1959 and January 1960).

28. Smith 1959, esp. Chapters 9–11.

29. Nakabe Yoshiko, *Kinsei toshi no seiritsu to kōzō* (Tokyo: Shinseisha, 1974).

30. Tsukada Kō, "Mushukunin," in Nishiyama, ed. 1943, 208–9.

31. Amino Yoshihiko, *Nihon chūsei no minshū zō: heimin to shoku nin* (Iwanami shoten, 1980), 107.

32. Toyoda Takeshi, *A History of Pre-Meiji Commerce in Japan* (Tokyo: Kokusai Bunka Shinkokai, 1969), 22.

33. Amino 1980, 131.

34. Toyoda 1969, 27–8.

35. William B. Hauser, "Za," in *The Kodansha Encyclopedia of Japan* (Tokyo, 1983), 8: 361.

36. Jansen, in Hall and Jansen, eds. 1968, 121.

37. Ogyū Sorai, *Ogyū Sorai* (Nihon shisō taisei, vol. 36, Iwanami shoten, 1973), 290.

38. Satō Shin'ichi and Ikeuchi Yoshimoto, eds., *Chūsei hōsei shiryō shū*, vol. 3: *Buke kahō*, part 1 (Tokyo: Iwanami shoten, 1965), 204–5, 215.

This code has been translated into German by Wilhelm Rohl. "Das Gesetz von Takeda Shingen's," *Oriens Extremus* (Hamburg), 2 (1959): 210–35.

39. Jansen, in Hall and Jansen, eds., 1968, 106.

40. Ōsaka shi shi hensan gakari, eds., *Ōsaka shi shi*, 8 vols. (1911–14), 5: 151, 153. I am indebted to Wakita Osamu of Osaka University for bringing this and the following reference to my attention.

41. Kobata Atsushi, ed., *Sakai shi shi* (Sakai Shiyakusho, 1971–76), Zoku hen, 5: 903.

42. Maki Hidemasa, *Koyō no rekishi* (Tokyo: Kobundō, 1977), 29–33.

43. Takagi Shūsaku, "Iwayuru 'mibun hōrei' to 'ikii' kinrei: 'samurai' wa 'bushi' de wa nai," in *Nihon kinsei shi ronsō*, 1 (1984).

44. Maki Hidemasa, *Jinshin baibai* (Tokyo: Iwanami shoten, 1971), 83–84.

45. Wakita Haruko with Susan B. Hanley, "Dimensions of Development: Cities in Fifteenth- and Sixteenth-Century Japan," in John Whitney Hall, Nagahara Keiji, and Kozo Yamamura, eds., *Japan Before Tokugawa: Political Consolidation and Economic Growth, 1500 to 1650* (Princeton, N.J.: Princeton University Press, 1981), 311.

46. Louis Frederic, *Daily Life in Japan at the Time of the Samurai, 1185–1603* (Tokyo and Rutland, Vt.: Charles E. Tuttle Co., 1973), 143.

47. Shibusawa Keizō, *Nihon jōmin seikatsu ebiki* (Heibonsha, 1966–67), 3: 108; 4: 146.

48. Wakita Osamu, *Kinsei hōken shakai no keizai kōzō* (Tokyo: Ochanomizu shobō, 1978), 278.

49. Quoted in J. R. McEwan, *The Political Writings of Ogyū Sorai* (Cambridge: Cambridge University Press, 1981), 98.

50. Honjō Eijirō, *Nihon keizai shi bunken* (Tokyo: Nihon hyōronsha, 1931–59), vol. 9.

51. Toyoda 1969, 41.

52. Wakita Osamu suggests that the Toyotomi regime at times assembled fifty thousand workers at one worksite, and during the reconstruction of Osaka Castle by the Tokugawa shogunate after 1615, "many tens of thousands of people made their livings solely by day-labor on Osaka Castle construction." "Kinsei shoki no toshi keizai," *Nihonshi kenkyū*, 200 (April 1974): 52–75.

53. Yoshida Nobuyuki, "Toshi minshū no seikatsu to henkaku ishiki," *Rekishigaku kenkyū*, no. 534 (Oct. 1984).

54. Ibid.

55. Takimoto Seiichi, ed., *Nihon keizai taiten dai ten*, vol. 9, (Tokyo: Shishi shuppansha, 1928), 487.

56. Maki 1971, 61f.

57. Ibid., 80–81.

58. Maki 1977, 92.

59. Ibid., 73–74.

60. Ibid., 94.

61. Ibid., 96.

62. Ibid., 100–101.

63. Takekoshi Yosaburō, *Economic Aspects of the History of the Civilization of Japan*, vol. 2 (London: Allen and Unwin Ltd., 1930), 61.

64. Maki 1977, 98.

65. According to a clause in the medieval code *Goseibai Shikimoku* (1232).

66. Maki 1977, 101–3.

67. Ōtake Hideo, *Kinsei koyō kankei shiron* (Tokyo: Yūzankaku, 1983), 9f.

68. Ibid., 24f.

69. Maki 1977, 83.

70. Ōtake 1983, 26.

71. This is Kitajima Masamoto's opinion, summarized in Ōtake 1983, 25.

72. Tokoro Rikio, "Edo no dekaseginin," in Nishiyama, ed., 1943, 270f.

73. See Chapter 6.

74. Takayanagi Shinzō and Ishii Ryōsuke, eds., *Ofuregaki Kanpō shūsei* (Tokyo: Iwanami Shoten, 1976), 401 (no. 718).

75. *Ofuregaki Kanpō shūsei*, 398 (no. 710).

76. *Ofuregaki Kanpō shūsei*, 406 (no. 727 and no. 728), 267–68 (no. 380).

77. Ōtake 1983, 19.

78. Ihara Saikaku's works are available in numerous editions, many with commentary and parallel modern Japanese translation. In these notes I will refer the reader to the work, section, and chapter (or story) number, rather than to any particular edition. This quotation is from *Saikaku oritome*, 5: 2.

79. Kawatake Mokuami, *The Love of Izayoi and Seishin: A Kabuki Play*, translated by Frank T. Motofuji (Tokyo and Rutland, Vt.: Charles E. Tuttle, Co., 1966), 91.

80. Maki 1977, 87–88.

81. Merry E. Wiesner, *Working Women in Renaissance Germany* (New Brunswick, N.J.: Rutgers University Press, 1986), 84.

82. Ann Kussmaul, *Servants in Husbandry in Early Modern England* (Cambridge: Cambridge University Press, 1981), 50.

83. Contracts, at least, typically specified ten-year terms. As shown in Chapter 3, however, workers often left before the term was completed. By the end of the period, the contractual apprenticeship term itself had been reduced to six or seven years. Sumiya Mikio, ed., *Nihon shokugyō kanren hattatsu shi*, I:76–77.

84. Smith 1959, *passim*.

85. *Nihon shisō taikei*, vol. 36: *Ogyū Sorai*, ed. Yoshikawa Kōjirō et al. (Tokyo: Iwanami, 1983), 290.

86. R. J. Kirby, trans., "Food and Wealth, an Essay by Dazai Jun," *Transactions of the Asiatic Society of Japan*, 355 (1908), 119.

87. Yamamoto Tsunetomo, *Hagakure zenshū*, ed. Nakamura Ikukazu (Tokyo: Satsuki shobō, 1978), *passim*.

88. Saku Tadashi, *Echizen kuni shūmon ninbetsu go-aratamechō* (Tokyo: Kogawa Kōbunkan 1973), 704, 743.

89. *Takayama Ichi no chō shūmon ninbetsu aratamechō* and *Takayama Ni no chō shūmon ninbetsu aratamechō* (MS, Takayama Kyōdokan).

90. *Okeyamachi genrai shūmon aratame fumie chō* (MS 316.11.1, Nagasaki Kenritsu Toshokan).

91. *Kyūshū shiryō sōsho, Nagasaki Hirado machi ninbetsuchō*, Kyūshū shiryō kankō kai, eds., 1955.

92. Haraguchi Torao et al., eds., *The Status System and Social Organization of Satsuma* (Honolulu: University Press of Hawaii, 1975), 79, 82.

93. Hayashi Reiko et al., eds., "Hōei ni-nen Kasamamachi machikata kenbetsu aratamechō," *Ibaraki-ken shiryō, Kinsei shakai keizai hen*, I (1971), 133–73. I am grateful to Professor Hayashi for drawing this document to my attention.

94. Hayashi et al. 1971, 166.

95. Ibid., 172.

96. Karl Marx, *Capital*, vol. 1 (Chicago: C. H. Kerr & Co., 1906), 689.

97. Thomas C. Smith, "Japanese Village in the Seventeenth Century," in Hall and Jansen eds., 1978, 278.

98. Thomas C. Smith, "Pre-modern Economic Growth: Japan and the West," *Past and Present*, 60 (1973).

99. Gilbert Rozman, "Edo's Importance in the Changing Tokugawa Society," *Journal of Japanese Studies*, 1, 1 (Autumn 1974): 91–112.

100. Smith 1959, 108f.

101. Rozman 1974, 100.

102. McEwan 1981, 56.

103. The "commodification" of servants' labor power is discussed in Cissie Fairchilds, *Domestic Enemies: Servants and Their Masters in Old Regime France* (Baltimore and London: Johns Hopkins University Press, 1984), and in Sarah Maza, *Servants and Masters in Eighteenth-Century France: the Uses of Loyalty* (Princeton, N.J.: Princeton University Press, 1983).

CHAPTER TWO
MASTER AND SERVANT POPULATIONS

1. See Thomas C. Smith, *Agrarian Origins of Modern Japan* (Stanford: Stanford University Press, 1959), 12–23.

2. For example, Tsuda Hideo, "Bakumatsu no kōyō rōdō ni tsuite," *Toshi seidoshigaku*, 8 (July 1960): 13–45.

3. However, James L. McClain has discussed urban *hōkōnin* in his *Kanazawa: a Seventeenth-Century Castle Town* (New Haven: Yale University Press, 1982).

4. Gilbert Rozman, "Edo's Importance in the Changing Japanese Society," *Journal of Japanese Studies*, VI, 1 (Autumn 1974). Sekiyama Naotarō estimates that at the end of the period some fifty thousand servants were employed by domain samurai alone. *Nihon Kinsei Nihon no jinkō* (Tokyo: Yoshikawa kōbunkan, 1958), 228. Henry D. Smith suggests that one-quarter of all Edo's "samurai" were in fact servants. "The Edo-Tokyo Transition: in Search of Common Ground," in Marius B. Jansen and Gilbert Rozman, *Japan in Transition: From Tokugawa to Meiji* (Princeton, N.J.: Princeton University Press, 1986), 351.

5. Nishiyama Matsunosuke et al., eds., *Edo gaku jiten* (Tokyo: Kōbundō, 1984), 698.

6. Saitō Osamu, "Changing Structure of Urban Employment and Its Effects on Migration Patterns in Eighteenth- and Nineteenth-Century Japan," *Institute of Economic Research Discussion Paper* no. 137 (Hitotsubashi University, Tokyo, March 1986).

7. Inui Hiromi, "Ōsaka chōnin shakai no kōzō: jinkō dōtai ni okeru," in Tsuda Hideo, ed., *Kinsei kokka no kaitei to kindai* (Tokyo: Hanawa Shobō, 1979).

8. Akiyama Kunizō and Nakamura Ken, *Kyōto 'chō' no kenkyū* (Hosei daigaku shuppan kyoku, 1975), 297.

9. Harada Tomohiko, *Harada Tomohiko ronshū*, vol. 3: *Toshi shakai shi* (1985), 321.

10. Ibid., 323.

11. Harada Tomohiko, *Harada Tomohiko ronshū*, vol. 2: *Toshi keitaishi kenkyū* (1985), 229.

12. Tanaka Yoshio, *Kaga han ni okeru toshi kenkyū* (Tokyo: Bun'ichi sōgō shuppan, 1978), 140.

13. Carlo Cipolla, *Before the Industrial Revolution* (New York: Norton, 1976), 36.

14. Sarah Maza, *Servants and Masters in Eighteenth-Century France* (Princeton, N.J.: Princeton University Press, 1983), 26–27; D. C. Coleman, "Labour in the English Economy of the Seventeenth Century," *Economic History Review*, second series, vol. 8 (1956): 291.

15. Lawrence Stone, *The Family, Sex and Marriage in England, 1500–1800*, abridged ed. (London: Penguin, 1979), 28, 84.

16. Cipolla 1976, 79; Merry E. Wiesner, *Working Women in Renaissance Germany* (New Brunswick, N.J.: Rutgers University Press, 1986), 92.

17. J. Jean Hecht, *The Domestic Servant Class in Eighteenth Century England* (London: Routledge and Paul, 1956), 5.

18. Cipolla 1976, 36; Hecht 1956, 5.

19. Hecht 1956, 5.

20. Cipolla 1976, 36; Hecht 1956, 5.

21. T. G. Tsukahira, *Feudal Control in Tokugawa Japan: The Sankin Kōtai System* (Cambridge: Harvard University East Asian Monographs, 1966), 62.

22. Hōsei-shi Gakkai, eds., *Tokugawa kinreikō*, vol. 4 (Tokyo: Yoshikawa Kōbunkan, 1931–1932), 528–29.

23. Kitajima Masamoto, *Edo bakufu no kenryoku kōzō* (Tokyo: Iwanami shōten, 1964), 407.

24. Maza 1983, 200–10.

25. Ihara Saikaku, *Nippon eitaigura*, I:4.

26 For example, Chikamatsu Monzaemon, *Chikamatsu jōruri shu*, 1, ed. Shigetomo Ki (Tokyo: Iwanami, 1976), 361.

27. Tsukahira 1966, 62.

28. Kitajima Masamoto, "Buke no hōkōnin," in *Edo jidai bushi no seikatsu* (Tokyo: Yūzankaku, 1984), 141.

29. Yamamura 1974, 122.

30. Minami Kazuo, *Edokko no sekai* (Tokyo: Kōdansha, 1980), 135.

31. Yamamura 1974, 132.

32. Minami 1980, 135–6.

33. Inui 1979, *passim*. Evidence published by Saitō Osamu in his "Changing Structure" article also suggests that the proportion of employer households was high in Osaka, at least in the latter days of the shogunate. In Amagasaki Itchōme in 1866, 83.5 percent of the households had servants; in Kajichō in 1864, 79.2 percent; and in Kōraibashi San-chōme the year after the Restoration, 48.6 percent. My own research on Sadoyamachi, meanwhile, shows that on average, 58 percent of the ward households employed a servant between 1832 to 1842.

34. *Minami-gumi Sadoyachō shakuya ninbetsuchō* (photocopies of manuscript at University of Osaka, Kokushi Kenkyūshitsu).

35. Akiyama and Nakamura 1975, 294.

36. *Taishiyamachō shūmon ninbetsu aratamechō, Hanagurumachō shūmon ninbetsu aratamechō* (manuscript, Kyōto-shi Shiryōkan).

37. Saitō 1980, 20.

38. Saitō 1980, 6–7.

39. Saitō Osamu, *Shōka no sekai uramise no sekai* (Tokyo: Ripuropotto, 1987), 91f. Unfortunately this work came to my attention too late for me to make full use of its insights.

40. Tsukahira 1966, 62.

41. Naramoto Tatsuya, ed., *Yomeru nenpyō: Edo hen*, 1 (Tokyo: Jiyū kokuminsha, 1983), 48.

42. George Sansom, *A History of Japan, 1615–1867* (Stanford: Stanford University Press, 1963), 13.

43. Endō Motoo, *Kinsei seikatsu nenpyō* (Tokyo: Yūzankaku, 1982), 309.

44. Kodama Kōta, *Genroku jidai* (Tokyo: Chūō kōronsha, 1984), 136.

45. Hayami Akira, "Kyōto machikata no shūmon aratamechō: Shijō tateuri nakanomachi," *Tokugawa rinsei shi kenkyū*, kenkyū kiyō, 1980.

46. *Hanagurumachō monjo* manuscript, J-1, 1. Kyoto Municipal Historical Archive.

47. Inui 1979, 23.

48. Ihara, *Seken munasanyō*, 2:3.

49. Sakamoto Heihachirō and Miyamoto Mataji, eds., *Ōsaka Kikuyachō shūshi ninbetsuchō* (1941–73), 1:6.

50. Ibid., 2:428.

51. Ibid., passim.

52. Ibid., 2:437.

53. Hayami 1980, 513.

54. Roy Porter, *English Society in the Eighteenth Century* (Harmondsworth: Penguin, 1982), 100.

55. Ishii Ryōsuke, *Edo jidai manpitsu*, 1 (Tokyo: Asahi sensho, 1979), 91.

56. Porter (1982), 100.

57. Ronald Dore, *Education in Tokugawa Japan* (Berkeley: University of California Press, 1975), 43.

58. Robert Bellah, *Tokugawa Religion: The Cultural Roots of Modern Japan* (Glencoe, Ill.: Free Press, 1957; 1985), 123–24.

59. Haraguchi Torao et al., eds., *The Status System and Social Organization of Satsuma* (Honolulu: University Press of Hawaii, 1975), 144.

60. Ikeda shōichirō, *Edo jidai yōgo kōshō jiten* (Tokyo: Shinjinbutsu ōraisha, 1984), 18.

61. Haraguchi et al. 1975, 18.

62. Takagi Shūsaku, "Iwayuru 'mibun hōrei' to 'ikii' kinrei: 'samurai' wa 'bushi' de wa nai," in *Nihon kinsei shi ronsō*, 1 (Tokyo, 1984): 117–18.

63. Ishii Ryōsuke & Takayanagi Shinzō, eds., *Ofuregaki Kanpō shūsei* (Tokyo: Iwanami shoten, 1936).

64. Kitajima 1984, 127.

65. For example, the lists in *Kaga han shoki no samurai chō* (1661). Facsimile published by Ishikawa-ken Toshokan Kyōkai (Kanazawa, 1942).

66. Kitajima 1984, 127f.

67. Kitajima 1984, 126.

68. Yamamoto Tsunetomo, *Hagakure zenshū*, ed. Nakamura Ikukazu (Tokyo: Satsuki shobō, 1978), 189.

69. R. H. Blyth, *Oriental Humour* (Tokyo: Hokuseidō, 1959), 358. I have altered the translation to conform with my servant terminology.

70. Michael Cooper, trans. and ed., *This Island of Japon: João Rodrigues' Account of 16th Century Japan* (Tokyo: Kodansha, 1973), 104.

71. Yamamoto 1978, 355.

72. Cooper 1973, 93.

73. Cooper 1973, 104.

74. Kodama Kōta, *Genroku jidai* (Tokyo: Chūō kōronsha, 1984), 78.

75. Fukuzawa Yukichi, *The Autobiography of Fukuzawa Yukichi* (New York: Columbia University Press, 1966), 23.

76. A. L. Sadler, *The Maker of Modern Japan: The Life of Tokugawa Ieyasu* (London: Allen and Unwin, 1937), 338.

77. Sansom 1963, 175.

78. Date Masamune (1567–1636), the lord of Sendai, and Iemitsu, the third Tokugawa shogun, were among the notables of the period owing their positions, at least in part, to the interventions of their nurses.

79. Sugimoto Etsuko, *Daughter of the Samurai* (Tokyo and Rutland, Vt.: Tuttle, 1955), 8–9.

80. Harada Tomohiko, *Harada Tomohiko ronshū*, vol. 3: *Toshi keitaishi kenkyū* (1985), 229.

81. Ihara, *Saikaku oritome*, 1:3.

82. Ihara, *Kōshoku ichidai otoko*, 5:6. See also Shikitei Sanba, *Ukiyoburo*, ed. Nakamura Michio (Tokyo: Iwanami shoten, 1957), 59–60, where the "detchi" Tsurukichi seems to serve as a footboy rather than an apprentice.

83. Kitajima Masamoto, *Edo jidai* (Tokyo: Iwanami shinsho, 1983), 112f.

84. Kitajima 1984, 113.

85. Ihara, *Saikaku oritome*, 1:1.

86. Ōkubo 1955, 161.

87. Hayami 1980, 513.

88. *Sanjō Koromontanachō monjo*, Kyōtō Machifure Kenkyū-kaisho shashin shiryō (Kyoto University, photocopied manuscript), vol. 2; *Taishiyama shūmon ninbetsu aratamechō*, Kyōto-shi Shiryō Kaikan, doc. J-1, 28; 26 (manuscript).

89. Ikegami Akihito, "Kōki Edo kasō chōnin no seikatsu," in Nishiyama Matsunosuke, ed., *Edo chōnin no kenkyū*, vol. 2 (Tokyo: Yoshikawa kōbunkan, 1972–73), 176.

90. Ihara, *Nippon eitaigura*, 2:5.

91. Nihon meichō zenshū kankōkai, eds., *Nihon meichō zenshū* (1926–29), 9: 768.

92. A *kara-usu* was a mortar used for hulling rice, the pestle of which was worked by foot.

93. Ihara, *Saikaku oritome*, 5:2.

94. Ibid., 6:2.

95. Charles J. Dunn, *Everyday Life in Traditional Japan* (Tokyo and Rutland Vt.: Charles E. Tuttle, 1969), 165.

96. Ihara, *Saikaku oritome*, 6:3.

97. Mary Martin McLaughlin, "Survivors and Surrogates: Children and Parents from the Ninth to Thirteenth Centuries," in Lloyd deMause, ed., *The History of Childhood* (New York: Harper Torchbooks, 1974), 116; Fairchilds 1984, 196; Charlotte Furth, "Concepts of Pregnancy, Childbirth and Infancy in Ch'ing Dynasty China," *Journal of Asian Studies*, 46, 1 (February 1987): 22.

98. Furth 1987, 22.

99. Christiane Klapisch-Zuber, "Women Servants in Florence during the Fourteenth and Fifteenth Centuries," in Barbara A. Hanawalt, *Women and Work in Preindustrial Europe* (Bloomington, Ind.: Indiana University Press, 1986), 141.

100. Ihara, *Saikaku oritome*, 6:3.

101. Furth 1987, 43.

102. Ihara, *Saikaku oritome*, 6:3.

103. Dunn 1969, 96.

104. See the 1642 Chōnin Code of Kanazawa, translated in McClain, 1982, 160.

105. Wakayama-shi shi hensan iinkai, eds., "Gejo kyūgin kashi hikaechō," in *Wakayama-shi shi* (1975), 5: 173–98.

106. Ibid., 182.

107. Ibid., 192.

108. Ibid., 194.

109. This description based primarily on Dunn, Saikaku's stories about merchant households, and the Numano wagebook.

110. Thorstein Veblen, *The Theory of the Leisure Class: An Economic Study of Institutions* (New York: Modern Library, 1931), 78.

111. Minami Kazuo, "Edo no chūgin kyūkin kō," *Nihon rekishi*, 204, 5 (May 1965): 82.

112. Ibid., 82.

113. Gordon T. Bowles, "Japanese people, physical characteristics," *Kōdansha Encyclopedia of Japan* (Tokyo: Kōdansha, 1983), 4: 37.

114. Ronald E. Rainey, *Sumptuary Legislation in Renaissance Florence* (Ph.D. diss., Columbia University, 1985), 216–18.

115. Donald H. Shively, "Sumptuary Regulation and Status in Early Tokugawa Japan," *Harvard Journal of Asiatic Studies*, 25 (1964–65): 43.

116. Wilfred Hooper, "The Tudor Sumptuary Laws," *English Historical Review*, 30 (1915): 439.

117. Shively 1964–65, 43.

118. McClain 1982, 72, 93.

119. Ishii and Takayanagi 1936, 561.

120. *Nihon meichō zenshū kankōkai*, eds., 9:768.

121. Blyth 1959, 324.

122. Ibid.

123. Ihara, *Kōshoku ichidai otoko*, 5:6.

124. Shively 1964–65, 123–64.

125. Ibid., 128–9.

126. Endō 1958, 115.

127. Apparently the bakufu never attempted to reduce such pretension by placing a *tax* on servants, such as was proposed in England in the late eighteenth century. E. S. Turner, *What the Butler Saw: 200 Years of the Servant Problem* (London: M. Joseph, 1962), 79.

128. Cipolla 1976, 94.

129. *Hanaguruma monjo*, Kyōto Rekishi Shiryōkan, doc. J-I, 27; J-I, 30 (manuscript).

130. "Hōei ni nen Kasamamachi machikata kenbetsu aratamechō," in Hayashi Reiko et al., eds., *Ibaraki-ken shiryō: Kinsei shakai keizai hen*, 1 (1971); Fukushima-shi shi hensan iinkai, eds., *Fukushima-shi shi: Kinsei shiryō*, 2 (Fukushima: Nichirento insatsujo, 1968), 317–333.

All figures on ages are according to the old Japanese system of reckoning, which added one or two years to the person's actual age from birth.

131. Inui Hiromi, *Naniwa Ōsaka Kikuyachō* (Kyoto: Yanagiwara shoten, 1977), 301.

132. Wakayama-shi shi hensan iinkai 1975, *passim*.

133. The employment of young children might also serve a display purpose. To pamper, dress up and support a helpless child might in fact be the ultimate in conspicuous consumption.

134. Kitajima 1983, 113.

135. Kurowa Heijirō, ed., *Ōsaka shōgyō shiryō shūsei*, 1 (Osaka: Ōsaka Shiritsu Daigaku Keizai Kenkyūjo, 1934), 75.

136. Philippe Ariès observed that in fifteenth-century France the word *enfant* might be synonymous with *valet*, and in the seventeenth century a *garçon* "was not necessarily a child but a young servant." *Centuries of Childhood* (Harmondsworth: Penguin, 1973), 24.

137. Maza 1983, 63.

138. Akiyama and Nakamura 1975, 297.

139. Harada, 2 (1985): 229.

140. Fairchilds 1984, 15–16; Maza 1983, 277–78.

141. Saitō Osamu, "Shōka hōkōnin to zatsugyōsha," *Keizai kenkyū*, 36, 3 (1985): 252, 255.

142. Inui 1979, 33.

143. Shinshū Ōsaka-shi shi hensan iinkai, comp., *Shinshū Ōsaka-shi shi*, 3 vols. (Kawakita insatsu, 1988–89), 3: 840.

144. Inui 1979, 25.

145. Hayami Akira, "Tokugawa kōki jinkō hendō no chiikiteki tokusei," *Mita gakkai zasshi*, nos. 64–68 (1971).

146. Nishiyama, ed. 1984, 157.

147. Higuchi Kiyoyuki, *Nihon josei no seikatsushi* (Tokyo: Kōdansha, 1977), 159.

148. Nishiyama Matsunosuke, *Iemoto no kenkyū* (Tokyo: Yoshikawa kō-bunkan, 1982), 495.

149. Shikitei Sanba, *Ukiyoburo*, ed. Nakamura Michio (Tokyo: Iwanami shoten, 1957), 185.

150. Shibata Kyūō, *Kyūō dōwa* (Tokyo: Heibonsha, 1970), 11–12.

151. Hayami Akira, "Labor Migration in a Pre-industrial Society: A Study Tracing the Life Histories of the Inhabitants of a Village," *Keio Economic Studies*, X, 2 (1973).

152. Dore 1975, 254.

153. Shikitei 1957, 185.

154. Quoted in Honjō Eijirō, *Social and Economic History of Japan* (New York: Russell & Russell, 1935), 171–72.

155. Lafcadio Hearn, *Japan: An Attempt at Interpretation* (Tokyo and Rutland, Vt.: Charles E. Tuttle Co., 1955), 407.

156. L. L. Cornell, "Life Cycle Service, Age at Marriage, and Household Formation in the Industrialization of Japan," in *Preconditions to Industrialization in Japan*, organized by Hayami Akira, Ninth International Economic History Congress, International Research, section D-15 (Bern, 1986), 4.

CHAPTER THREE
MASTER-SERVANT RELATIONS

1. Ikegami Akihito, "Kōki Edo kasō chōnin no seikatsu," in Nishiyama Matsunosuke, ed., *Edo chōnin no kenkyū* (Tokyo: Toshikawa kōbunkan, 1972–73), 2: 177–226.

2. Inui Hiromi, *Naniwa Ōsaka Kikuyachō* (Kyoto: Yanagiwara shoten, 1977), 301.

3. Matsumoto Shirō, *Nihon kinsei toshi ron* (Tokyo: Tōkyō Daigaku shuppankai, 1983), 99–100.

4. Ihara, *Kōshoku ichidai onna*, 4:4.

5. D. C. Coleman, "Labour in the English Economy in the Seventeenth Century," *Economic History Review*, 2d ser., VIII (1956), 280.

6. George B. Sansom, *A History of Japan, 1615–1867* (Stanford: Stanford University Press, 1963), 166.

7. Ogyū Sorai, *Nihon shisō taisei*, vol. 36: *Ogyū Sorai* (Tokyo: Iwanami shoten, 1983), 34.

8. Honjō Eijirō, *The Social and Economic History of Japan* (New York: Russell & Russell, 1965), 215–16.

9. Ibid., 171–72.

10. Ibid., 172.

11. See Harold Bolitho's review of Susan Hanley and Kozo Yamamura, *Economic and Demographic Change in Preindustrial Japan* (1977), in *Harvard Journal of Asiatic Studies*, 39, 2 (December 1979).

12. Shikitei Sanba, *Ukiyoburo*, ed. Nakamura Michio (Tokyo: Iwanami shoten, 1957), 121.

13. Ibid., 128–29.

14. Ogyū Sorai, in Takimoto Seiichi, ed., *Nihon keizai taiten*, vol. 9 (Tokyo: Keimeisha, 1928), 141.

15. Ikegami 1974, 177f.

16. Thomas C. Smith, *The Agrarian Origins of Modern Japan* (Stanford: Stanford University Press, 1959), 162.

17. J. R. McEwan, *The Political Writings of Ogyū Sorai* (Cambridge: Cambridge University Press, 1981), 11.

18. For examples of contracts in which such terms appear, see John Henry Wigmore, ed., *Law and Justice in Tokugawa Japan*, vol. VIII-B (Japan Foundation, 1983), 73f.

19. McEwan 1981, 130.

20. Ogyū 1928, 11.

21. Wigmore 1983, 73.

22. Takekoshi Yosaburō, *The Economic Aspects of the History of the Civilization of Japan*, vol. II (London: George Allen and Unwin, 1930), 359.

23. Ihara, *Saikaku oritome*, 5:2.

24. On the *bureaux d'adresse* in France, see Howard Solomon, *Public Welfare, Science and Propaganda in Seventeenth-Century France: The Innovations of Theophraste Renaudot* (Princeton, N.J.: Princeton University Press, 1972), 21f.

On English placement offices, see Dorothy George, "The Early History of Registry Offices," *Economic Journal* (January, 1929).

25. *Dai Nihon hyakka jiten*, vol. 13 (Shogakkan, 1970), 615.

26. Maki Hidemasa, *Koyō no rekishi* (Tokyo: Kobundō, 1977), 129; Wigmore, vol. VII (1981), 105.

27. Wakayama-shi shi hensan iinkai, eds., "Gejo kyūgin kashi hikaechō," in *Wakayama-shi shi* (1975), 5: 177f.

28. Nishiyama Matsunosuke et al., eds., *Edo gaku jiten* (Tokyo: Kōbunkan, 1984), 156.

29. Ihara, *Saikaku oritome*, 6:2.

30. Takizawa Bakin, *Bakin nikki*, ed. Teruoka Yasutaka et al. (Tokyo: Chūō kōronsha, 1968).

31. Ronald P. Dore, *Education in Tokugawa Japan* (Berkeley: University of California Press, 1975), 230–31.

32. *Tōryō Ōguri hyōkan*, cited in Kitajima Masao, *Edo jidai* (Tokyo: Iwanami shoten, 1958), 117.

33. Chikamatsu Monzaemon, *Chikamatsu jōruri shū*, ed. Shigetomo Ki (Tokyo: Iwanami shoten, 1958), 1: 24.

34. Ishida Baigan, *Dialogues of Town and Country*, trans. Matsuo Akira (Osaka: Ōsaka Kyōiku Tosho, 1985), 66.

35. Joseph Spae, *Itō Jinsei: A Philosopher, Educator, and Sinologist of the Tokugawa Period* (Peking: Catholic University of Peking, 1967).

36. Cited in Dore 1965, 36.

37. Sidney Crawcour, trans., "Some Observations on Merchants: A Transla-

tion of Mitsui Takafusa's *Chōnin Kōken Roku*," in *Transactions of the Asiatic Society of Japan*, 3d ser., 8 (1961).

38. Howard Hibbett, *The Floating World in Japanese Fiction* (Tokyo & Rutland, Vt.: Charles E. Tuttle Co., 1975), 49.

39. Ihara, *Yorozu no fumihōgu*, 1:2.

40. Cissie Fairchilds, *Domestic Enemies: Servants and Their Masters in Old Regime France* (Balitmore and London: Johns Hopkins University Press, 1984), 138.

41. Cited in Yoshida Nobuyuki, "Chōnin to chō," in *Kōza Nihon rekishi*, 5: *Kinsei*, 1 (Tōkyō daigaku, 1985), 170.

42. Johannes Hirschmeier and Yui Tsunehiko, *The Development of Japanese Business, 1600–1973* (Cambridge: Harvard University Press, 1975), 63.

43. Louis Frederic, *Daily Life in Japan at the Time of the Samurai, 1185–1603* (Tokyo & Rutland, Vt.: Charles E. Tuttle Co., 1973), 49.

44. Maki 1981, 47.

45. David John Lu, *Sources of Japanese History*, vol. 1 (New York: McGraw-Hill, 1974), 213; Ōkubo Toshiaki et al., *Shiryō ni yoru Nihonshi no ayumi* (Yoshikawa kōbunkan, 1955), 105–6.

46. Lu 1974, 212; Ōkubo 1955, 108; see also Dan Fenno Henderson, *Conciliation and Japanese Law*, vol. 1 (Seattle and Tokyo: University of Washington Press and University of Tokyo Press, n.d.), 119.

47. Fairchilds 1984, 128.

48. Henderson, 120; *Osadamegaki*, article 65, section 3.

49. Henderson, 67, 127f.

50. Michiko Y. Aoki, "The Judge Ōoka Tales," in Aoki and Margaret B. Darders, *As the Japanese See It: Past and Present* (Honolulu: University of Hawaii Press, 1981).

51. This is in contrast to China, where the killing of one's father outweighed all other crimes.

52. Maki 1981, 48.

53. Fairchilds 1984, 131; Merry E. Wiesner, *Working Women in Renaissance Germany* (New Brunswick, N.J.: Rutgers University Press, 1986), 90.

54. J. Victor Koschmann, *The Mito Ideology: Discourse, Reform, and Insurrection in Late Tokugawa Japan, 1790–1864* (Berkeley: University of California Press, 1987), 155.

55. Arai Hakuseki, *Told Around a Brushwood Fire: The Autobiography of Arai Hakuseki*, trans., with introduction by Joyce Ackroyd (Tokyo: University of Tokyo, 1979), 70–71.

56. Naramoto Tatsuya, gen. ed., *Yomeru nenpyō*, 5: *Edo-hen* (Jiyūkokumin-sha, 1982), 1: 117.

57. Yamamoto Tsunetomo, *Hagakure zenshū* (Satsuki shobō, 1978), 17.

58. Ibid., 69.

59. Arai 1979, 71.

60. Text of the *Ishida sensei jiseki* in Robert Bellah, *Tokugawa Religion: The Cultural Roots of Modern Japan* (Glencoe, Ill.: Free Press, 1957), 199–215. This quote on p. 207.

61. Leon Zolbrod, *Takizawa Bakin* (1967), 102.

62. Sugimoto (Inagaki) Etsu, *Daughter of the Samurai* (Tokyo and Rutland, Vt.: Charles E. Tuttle Co., 1966), 8.

63. Yamamoto 1978, 57–58.

64. Wakayama-shi shi hensan iinkai, eds., "Gejo kyūgin kashi hikaechō," in *Wakayama-shi shi* (1975), 5:173–98.

65. Fairchilds 1984, 157; J. Jean Hecht, *The Domestic Servant Class in Eighteenth Century England* (London: Routledge and Paul, 1956), 90–95.

66. Ikegami Akihito, "Kōki Edo kasō chōnin no seikatsu," in Nishiyama Matsunosuke, ed., *Edo chōnin no kenkyū*, 2 (Tokyo: Yoshikawa kōbunkan, 1972–73), 177–226.

67. Hayashi Reiko, "Chōka josei no sonzai keitai," in *Nihon josei-shi*, vol. 3: *Kinsei* (Tokyo: Tōkyō Daigaku shuppankai, 1982), 118.

68. Ikegami 1974, 177.

69. Inui Hiromi, *Naniwa Ōsaka Kikuyachō* (Kyoto: Yanagiwara shoten, 1977), 181–83.

70. Endō Motoo, *Kinsei seikatsu nenpyō* (Tokyo: Yūzankaku, 1982), 182, 218.

71. Kanai Madoka, *Kinsei daimyō ryō no kenkyū: Shinano Matsumoto han chūshin toshite* (Tokyo: Meicho shuppan, 1981), 372. Chūgen, kachi, koshō, komono and gejo are mentioned in daimyo wills.

72. "Bekke tedai no yuigonjo to atoshiki kankei shiryō," *Mitsui bunko ronsō*, 18 (1984), 411.

73. Ihara, *Honchō oin hiji*, 3:7. See also 4:5.

74. "Bekke," 434, 340.

75. Yasuoka Shigeaki, "Kinsei Kyōto shōnin no kagyō to sōzoku," in *Kyōto shakaishi kenkyū*, ed. Nakamura Shūsaku (Kyoto: Hōritsu bunkasha, 1971), 320 (chart).

76. R. H. Blyth, *Japanese Life and Character in Senryū* (Tokyo: Hokuseido Press, 1960), 85. My translation of this An'ei period (1772–80) poem.

77. Fukawa Kiyoshi, *Kinsei fūzoku no igi to seikatsu* (Tokyo: Nōsangyōson bunka kyōkai, 1984), 40.

78. Kodama Kōta, *Genroku jidai* (Tokyo: Chūō kōronsha, 1984), 125; Maki 1977, 534.

79. Yamamoto 1978, 294.

80. Kodama 1984, 125–26.

81. Ishida 1957, 48–49.

82. Inui 1977, 156.

83. Endō 1982, 146.

84. Yamamoto 1978, 302.

85. James McClain, *Kanazawa: A Seventeenth-Century Japanese Castle Town* (New Haven: Yale University Press, 1982), 96.

86. Nishiyama et al. 1984, 574.

87. McClain 1982, 99; Naramoto 1982, 75.

88. Conrad Totman, *Tokugawa Ieyasu, Shōgun* (San Francisco: Heian Books, 1973), 65.

89. Ueda Akinari, *Tales of Moonlight and Rain: Japanese Gothic Tales*, trans. Kengi Hamada (Tokyo: University of Tokyo Press, 1974).

90. Ishida 1957, 53.

91. Yamamoto 1978, 288.

92. Ihara, *Saikaku oritome*, 5:2.

93. Henry Faulds translated an extract from what he describes as a Bakin work written in 1809–10. I have not been able to find the original, and have relied on Fauld's version. *Nine Years in Nipon: Sketches of Japanese Life and Manners* (London: A. Gardner, 1885) 217–24.

94. Fairchilds 1984, 194–200; Joseph E. Illick, "Child-Rearing in Seventeenth-Century England and America," in Lloyd deMause, ed., *The History of Childhood* (New York: Harper Torchbooks, 1974), 309; Lawrence Stone, *The Family, Sex and Marriage in England*, abridged ed. (London: Penguin, 1979), 272.

95. Chikamatsu Monzaemon, *Chikamatsu jōruri shū*, 1, ed. Shigetomo Ki (Tokyo: Iwanami shoten, 1976), 96.

96. Ihara, *Saikaku oritome*, 6:3.

97. Ibid.

98. Hidemura Senzō, "Genin ni kansuru shiryō oboegaki sandai: shiryō no shōkai to gimon," *Kyūshū keizaishi ronshū*, vol. 2, ed. Miyamoto Mataji (Fukuoka, Fukuoka shōkōjo kaigijo, 1954–58), vol. 2, chart facing 168.

99. Minami Kazuo, "Edo no chūgin kyūkin kō," *Nihon rekishi*, 204, 5 (May 1965), 81.

100. Ogyū Sorai, *Seidan*, in *Nihon keizai taiten* (Tokyo: Keimeisha, 1928), 86.

101. Wakayama-shi shi hensan iinkai, eds. 1975, 187.

102. *Kawachiya no genin Teisuke shūjin no shohindai mochinige* (Kikuyachō monjo, cat. no. 251, Nakanoshima Library, Osaka).

103. Sometimes such "theft" was indirect. In *Sonezaki shinjū* Tokubei flees without repaying two ryō which his master had given the clerk's stepmother. The money was supposed to be the dowry for the master's niece, whose hand Tokubei indignantly refuses.

104. Again, this seems to have been a universal phenomenon. Steve Ozment, *When Fathers Ruled: Family Life in Reformation Europe* (Cambridge: Harvard University Press, 1983), 151–52; Patricia Buckley Ebrey, trans., *Family and Property in Sung China* (Princeton, N.J.: Princeton University Press, 1984), 207–8.

105. Sakai Atsuhara, "Kaibara Ekiken and 'Onna Diagaku,' " *Cultural Nippon*, 7, 4 (1939): 55.

106. Ishida 1972, 66–67.

107. Wakayama-shi shi hensan iinkai, eds. 1975, 178, 182, 189.

108. Hayashi Reiko, "Edodana no seikatsu," in Nishiyama Matsunosuke, *Edo chōnin no kenkyū*, 2: 130 (chart).

109. Hecht 1956, 82.

110. Inui Hiromi, "Ōsaka chōnin shakai no kōzō," in Tsuda Hideo, ed., *Kinsei kokka no tenkai* (Tokyo: Kōshobō, 1980), 11–64.

111. Smith 1959, 149.

112. McEwan 1981, 51.

113. Tsunoda Ryūsaku et al., *Sources of Japanese Tradition* vol. 1 (New York: Columbia University Press, 1958), 492.

114. Ihara, *Saikaku oritome*, 5:2.

115. Ishii Ryōsuke, *Edo jidai manpitsu* vol. 1 (Tokyo, 1979), 95.

116. Fairchilds 1984, 110.

117. Sakamoto Heihachirō and Miyamoto Mataji, eds., *Ōsaka Kikuyachō shūshi ninbetsuchō* vol. 1 (Tokyo: Yoshikawa kōbunkan, 1971–77).

118. Blyth 1959, 545. My translation.

119. Ihara, *Saikaku oritome*, 1:3.

120. See for example the amusing episode in *Hizakurige* in which Kitahachi is mistaken for a servant because of his blue *kanban* coat. Jippensha Ikku, *Tōkai-dōchū hizakurige* vol. 2 (Tokyo: Iwanami shoten, 1973), 227.

121. Ihara, *Kōshoku ichidai onna*, 1:3.

122. Miyamoto Mataji, *Kinsei Ōsaka no keizai to chōsei* (Tokyo: Bunken shuppan, 1985), 254.

123. "The willingness to have an economy where many servants were not expected to marry has existed in many societies nurturing the class belief that only people of a given status are persons." John J. Noonan, Jr., "Intellectual and Demographic History," in D. V. Glass & Robert Revell, eds., *Population and Social Change* (London: E. Arnold, 1972).

124. Sugawara Kenji, "Kinsei Kyōto no chō to sutego," *Rekishi hyōron*, 422 (June 1985), 41.

125. Ihara, *Nanshoku ōkagami*, 5:2. This translation by Paul Gordon Schalow, *The Great Mirror of Male Love* (Stanford: Stanford University Press, 1990), 198.

126. Olof G. Lidin, *The Life of Ogyū Sorai: A Tokugawa Confucian Philosopher* (Sweden: Studentlitteratur, 1973), 168.

127. Suzuki Katsutada, *Senryū zappai kara mita Edo seimin fūzoku* (Okazaki: Yūzankaku, 1978), 183.

128. R. H. Blyth, *Oriental Humour* (Tokyo: Hokuseidō, 1959), 325.

129. Ibid., 407, 387.

130. Kosaka Jirō, *Genroku go-tatami bugyō no nikki: Owari han samurai no mita ukiyō* (Tokyo: Chūō kōronsha, 1984), 141–43.

131. A. L. Sadler, *The Maker of Modern Japan: The Life of Tokugawa Ieyasu* (London: Allen and Unwin, 1937), 96; Totman 1973, 40–41.

132. Kodama 1984, 126; Maki 1977, 53–54. As late as 1918 the judiciary tended to concede employers' rights to the sexual favors of their servants. In that year, a sixteen-year-old Yokohama girl was contracted to work as a waitress in Ibaraki-ken but was sent to work instead as a bar prostitute. The Japan Women's Christian Temperance Union brought the case to the attention of the local prosecutor, who found it unworthy of consideration. So did other courts up to the Imperial High Court. Albert Novack, "The Japanese Looking Glass: Prostitution and Japanese Women (7)," *The Daily Yomiuri*, August 27, 1986, 7.

133. Ihara Saikaku, *Five Women Who Loved Love*, trans. Theodore de Bary (Tokyo and Rutland, Vt.: Charles E. Tuttle Co., 1956), 251.

134. See, for example, Article 36 of the "Hundred Article Code of Chosokabe Motochika," in Marius B. Jansen, "Tosa in the Seventeenth Century: The Establishment of Yamauchi Rule," in John W. Hall and Jansen, eds., *Studies in the Institutional History of Early Modern Japan* (Princeton, N.J.: Princeton University Press, 1968), 106. Although this code predates the Tokugawa era, it expresses a of female chastity applied to samurai women through the next several hundred years. See also Yamamoto 1978, 445–46.

135. Donald Keene, *Major Plays of Chikamatsu* (New York: Columbia University Press, 1959), 76.

136. Lu 1974, 213; Ōkubo 1955, 108.

137. For example, Ihara, *Kōshoku ichidai onna*, 3:1.

138. Ueda Akinari, *Ugetsu Monogatari: Tales of Moonlight and Rain* (Tokyo and Rutland, Vt.: Charles E. Tuttle Co., 1977), 24.

139. Naramoto 1982, 1: 117.

140. Kosaka 1984, 141–43.

141. Endō 1982, 179.

142. Ishii 1979, 1: 267–71.

143. Hashimoto Seiji, ed., *Himeji-shi shi* (1973), 2: 155–56.

144. Ihara 1956 (trans. de Bary), 242.

145. Wakita Osamu, *Kinsei Ōsaka no chō to hito* (Jinbun shoin, 1986), 182; for other cases, Naramoto 1982, 103.

146. Wakayama-shi shi hensan iinkai, eds. 1975, 189, 180.

147. Fukawa 1984, 40–41.

148. McClain 1982, 93.

149. Naramoto, vol. 1, 1982, 105.

150. Robert W. Malcolmson, *Popular Recreations in English Society, 1700–1850* (Cambridge: Cambridge University Press, 1973), 78–79.

151. Ihara, *Kōshoku ichidai otoko*, 3:3.

152. Richard Rubinger, *Private Academies of Tokugawa Japan* (Princeton, N.J.: Princeton University Press, 1982), 21.

153. Ihara, *Saikaku oritome*, 6:3.

154. Chikamatsu Monzaemon, *Masterpieces of Chikamatsu*, trans. Miyamori Asatarō (Toseido, n.d.), 67.

155. Wakayama-shi shi hensan iinkai, eds. 1975, 187.

156. C. Andrew Gerstle, *Circles of Fantasy: Convention in the Plays of Chikamatsu* (Council on East Asian Studies, Harvard University, 1986), 41; Hironaga Shuzaburō, *The Kabuki Handbook* (Tokyo: Maison des Arts, 1976), 170–76.

157. The standard Japanese work on the topic is Iwata Jun'ichi, *Honchō nanshoku kō*, written in the 1930s and republished in 1974. Unfortunately the study does not cover the Tokugawa period. But see Watanabe Tsuneo and Iwata Jun'ichi, *The Love of the Samurai: A Thousand Years of Japanese Homosexuality* (London: Gay Men's Press, 1989).

158. Michel Foucault, *The Uses of Pleasure: The History of Sexuality, Volume Two*, trans. Robert Hurley (New York: Vintage Books, 1986), 215.

159. Alan Bray, *Homosexuality in Renaissance England* (London: Gay Men's Press, 1982), 49.

160. "Nanshoku is the pastime of the samurai," declares a character in one of Ejima Kiseki's works. "How could it possibly be a hindrance to good government?" Nihon meichō zenshū kankōkai, eds., *Nihon meicho zenshū* vol. 9 (1926–29), 619.

161. Yamamoto 1978, 69.

162. Suzuki 1978, 182.

163. Kitamura Nobuyo, *Kiyū shoran*, in *Nihon zuihitsu taisei* vol. 2 (2nd ser., 1929), 394–406.

164. Takekoshi 1930, vol. 2, 196; Nishiyama et al. 1984, 557; Kodama

1984, 78; Kaga Jushirō, *Genroku kakyū bushi no seikatsu* (Tokyo: Yūzankaku, 1970), 41.

165. On Ieyasu (r. 1603–5), see Nishigori Takeo, *Yūjo to gaishō: Kōto o chū-shin toshite baishun shi* (Tokyo: Keibunkan, 1964), 83–84 and Saiki Kazuma, "Tokugawa shōgun seibo narabi saisho kō," in *Rekishi to jinbutsu*, ed. Nihon rekishi gakkai (Tokyo: Yoshikawa kōbunkan, 1964), 421–26. On Iemitsu (1623–51), see Francois Caron, *A Description of the Mighty Kingdom of Japan and Siam* (London, 1671), 24. On Tsunayoshi (r. 1680–1709), see Donald Shively, "Tokugawa Tsunayoshi, the Genroku Shogun," in *Personality in Japanese History*, ed. Albert Craig and Donald Shively (Berkeley, University of California, 1970). Also see Koike Tōgorō, *Kōshoku monogatari* (Tokyo: Kamakura insatsu, 1963), 180.

166. Naramoto, ed. 1982, 44.

167. Ibid., 50.

168. Shively 1970, 246.

169. Yamamoto 1978, 288.

170. See the jocular reference in Jippensha, vol. 1, 105.

171. Ihara, *Kōshoku gonin onna*, 4:1; see also Ishikawa Masamochi, *Hida takumi no monogatari* (1808).

172. Ihara, *Kōshoku ichidai onna*, 4:4.

173. Sakamoto and Miyamoto, vol. 2, 26.

174. Kitajima Masamoto, *Edo bakufu no kenryoku kōzō* (Tokyo: Iwanami, 1964), 414.

175. Kitajima Masamoto, "Buke no hōkōnin," in *Edo jidai bushi no seikatsu* (Tokyo: Yūzankaku, 1984), 140; McClain 1982, 109.

176. Ishii Ryōsuke, *Edo jidai manpitsu* (Tokyo: Asahi shinbunsha, 1982), vol. 1, 97.

177. Conversation with Wakita Osamu.

178. Wakayama-shi shi hensan iinkai, eds. 1975, 189, 180.

179. Ishida Baigan, *Ishida Baigan zenshū*, vol. 1, ed. Shibata Makoto (Osaka: 1972), 155.

180. Hayashi Reiko, *Edodana hankachō* (Tokyo: Yoshikawa kōbunkan, 1982), 34–35.

181. Hayashi 1982, 35.

182. Yasuoka Shigeaki, "Kyōhō ni okeru shōka hōkōnin no seikatsu: Kōnoike-ke no baai," *Ōsaka no kenkyū*, ed. Miyamoto Mataji, 5 vols. (Osaka: Seibundō, 1968–70), vol. 3, 252–56.

183. Ibid., 253.

184. Wakayama-shi shi hensan iinkai, eds. 1975, 178.

185. Ibid., 177.

186. Kozo Yamamura, *A Study of Samurai Income and Entrepreneurship* (Cambridge: Harvard University Press, 1974), 45.

187. Cited in Hanley and Yamamura 1977, 122.

188. Rice prices taken from Miyamoto Mataji, *Kinsei Ōsaka no bukka to rishi* (Ōsaka: Sōbunsha, 1963), 122–24.

I have also evaluated the Numano maidservants' wages in terms of the spring, summer, and winter prices listed in Yamamura (1974), 49–53. The yearly wages expressed in rice purchased at the average of these three prices have nearly the same purchasing power as the chart based on Miyamoto's data suggests: chambermaids, 1.34 *koku*; parlormaids, 1.34; nursemaids, 1.14; scullery maids, 1.19. In this case, twenty out of the seventy-nine servants (25%) have a purchasing power of over 1.4 *koku*.

189. Sepp Linhart, "Some Observations on the Development of 'Typical' Japanese Attitudes Towards Working Hours and Leisure," in Gordon Daniels, ed., *Europe Interprets Japan* (London: European Association for Japanese Studies, 1984), 212.

190. In Ki no Kaion's 1711 bunraku play *Imamiya shinjū marukoshi renrimatsu*, two lovers employed in the same shop are granted a few days off, the maidservant Okisa ostensibly to recover from a cold, and the clerk Jirobei to visit his parents. In reality they spend their time together. *Ki no Kaion zenshū* vol. 1 (Osaka: Seibundō, 1977), 162f.

191. Wakayama-shi shi hensan iinkai, eds., 1975, 187.

192. Fukushima-shi shi hensan iinkai, eds., vol. 9, 177–182.

193. Ihara, *Saikaku oritome*, 5:4.

CHAPTER FOUR
SERVANTS IN SOCIETY

1. See for example Kawatake Mokuami's *sewamono Kichisama mairu yukari no otozure*, in which the maidservant Osugi heroically undergoes torture and commits suicide rather than betray her master.

2. Sarah Maza, *Servants and Masters in Eighteenth-Century France: The Uses of Loyalty* (Princeton, N.J.: Princeton University Press, 1983), 229.

3. Sakanishi Shio, *Japanese Folk-Plays: The Ink-Smeared Lady and Other Kyōgen* (Tokyo and Rutland, Vt.: Charles E. Tuttle Co., 1960), 19–20.

4. Shinmura Izuru et al., *Kōjien* (Tokyo: Iwanami shoten, 1981), 1527.

5. R. H. Blyth, *Japanese Life and Character in Senryū* (Tokyo: Hokuseidō Press, 1959), caption facing p. 544.

6. R. H. Blyth, *Oriental Humour* (Tokyo: Hokuseidō Press, 1959), 411.

7. Ogyū Sorai, *Seidan*, in *Nihon keizai taiten* (Tokyo: Keimeisha, 1928), 86.

8. Mishima Kichitarō, ed., *Gamō Kunpei zenshū* (Tōkyō: Shuppansha, 1911).

9. E. H. Norman, *Andō Shōeki and the Anatomy of Japanese Feudalism*. (Transactions of the Asiatic Society of Japan, 3d ser., vol. 2 (Tokyo: Kenkyūsha Press, 1949), 108. Also see p. 78.

10. J. Victor Koschmann, *The Mito Ideology: Discourse, Reform, and Insurrection in Late Tokugawa Japan, 1790–1864* (Berkeley: University of California Press, 1987), 102.

11. Ogyū 1928, 86.

13. Naramoto Tatsuya, *Yomeru nenpyō, 5: Edo-hen* (Tokyo: Jiyūkokuminsha, 1982), 1: 48.

14. Minami Kazuo, "Edo no chūgen kyūkin kō," *Nihon rekishi*, 204, 5 (May 1965): 81.

15. Jippensha Ikku, *Tōkaidōchū hizakurige*, vol. 2 (Tokyo: Iwanami shoten, 1973), 227.

16. Yamamoto Tsunetomo, *Hagakure zenshū* (Tokyo: Satsuki shobō, 1978), 302.

17. Ihara, *Nanshoku ōkagami*, 3:2.

18. Chikamatsu Monzaemon, *Major Plays of Chikamatsu*, trans. Donald Keene (New York: Columbia University Press, 1961), 287–88.

19. Blyth, *Japanese Life* 1959, 560.

20. Ihara, *Saikaku oritome*, 3:1.

21. Chikamatsu Monzaemon, *Chikamatsu jōruri shū*, vol. 1 (Tokyo: Iwanami, 1976), 60.

22. Ishida Baigan, *Ishida Baigan zenshū*, vol. 1, ed. Shibata Minoru (Osaka: Seibundō Shuppan, 1972), 66.

23. Blyth 1959, *Japanese Life*, 614.

24. Shikitei Sanba, *Ukiyoburo* (Tokyo: Iwanami, 1985), 159.

25. Shibata Kyūō, *Kyūō dōwa* (Tokyo: Heibonsha, 1970), 36–37.

26. Mutō Sadao, *Edo kobanashi jiten* (Tokyo: Tōkyōdō, 1965), 217.

27. Ihara, *Yorozu no fumihogu*, 2:3.

28. Chikamatsu Monzaemon, *Masterpieces of Chikamatsu*, trans. Miyamori Asatarō (Tokyo: Toseido, n.d.), 186.

29. Mutō 1965, 181.

30. Shibata 1970, 34–35.

31. Mutō 1965, 333.

32. Ibid., 197.

33. Blyth 1959, 515.

34. Ihara, *Kōshoku gonin onna*, 3:2.

35. Blyth 1959, 337.

36. Ibid., 387.

37. Margaret Spufford, *Small Books and Pleasant Histories: Popular Fiction and Its Readership in Seventeenth Century England* (Cambridge: Cambridge University Press, 1981), 59.

38. Henry Faulds, *Nine Years in Nipon: Sketches of Japanese Life and Manners* (1885; New York: Scholarly Resources, 1973), 215.

39. Mutō 1965, 117.

40. Charles H. Dunn, *Everyday Life in Traditional Japan* (Tokyo and Rutland, Vt.: Charles E. Tuttle Co., 1969), 120.

41. Shikitei 1985, 189–91.

42. An Edo edict issued in 1682, which explicitly forbade servants to approach the scene of a fire, suggests that they were a principal element in the gawking crowds that collected whenever fires broke out. Endō 1982, 112; Ishii and Takayanaga 1936, 776.

43. Susan Hanley, "The Material Culture: Stability in Transition," in Marius B. Jansen and Gilbert Rozman, eds., *Japan in Transition: Tokugawa to Meiji* (Princeton, N.J.: Princeton University Press, 1986), 450.

44. Fairchilds 1984, 47–54; Lawrence Stone, *The Family, Sex and Marriage in England, 1500–1800*, abridged ed. (London: Penguin, 1979), 169–70.

45. Chikamatsu n.d. (trans. Miyamori), 186.

46. Shikitei 1985, 190.

47. Saikaku, *Yorozu fumihōgu*, 2:1.

48. Hirai Kiyoshi, *Nihon jūtaku no rekishi* (Tokyo: NHK Books, 1974), 163 (chart of Edo mansion of the Uwajima daimyō).

49. Englebert Kaempfer, *The History of Japan*, vol. 2 (Glasgow: James MacLehose & Sons, 1906), 306.

50. McClain 1982, 81.

51. Dunn 1969, 150.

52. Ihara, *Saikaku oritome*, 1:3.

53. Mark Fruin, *Kikkoman: Company, Clan and Community* (Cambridge: Harvard University Press, 1984), 20.

54. Dunn 1969, 154.

55. See for example Blyth 1959, 509.

56. William Elliot Griffis, *The Mikado's Empire* (New York: Harper & Bros., 1876), 443.

57. Minami 1985, 1, 11–12.

58. Chikamatsu Monzaemon, *Four Major Plays of Chikamatsu*, trans. Donald Keene (New York: Columbia University Press, 1961), 186.

59. See illustration in Kitajima Masao, "Buke no hōkōnin," in Shinshi Keikan, ed., *Edo jidai bushi no seikatsu* (Tokyo: Yūzankaku, 1984), 143.

60. Yamakawa Kikue, *Buke no josei* (Tokyo: Iwanami, 1983), 23.

61. Fukuzawa Yukichi, *The Autobiography of Fukuzawa Yukichi* (New York: Columbia University Press, 1966), 11.

62. Shikitei 1957, 47.

63. William Elliot Griffis, ed., *Townsend Harris: First American Envoy in Japan* (Boston and New York, Houghton Mifflin, 1985), 80.

64. Shikitei 1957, esp. Book II, part 2, section 4.

65. See plot summary in Hironaga Shuzaburō, *The Bunraku Handbook* (Tokyo: Maison des Arts, 1976), 306–11.

66. Ihara, *Saikaku oritome*, 1:3.

67. Donald Shively, "*Bakufu* versus *Kabuki*," in John W. Hall & Marius B. Jansen, eds., *Studies in the Institutional History of Early Modern Japan* (Princeton, N.J.: Princeton University Press, 1968), 249.

68. John Dover Wilson, comp., *Life in Shakespeare's England: A Book of Elizabethan Prose* (Cambridge: Cambridge University Press, 1956), 177.

69. Shively 1968, 232.

70. Ronald Dore, *Education in Tokugawa Japan* (Berkeley: University of California Press, 1975), 48.

71. Shively 1968, 256–58.

72. Richard Burridge, *A Scourge for the Play-Houses* (London, 1702), cited in Emmett L. Avery, "The Audience," in Charles Beecher Hogan, ed., *The London Stage, 1660–1800: A Critical Introduction*, vol. 1 New York: (Columbia University Press, 1968), cix–clxi.

73. Shively 1968, 243.

74. McClain 1982, 112.

75. Avery 1968, clxviii.

76. Yamamoto 1978, 288.

77. Shively 1968, 246.

78. Ihara, *Saikaku oritome*, 1:3.

79. Mutō 1965, 231.

80. *Nikki kōki shū*, vol. 36 (Tokyo: Yūhodō bunko, 1929), 645–46.

81. Minami Kazuo, *Edokko no sekai* (Tokyo: Kōdansha, 1980), 105.

82. Ibid., 106.

83. Takeda Izumo, Miyoshi Shōraku and Namiki Senryū, *Chūshingura, The Treasury of Loyal Retainers*, trans. Donald Keene (New York: Columbia University Press, 1971), 38.

84. Minami 1980, 105.

85. Hayashi Reiko, *Edodana hankachō* (Tokyo: Yoshikawa kōbunkan, 1982), 129–31.

86. *Iyo-ya Kinzō genin bakuchi no ken* (Bunka 7), catalogue no. 109, Nakanoshima Prefectural Library, Osaka.

87. Minami 1980, 104.

88. Inui Hiromi, "Ōsaka chōnin shakai no kōzō: jinkō dōtai ni okeru," in Tsuda Hideo, ed., *Kinsei kokka no tenkai* (Tokyo: Kōshobō, 1980), 56.

89. Herbert P. Bix, *Peasant Protest in Japan, 1590–1884* (New Haven: Yale University Press, 1986), 207–8. In eighteenth-century France servants were even less likely to join in collective actions. See Maza 1983, 308.

90. Anne Walthall, *Social Protest and Popular Culture in Eighteenth-Century Japan* (Tucson: University of Arizona Press, 1986), 141f.

91. Takizawa Matsuyo, *The Penetration of Money Economy in Japan and Its Effects Upon Social and Political Institutions* (New York: Columbia University Press, 1927), 105.

92. Ikegami Akihito, "Kōki Edo kasō chōnin no seikatsu," in Nishiyama Matsunosuke, ed., *Edo chōnin no kenkyū*, vol. 2 (Tokyo: Yoshikawa kōbunkan, 1974), 176–226.

93. Tetsuo Najita, *Visions of Virtue in Tokugawa Japan: The Kaitokudō Merchant Academy of Osaka* (University of Chicago Press, 1987), 226.

94. Dore 1975, 257.

95. Kozo Yamamura, *A Study of Samurai Income and Entrepreneurship* (Cambridge: Harvard University Press, 1974), 144.

96. Haraguchi Torao et al., eds., *The Status System and Social Organization of Satsuma* (Honolulu: University Press of Hawaii, 1975), 33.

97. Dore 1975, 179.

98. Ibid., 182.

99. Donald Keene, *World Behind Walls: Japanese Literature of the Pre-Modern Era, 1600–1867* (New York: Grove Press, 1976), 73.

100. Yamamoto 1978, 12.

101. Kenneth P. Kirkwood, *Renaissance in Japan: A Cultural Survey of the Seventeenth Century* (Tokyo and Rutland, Vt.: Charles E. Tuttle Co., 1970), 227.

102. Keene 1976, 245.

103. Ibid., 424.

104. Daniel Roche, *The People of Paris: An Essay in Popular Culture in the Eighteenth Century*, trans. Marie Evans and Gwynne Lewis (Berkeley: University of California Press, 1987), 94.

105. L. Broom and J. H. Smith, "Bridging Occupations," *British Journal of Sociology*, 14, 4 (December 1963), 324–26.

106. Nihon meichō zenshū kankōkai, eds., *Nihon meichō zenshū* 9 (1926–69): 763.

107. Ibid., 793.

108. Quoted in Shively 1968, 158.

109. Quoted in Bridget Hill, ed., *Eighteenth Century Women: An Anthology* (London: Allen and Unwin, 1984), 238.

Ogyū Sorai complained that the leaders of society were even imitating the habits of female and male prostitutes. See McEwan 1981 (trans.), 55.

110. Hill 1976, 239.

Chapter Five
Casual Laborers

1. Saitō Osamu, "Changing Structure of Urban Employment and Its Effects on Migration Patterns in Eighteenth- and Nineteenth-Century Japan," *Institute of Economic Research Discussion Paper* no. 137 (Hitotsubashi University, Tokyo, March 1986), 6.

2. Wakita Haruko, with Susan B. Hanley, "Dimensions of Development: Cities in Fifteenth- and Sixteenth-Century Japan," in *Japan Before Tokugawa*, ed. John W. Hall, Nagahara Keiji and Kozo Yamamura (Princeton, N.J.: Princeton University Press, 1981), 301.

3. Gilbert Rozman, *Urban Networks in Ch'ing China and Tokugawa Japan* (Princeton, N.J.: Princeton University Press, 1975), 265.

4. Hayashi Reiko et al., eds., *Hōei ni-nen Kasamamachi machikata kenbetsu aratamechō, Ibaraki-ken shiryō, Kinsei shakai keizai hen*, I (1971), 133–73.

5. Nagasaki-ken shihenshū iinkai, *Nagasaki-ken shi, han-sei hen* (Tokyo: Yoshikawa kōbunkan, 1973), 465; Chihōshi kenkyūkai kyōgikai, eds., *Nihon no toshi to machi sono rekishi to genjō* (Tokyo: Yūzankaku, 1982), 189.

6. Hyōgo-ken shi henshū senmon iinkai, eds., *Hyōgo-ken shi*, vol. 4 (Kobe: Hyōgo-ken bunka kyōkai, 1980), 195.

7. Wakita Osamu, *Genroku no shakai* (Tokyo: Kōshobō, 1980), 175.

8. James McClain, *Kanazawa: A Seventeenth-Century Japanese Castle Town* (New Haven: Yale University Press, 1982), 84.

9. Matsumoto Shirō, *Nihon kinsei toshi ron* (Tokyo: Tōkyō Daigaku shuppansha, 1983), 204–5.

10. Nishiyama Matsunosuke et al., eds., *Edo gaku jiten* (Tokyo: Kōbunkan, 1984), 284.

11. Englebert Kaempfer, *The History of Japan* vol. 2 (Glasgow: James MacLehose & Sons, 1906), 174.

12. William Elliot Griffis, *The Mikado's Empire* (New York: Harper & Bros., 1876), 355; Sir Rutherford Alcock, *The Capital of the Tycoon: A Narrative of Three Years' Residence in Japan* vol. 2 (New York: Harper and Brothers, 1863), 293f.; Jean-Pierre Lehman, *The Image of Japan: From Feudal Isolation to World Power, 1850–1905* (London: Allen and Unwin, 1978), 43.

13. Quoted in Honjo Eijirō, *The Social and Economic History of Japan* (New York: Russell & Russell, 1965), 71.

14. Ihara, *Honchō nijū fukō*, 1:1.

15. Ihara, *Saikaku oritome*, 3:4.

16. J. R. McEwan, *The Political Writings of Ogyū Sorai* (Cambridge: Cambridge University Press, 1962), 27.

17. Quoted in Yazaki Takeo, *Social Change and the City in Japan* (Tokyo: Japan Publications, 1968), 212.

18. Takizawa Matsuyo, *The Penetration of Money Economy in Japan and Its Effects Upon Social and Political Institutions* (New York: Columbia University Press, 1927; reprinted by AMS Press, 1968), 105.

19. Ihara, *Irozato sansho setai*, 2:1.

20. John Fitchen, *Building Construction Before Mechanization* (Cambridge: MIT Press, 1986), 172.

21. Ikeda Shō ichiro, *Edo jidai yōgo kōsho jiten* (Shin jinbutsu ōrai sha, 1984), 337.

22. Koda Shigetomo, *Edo to Ōsaka* (1934), 135f.; English translation in Neil Skene Smith, ed., "Materials on Japanese Social and Economic History: Tokugawa Japan (1)," *Transactions of the Asiatic Society of Japan*, 2d ser., XIV (1937).

23. Ikeda 1984, 263.

24. *Kago* or *norimono* might be rendered by a more familiar-sounding English word such as "litter," and since the latter were still commonly used in Europe in the seventeenth century, it is curious that the Portuguese—who derived their term *palanquim* from the Javanese *pelanki*—should have felt the need to borrow a Japanese word. Perhaps the Japanese model struck the Europeans as a less luxurious version of their own, which being well-cushioned, served as a portable bed.

25. Facsimile edition, *Vocabulario de Iapon Declarado primero en portugues por les padres* . . . [Manila, 1630] (Tokyo: Tenri Central Library, 1972), 342.

26. Litters in ancient Rome were in theory reserved for the use of emperors and senators' wives.

27. Endō 1982, 141.

28. Ikeda 1984, 297.

29. Kaempfer, vol. 2, 1906, 288–90.

30. Ibid., 336.

31. The Five Highways (*Gokaidō*) were: Tōkaidō: Edo to Kyoto (514 km); Nakasendō: Edo to Kyoto through the Japan Alps (542 km); Nikkō-kaidō: Edo to Nikkō (146 km); Kōshū-kaidō: Edo to Kōfu (139 km); and Ōshū-kaidō: Edo to Aomori (786 km).

32. Constantine N. Vaporis, "Post Stations and Assisting Villages: Corvee Labor and Peasant Contention," *Monumenta Nipponica*, 41, 4: (1986) 383f.

33. Vaporis 1986, 380.

34. Vaporis 1986, 394.

35. Translated by Donald Keene in *Major Plays of Chikamatsu* (New York: Columbia University Press, 1961), 92–130.

There are numerous versions of the Yosaka story, apparently based on an actual incident that occurred in the mid-seventeenth century. A samurai lost his status after an illicit love affair and became a packhorseman, later receiving a pardon and restoration to his post.

36. Kaempfer, vol. 2, 1906, 345.

37. Chikamatsu Monzaemon, *Chikamatsu jōruri shū*, vol. 2 ed. Shigetomo Ki (Tokyo: Iwanami shoten, 1958), 96.

38. Jippensha Ikku, *Tōkaidōchū hizakurige* vol. 1, (Tokyo: Iwanami shoten, 1973), 76–77.

39. Ibid., 266.

40. Ibid., 258–60.

41. J. C. Hall, "Japanese Feudal Laws," *Transactions of the Asiatic Society of Japan*, 33 (1910–12), 324.

42. Jippensha 1973, 233.

43. Charles David Sheldon, *The Rise of the Merchant Class in Tokugawa Japan* (Institute for Pacific Relations, 1958), 28.

44. Joyce Ackroyd, *Told Around a Brushwood Fire: The Autobiography of Arai Hakuseki* (Tokyo: University of Tokyo, 1979), 157–58.

45. Jippensha 1973, 66.

46. Keene 1976, 92. A daimyo's horse-drivers "are accomplished ballad-singers, chosen, with no expenses spared, for their good looks and fine voices."

47. Jippensha 1973, vol. 2, 13.

48. Patia R. Isaku, *Mountain Storm, Pine Breeze: Folk Songs in Japan* (Tucson: University of Arizona Press, 1981), 54.

49. Jippensha 1973, vol. 2, 14.

50. Koda 1985, 135f.

51. Jippensha 1973, vol 1, 141.

52. Smith 1979, 69.

53. *Manners and Customs of the Japanese in the Nineteenth Century from the Accounts of Dutch Residents in Japan and from the German Work of Dr. Philipp Franz von Siebold* (1841; Tokyo and Rutland, Vt.: Charles E. Tuttle Co., 1973), 229; Alcock 1983, vol. 2, 142.

54. Smith 1979, 71.

55. Satō Ubei, ed., *Tsūzoku keizai bunko* vol. 1 (1916), 224.

56. Ibid., 224.

57. Ihara, *Nippon eitaigura*, 1:3.

58. Satō 1916, 224.

59. Ibid., 224.

60. In modern times the word *anko* has continued to be applied to casual dockworkers. Mori Hideto, "The Longshoremen of Kobe Harbor," in Maurice Schneps and Alvin D. Coox, eds., *The Japanese Image* (Tokyo and Philadelphia: Orient/West, 1965).

61. *Chikamatsu zenshū*, vol. 7, ed. Fujii Otō (Osaka: Asahi Shinbunsha, 1926), vol. 7, 218.

62. Nishiyama Matsunosuke et al., eds., *Edo gaku jiten* (Tokyo: Kōbundō, 1984), 580.

63. G. V. Blackstone, *A History of the British Fire Service* (London, Routledge and Kegan Paul, 1957), 48–49.

64. Honjō Eijirō, comp., *Nihon keizaishi jiten* (Tokyo: Nihon hyōronsha, 1940), 1368.

65. Ōsaka shiyakusho, *Osaka-shi shi*, vol. 2 (1978), 56–57.

66. Kaempfer, vol. 3, 1906, 72.

67. Toyoda Takeshi and Sugiyama Hiroshi, with V. Dixon Morris, "The Growth of Commerce and the Trades," in John W. Hall and Toyoda Takeshi, eds., *Japan in the Muromachi Age* (Berkeley: University of California Press, 1977), 142.

68. Nagahara Keiji and Kozo Yamamura, "Shaping the Process of Unification: Technological Progress in Sixteenth- and Seventeenth-Century Japan," *Journal of Japanese Studies*, 14, 1 (1988), 91.

69. McEwan 1981, 48.

70. Michael J. Cooper, ed. and trans., *This Island of Japon: Joao Rodrigues' Account of 16th-Century Japan* (Tokyo: Kōdansha International, 1973), 84; see also 308.

71. He did not, however, appreciate the simple qualities of Japanese architecture and found the streets of Edo "miserable-looking." Alcock 1863, vol. 2, 280.

72. Ihara, *Nippon eitaigura*, 3:1.

73. Ikeda Masaichirō, *Edo jidai yōgo kōsho jiten* (1984), 294.

74. Ikegami Akihito, "Kōki Edo kasō chōnin no seikatsu," in Nishiyama Matsunosuke, ed., *Edo chōnin no kenkyū*, vol. 2 (Tokyo: Yoshikawa Kōbunkan, 1974), 177–226.

75. Alice Clark, *Working Life of Women in the Sixteenth Century* (New York: Harcourt, Brace & Howe, 1920); Louis A. Tilly and Joan W. Scott, *Women, Work and Family* (New York: Holt, Rinehart and Winston, 1978).

76. Ihara, *Yorozu no fumihōgu*, 2:3.

77. Charles J. Dunn, *Everyday Life in Traditional Japan* (Tokyo and Rutland, Vt.: Charles E. Tuttle Co., 1969), 55.

78. Ihara, *Saikaku shokoku banashi*, 1:2.

79. Tema Kenkyūjo, eds., *Sado kinzan* (Shinsho, 1985), 141.

80. Ibid., 138–39.

81. Hayashi Reiko et al., eds., *Ibaraki-ken shiryō, Kinsei shakai keizai hen*, I (1971), 133–73.

82. Ikegami 1974, 177–226.

83. Ibid., 186, 202, 204.

84. Hayashi et al., 1971, 133–73.

85. McEwan 1981, 56.

86. Ihara, *Nippon eitaigura*, 5:6.

87. Ueda Akinari, "Kanpekitan," in *Ueda Akinari zenshū* (Tokyo: Kokusho kankō kai, 1917–18), vol. 7.

88. Griffis 1877, 356.

89. Toyoda Takeshi, *A History of Pre-Meiji Commerce in Japan* (Tokyo: Kokusai bunka shinkōkai, 1969), 78–84.

90. Toyoda 1969, 78.

91. Takekoshi Yosaburō, *Economic Aspects of the History of the Civilization of Japan* (London: Allen and Unwin Ltd., 1930), vol. 3, 243.

92. Takekoshi 1930, 245.

93. Ishino Iwao, "The Oyabun-Kobun: A Japanese Ritual Kinship Institution," *American Anthropologist*, vol. 55 (1953), 695.

94. See "A Story of the Otokodate of Yedo," and other *otokodate* tales in A. B. Mitford, *Tales of Old Japan* (1871; Tokyo and Rutland, Vt.: Charles E. Tuttle Co., 1966).

95. Mitford 1966, 91.

96. Nishiyama et al. 1984, 582–83.

97. Robert W. Leutner, *Shikitei Sanba and the Comic Tradition in Edo Fiction* (Cambridge: Harvard University Press, 1985), 29–30; Donald Keene, *World Within Walls: Japanese Literature of the Pre-modern Era, 1600–1867* (New York: Grove Press, 1976), 414.

98. Leutner 1985, 30.

99. Howard Solomon, *Public Welfare, Science and Propaganda in Seventeenth-Century France: The Innovations of Theophraste Renaudot* (Princeton, N.J.: Princeton University Press, 1972), 41.

100. Ihara, *Seken munezanyo*, 3:2.

101. Ishino 1953, 696.

102. Ibid., 704.

103. Richard Storry, *The Double Patriots* (Boston: Houghton and Mifflin, 1957), 27f.

104. Chester W. Hepler, "The Labor Boss System in Japan," *Monthly Labor Review* (January 1949), 47.

105. Thomas P. Rohlen, "Oyabun-kobun," in *Kōdansha Encyclopedia of Japan* vol. 6 (Kōdansha, 1983), 137.

106. E. S. Crawcour, "Kawamura Zuiken: A Seventeenth-Century Entrepreneur," *Transactions of the Asiatic Society of Japan*, 3d ser., vol. 9 (May 1966), 31.

107. Yanagita Kunio, *Manners and Customs of the Japanese in the Meiji Era* (Tokyo: Ōbunsha, 1957) 116–17.

108. Andrew Gordon, *The Evolution of Labor Relations in Japan: Heavy Industry, 1853–1955* (Cambridge: Harvard University Press, 1985), 38.

109. Gordon 1985, 49–54.

110. Miyamoto Musashi, *The Book of Five Rings*, trans. Victor Harris (Woodstock, N.Y.: Overlook Press, 1974), 41.

111. *Kōda Rohan zenshū* (Tokyo: Iwanami, 1951), 185–272.

112. Chikamatsu Monzaemon, *Chikamatsu jōruri shū*, 1, ed. Shigetomo Ki (Tokyo: Iwanami, 1976), 111.

113. But see Endō 1982, 154.

114. These existed in early modern Italy and China; see Richard A. Goldwaite, *The Building of Renaissance Florence: An Economic and Social History* (Baltimore: Johns Hopkins University Press, 1980), 297, and Shih Min-hsiung, *The Silk Industry in Ch'ing China*, trans. E-tu Zen Sun (University of Michigan Center for Chinese Studies, 1976), 37.

115. Nagaoka Hakao, *Kaga Nōto no seikatsu to minzoku* (Tokyo: Keiyūsha, 1983), 194f.

116. Ihara, *Kōshoku ichidai onna*, 6:3.

117. Cited in Shinmura Izuru et al., *Kōjien* (Tokyo: Iwanami, 1981), 1524.

118. Endō Motoo, *Shokunin no rekishi* (Tokyo: Shibundō, 1958), 109. Note that according to the old system of reckoning time, the twelve hours of the day constituted a strange discontinuous sequence. Thus, the sixth hour (sunrise) was followed by the fifth hour of morning, then the fourth hour of morning, the ninth hour of noon, etc.

119. Cumbersome as the system seems, the Japanese modified Western-made

clocks, introduced during the sixteenth century, to indicate their own more complex system of time measurements. Examples are on display at the Japanese National Museum in Ueno Park, Tokyo.

120. R. H. Tawney and Eileen Power, *Tudor Economic Documents*, 3 vols. (London: Longmans, Green and Co., 1924), 1: 115–16.

121. Jeffrey Kaplow, *The Names of Kings: The Parisian Laboring Poor in the Eighteenth Century* (New York: Basic Books, 1972), 52.

122. Endō 1958, suggests that these short working hours were observed in most towns and cities.

123. Thomas C. Smith, *The Agrarian Origins of Modern Japan* (Stanford: Stanford University Press, 1959), 110, 124–25.

124. Meiji-period workdays, in contrast, were typically fifteen hours or more. See Jon Halliday, *A Political History of Japanese Capitalism* (New York: Random House, 1975), 67; Gordon 1985, 27.

125. Yoshida Nobuyuki, "Chōnin to machi," in *Kōza Nihonshi, 5: Kinsei*, 1 (Tokyo: Tōkyō Daigaku, 1985), 151–88.

126. Yazaki 1978, 217.

127. Takizawa 1968, 217.

128. Owada Tetsuo, in his *Shiro to jōkamachi* (Tokyo: Kyōikusha, 1979) provides a chart showing wards in present-day cities of castle-town origins bearing names of occupations. They include: Kaji-machi (Blacksmiths' Wards), 76; Konya-machi (Dyers' Wards), 50; Daiku-machi (Carpenters' Wards), 41; Okeyama-chi (Barrel-makers' Wards), 22.

129. McClain 1982, 84.

130. Ikegami 1974, 171–226.

131. Population densities in the commoner wards near the shogun's castle in Edo were the "highest population densities ever recorded for regular habitation— 67,317 persons per square kilometer, five times the present Tokyo average." Andrew Fraser, "Town-ward Administration in Eighteenth-Century Edo," *Papers in Far Eastern History* (Australian National University), vol. 27 March 1984), 131–41.

132. Ihara, *Nippon eitaigura*, 6:5.

133. Ihara, *Seken munezanyo*, 1:2.

134. *Nihon kinsei shomin seikatsu shiryō shūsei* vol. 7 (Tokyo: Heibonsha, 1970), 722.

135. Osaka-shi shi hensangakari, eds., *Ōsaka-shi shi*, 8 vols. (1901–29), 2: 806.

136. Ueda Akinari, 1918, vol. 7.

137. Ihara, *Seken munezanyo*, 6:5.

138. McEwan 1981, 44.

139. Pompe van Meerdervoort, *Doctor on Desima: Selected Chapters from JHR J. L. C. Pompe van Meerdervoort's Vijf Jaren in Japan (Five Years in Japan (1857–1863))*, trans. and annotated by Elizabeth P. Wittermans and John Z. Bowers (Tokyo: Sophia University, 1970), 55.

140. Roy Chapman Andrews, "The Worst Slums," in Michael Wise, comp., *Travellors' Tales of Old Japan* (Singapore: Time Books International, 1985), 214–16.

141. Miyamoto 1974, 41.

142. Nakamura Hajime, "Suzuki Shōsan, 1579–1655, and the Spirit of Capitalism in Japanese Buddhism," trans. William Johnson, *Monumenta Nipponica*, 22, 1 (1967): 6.

143. Robert Cornell Armstrong, *Just Before the Dawn: The Life and Works of Ninomiya Sontaku* (New York: Macmillan, 1912), 147.

144. *Ishida Baigan zenshū*, ed. Shibata Minoru (Osaka: Seibundō Shuppan, 1972), 153.

145. On the other hand, the British physician Faulds, in Japan during the Meiji period, paid tribute to the "great temperance" of Japanese carpenters "as opposed to our own workmen." Henry Faulds, *Nine Years in Nipon: Sketches of Japanese Life and Manners* (1885; Wilmington, Del., Scholarly Resources, 1973), 68.

146. Kōda 1951, 185–272.

147. Armstrong 1912, 147.

148. Gordon 1985, 29.

149. Chikamatsu 1976, 107.

150. Naramoto 1982, vol. 1.

151. See for example, Teruko Craig, *Musui's Story: The Autobiography of a Tokugawa Samurai* (Tucson: University of Arizona Press, 1988), 46–48.

152. Tanaka Yoshio, *Kaga hyakumangoku* (Tokyo: Kōikusha, 1980), 235–36.

153. Stephen Vlastos, *Peasant Protests and Uprisings in Tokugawa Japan* (Berkeley: University of California Press, 1986), 46.

154. Yazaki 1978, 258–59.

155. Dunn 1969, 179.

156. Walthall 1986, 141.

157. Herbert P. Bix, *Peasant Protest in Japan, 1590–1884* (New Haven: Yale University Press, 1986), 174f.

158. Bix 1986, 208.

159. Walthall 1986, 222.

160. E. H. Norman, *Origins of the Modern Japanese State: Selected Writings of E. H. Norman*, ed. John W. Dower (New York: Random House, 1974), 344–46.

161. Bix 1986, 171.

162. Norman 1974, 344, 346.

163. Takekoshi 1930, vol. 2, 486–87.

164. Tanaka Keiichi, *Sado kinzan* (Tokyo: Kyōikusha, 1980), 190–94.

165. Ihara, *Nippon eitaigura*, 2:5.

166. Ronald Dore, *Education in Tokugawa Japan* (Berkeley: University of California Press, 1975, 248.

167. McEwan 1981, 71.

168. Takekoshi 1930, vol. 3, 243.

169. Sansom 1963, vol. 3, 178.

170. Pompe van Meerdervoort 1970, 57.

171. *Chikamatsu zenshū* 1926, vol. 11, 260.

172. Nihon meichō zenshū kankōkai, eds., *Nihon meichō zenshū* vol. 9 (1926–29), 619.

173. Barry Jackman, trans., *Tales of the Spring Rain: Harusame Monogatari bu Ueda Akinari* (Tokyo: The Japan Foundation, 1975), 117–32.

174. McEwan 1981, 56.
175. L. Broom and J. H. Smith, "Bridging Occupations," *British Journal of Sociology*, 14, 4 (December 1963), 330.
176. McEwan 1981, 56.

CHAPTER SIX
STRATEGIES FOR THE CONTROL OF CASUAL LABORERS

1. Frederick L. Nussbaum, *A History of the Economic Institutions of Modern Europe: An Introduction to Der Moderne Kapitalismus* (New York: F. S. Crofts & Co., 1933), 108–9.
2. R. H. Tawney, *Religion and the Rise of Capitalism* (New York: Harcourt, Brace and World, 1926), 217.
3. Max Weber, *The Protestant Ethic and the Spirit of Capitalism* (New York: Charles Scribner's Sons, 1958), 177.
4. In the seventeenth century, English rulers "were apparently quite unconscious that there might be any other cause of poverty than the moral failings of the poor," while Parisian authorities "clung to conceptions which explained poverty and misery as the consequences of sin and man's fallen nature." Tawney, 1926, 265; Orest Ranum, *Paris in the Age of Absolutism: An Essay* (Bloomington, Ind.: Indiana University Press, 1968), 242.
5. Karl Marx, *Capital* vol. 1 (Chicago: Charles H. Kerr, 1908), vol. I, 689.
6. Ibid., 686. Sombart similarly stressed the "unnatural" character of capitalism. *The Quintessence of Capitalism: A Study of the History and Psychology of the Modern Business Man* (New York: E. P. Dutton and Co., 1915), 13f.
7. Christopher Hill, *Change and Continuity in 17th Century England* (Cambridge: Harvard University Press, 1975), 221.
8. Christopher Hill, "William Perkins and the Poor," *Puritanism and Revolution* (London: Mercury Books, 1958), 222.
9. Alexander Gerschenkron, "Economic Backwardness in Historical Perspective," in Bert F. Hoselitz, ed., *The Progress of Underdeveloped Areas* (Cambridge: Belknap Press of Harvard University Press, 1962), 7.
10. Johannes Janssen, *History of the German People after the Close of the Middle Ages* vol. 15 (London: K. Paul Trench, 1910), 504.
11. Araki Moriaki, "Taikō kenchi no rekishiteki zentei," *Rekishigaku kenkyū*, 163, 164 (1953).
12. Sasaki Junnosuke with Ronald P. Toby, "The Changing Rationale of Daimyo Control in the Emergence of the Bakufu State," in *Japan Before Tokugawa: Political Consolidation and Economic Growth*, edited by John Whitney Hall et al. (Princeton, N.J.: Princeton University Press, 1981), 275.
13. Honjō Eijirō, *The Social and Economic History of Japan* (New York: Russell and Russell, 1965), 173–74.
14. Hayami Akira, "Labor Migration in a Pre-industrial Society: A Study Tracing the Life Histories of the Inhabitants of a Village," *Keio Economic Studies*, vol. X, 2 (1973), 6.
15. Hayami 1973, 6.
16. Susan Hanley and Kozo Yamamura, *Economic and Demographic Change*

in Preindustrial Japan, 1600–1868 (Princeton, N.J.: Princeton University Press, 1977), 97.

17. Honjō 1965, 174.

18. Marius Jansen, "Tosa in the Seventeenth Century," in John W. Hall et al. 1968, 121.

19. Noma Kenshin, "Miyako no Nishiki gokuchu gokkai," part 1, *Kokugo kokubun*, vol. 17, 8 (1948), 456; Ishii Ryōsuke, *Edo jidai manpitsu* vol. 1 (Tokyo: Asahi shinbunsha, 1979), 38–41.

20. Honjō 1955, 42.

21. Matsumoto Shigeru, *Motoori Norinaga, 1730–1801* (Cambridge: Harvard University Press, 1970), 148.

22. Yoshida Nobuyuki, "Edo machi kaisho kinkashitsuke ni tsuite," *Shigaku zasshi*, vol. LXXXVI, 1 (January 1977): 33–59.

23. According to the Legacy of Ieyasu, "kindness must be shown" to eta, beggars, and the blind. "From ancient days benevolent rule began with this." Quoted in A. L. Sadler, *The Maker of Modern Japan: The Life of Tokugawa Ieyasu* (London: Allen and Unwin, 1937), 392.

24. A 1635 proclamation issued by the Nagasaki bugyo, for example, specified that no more than two mace were to be given to beggars "no matter how impoverished." Robert LeRoy Innes, *The Door Ajar: Japan's Foreign Trade in the Seventeenth Century* (Ph.D. diss., University of Michigan 1980), 147.

25. Buraku mondai kenkyūkai, eds., *Buraku no rekishi to kaiho undo* (Tokyo: Buraku Mondai Kenkyūjo, 1985), 244–45.

26. James McClain, *Kanazawa: A Seventeenth-Century Japanese Castle Town* (New Haven: Yale University Press, 1982), 131.

27. For example, Ihara, *Nippon eitaigura*, 2:3.

28. James Murdoch, *A History of Japan*, 3 vols. (London: H. Paul, Trench, Truber and Co., 1925–26), 3: 39.

29. Quoted in V. A. Casal, "The Yamabushi," in *Mitteilungen der Deutschen Gesellschaft fur Natur-und Volkerkunde Ostasiens*, vol. 49 (1965), 11.

30. Ihara *Seken munezanyo*, 1:4.

31. Wakita Osamu, *Kinsei hōken shakai no keizai kozo* (Tokyo: Ochanomizu, 1978), 245–46.

32. Takayanagi Shinzō and Ishii Ryosuke, *Ofuregaki Kanpō shūsei* (Tokyo: Iwanami shoten, 1976), no. 2343.

33. Osaka shi shi hensangakari, eds., *Osaka-shi shi*, vol. 3 (1928), 58.

34. Yoshida Nobuyuki, "Edo no hiyoza to hiyo = mibun," in Bito Masahide sensei kanreki kinen-kai, eds., *Nihon kinsei shi ronso*, vol. 1 (Tokyo: Yoshikawa kōbunkan, 1984), 372.

35. Yoshida 1984, 371–72.

36. Yazaki Takeo, *Social Change and the City in Japan* (Tokyo: Japan Publications, 1978), 140.

37. Oana Yoshimi, "Shomin to tojiba," in Ōishi Shinzaburō, ed., *Edo to chihō bunka* (Tokyo: Bun'ichi Sōgō, 1977), 231.

38. Robert Sakai et al., eds., *The Status System and Social Organization of Satsuma: A Translation of the Shūmon Aratame Jōmoku* (Honolulu: University Press of Hawaii, 1981), frontispiece photograph.

39. *Ofuregaki Kanpō shūsei* 1936, no. 2350.

40. Ibid., no. 2344.

41. Ibid., no. 2345.

42. Or *hiyō-za*. "Day Laborers' *Guild*" might be a more literal rendering of this title, but the institution was clearly a registry rather than a merchant or craft association. *Ofuregaki Kanpō shūsei*, no. 2346.

43. *Ofuregaki Kanpō shūsei*, 1936, no. 2346.

44. *Ofuregaki Kanpō shūsei* 1936, nos. 2350, 2352, 2354, 2355, 2356, 2358, 2360, 2368.

45. Ibid., nos. 2347, 2348, 2351, 2352.

46. Ibid., no. 2351.

47. Ibid., no. 2353.

48. Ibid., no. 2358.

49. Nishiyama Matsunosuke et al., eds., *Edo gaku jiten* (Tokyo: Kobunkan, 1984), 187.

50. *Ofuregaki Kanpō shūsei* 1936, nos. 2350, 2366.

51. Yoshida 1984, 399.

52. Ibid., 400.

53. Howard M. Solomon, *Public Welfare, Science, and Propaganda in Seventeenth Century France: The Innovations of Theophraste Renaudot* (Princeton, N.J.: Princeton University Press, 1972), 40.

54. Solomon 1972, 44–5.

55. W. K. Jordan, *Men of Substance* (Chicago: University of Chicago Press, 1942), 250–52.

56. Noma 1948, 457.

58. McClain 1982, 127.

59. Sheldon 1958, 119.

60. Michel Foucault, *Madness and Civilization: A History of Insanity in the Age of Reason* (New York: Random House, 1965), 38.

61. For a discussion of the ambiguous character of these institutions, see Sidney and Beatrice Webb, *English Local Government. English Poor Law History: Part I: The Old Poor Law* (London: Longmans, Green and Co., 1927), 220; Maurice Bruce, *The Coming of the Welfare State* (London: B. T. Batsford, 1965), 61.

62. Tawney used the term "new medicine for poverty" to refer to the work-house movement in England. *Religion and the Rise of Capitalism* (New York: Harcourt, Brace and World, 1926), 264.

63. Michel Foucault, *The Birth of the Prison* (New York: Random House, 1977), 113.

64. Foucault 1965, 45–46.

65. Foucault 1977, 106.

66. Kuranami Seiji, *Hyakumangoku daimyō* (Tokyo: Hachiyo shuppan, 1965), 53.

67. McClain 1982, 127.

68. Kuranami 1965, 55.

69. Tanaka Yoshio, "Kaga-han hiningoya seiritsu to jijo ni tsuite," *Nihon rekishi*, vol. 183 (August 1963), 45–67.

70. Kuranami 1965, 56.

71. McClain 1982, 128.

72. Ibid., 189 (footnote 27).

73. Kuranami 1965, 56.

74. McClain 1982, 129.

75. Kuranami 1965, 57; Tanaka 1963, 67.

76. Tanaka Keiichi, *Sado kinzan* (Tokyo: Kyōikusha, 1980), 228–29.

77. Quoted in Solomon 1972, 25.

78. "Malthus," *Encyclopaedia Britannica* v. 11 (Chicago: Encyclopaedia Britannica Inc., 1983), 395.

79. Tanaka Keiichi 1980, 232.

80. Ibid., 233.

81. Isobe Kinzō, *Mushukunin: Sado kinzan hishi* (Tokyo: Jinbutsu ōrai, 1964), 226.

82. The forced labor of the Sado workhouse inmates was, unlike island exile, not included in the official punishment system. Isobe says it "was like 'peace-preservation confinement' [*hoan kokin*] in modern criminal law terminology." *Sado kinzan hishi*, 119.

83. Isobe 1964, 120.

84. Matsudaira Sadanobu, *Uge no hito goto: Shugoroku*, rev. ed. edited by Matsudaira Sadamitsu (Tokyo: Iwanami shoten, 1983), 118.

85. Shibusawa 1937, 189–90.

86. Nishiyama Matsunosuke et al., eds., 1984, 186.

87. Tanaka 1963, 67.

88. Matsudaira 1983, 117–18.

89. Nishiyama Matsunosuke et al. 1984, 186.

90. Shibusawa Eiichi, *Rakuō kōden* (Tokyo: Iwanami shoten, 1937), 189–90.

91. Matsudaira 1983, 118.

92. Takikawa Masajirō, *Nihon shakai shi* (Tokyo: Tōe shoin, 1948), 326.

93. Nishiyama Matsunosuke et al. 1984, 186.

94. Ibid.

95. Matsudaira 1983, 117.

96. Nishiyama Matsunosuke et al. 1984, 186.

97. E. Papinot, *Historical and Geographical Dictionary of Japan* (Tokyo and Rutland, Vt.: Charles E. Tuttle Co., 1972), 755.

98. Takikawa 1948, 326.

99. Nishiyama Matsunosuke et al. 1984, 186.

100. Ikeda 1984, 485.

101. J. Cunningham, *An Essay on Trade and Commerce, containing Observations of Taxes, etc.* (1770), quoted in Marx, *Capital*, 263.

102. Matthew Marryott, *Account of Several Workhouses for Employing and Maintaining the Poor* (1732), cited in Sidney and Beatrice Webb 1927, 244.

103. Matsudaira 1983, 118–19.

104. Robert Bellah, *Tokugawa Religion: The Values of Preindustrial Japan* (Glencoe, Ill.: Free Press, 1957), 171.

105. Ishikawa Ken, *Sekimen Shingaku shi no kenkyū* (Tokyo: Iwanami shoten, 1942), 1165f.

106. Bellah 1957, 173.

107. Mitsui Rokurō et al., eds., *Shin Nagasaki nenpyō*, 1 (1974), 365.

108. Nagasaki shishi nenpyō hensan iinkai, eds., *Nagasaki shishi nenpyō* (1981), 79.

109. Ōsaka shi shi hensangakari, eds., vol. 2, 561.

110. Tezuka Yutaka, "Nagaoka han no yoseba to Matsuyama han no tokei-sho," *Hōgaku kenkyū*, 31, no. 5 (1958).

111. Shirayama Tomomasa, "Ezochi no yoseba kō," *Hōseishi kenkyū* 13 (1962): 144–63.

112. Conceivably there was some European influence upon these institutions. Several works from the early nineteenth century described Dutch "hospitals," and Fukuzawa Yukichi's *Seiyo jijo*, in the closing years of the period, gave an eye-witness account of European "poorhouses."

113. "Interestingly enough, the closest approximation (to the factory in prein-dustrial England) is to be found in the municipal workhouses, established under a succession of Acts of Parliament and as part of various bursts of energy on the part of municipalities to 'set the poor on work.' " Peter Laslett, *The World We Have Lost: England Before the Industrial Age* (New York: Charles Scribner's Sons, 1984), 190.

114. Cited in Marx, *Capital*, 612n.

APPENDIX A

1. The most thorough discussion is probably L. L. Cornell and Hayami Akira, "The *Shūmon Aratame Chō:* Japan's Population Registers," *Journal of Family History*, 11, 4 (1986): 311–28. See also Susan B. Hanley and Kozo Yamamura, *Economic and Demographic change in Preindustrial Japan, 1600–1868* (Princeton, N. J.: Princeton University Press, 1977) 40–43.

2. Members of the warrior or samurai class were recorded in separate, less informative, logs throughout the period.

3. Hayami akira of Keio University heads a team of scholars presently collect-ing photocopies of all extant nibetsuchō, widely scattered in local archives, and subjecting their contents to computer-aided analysis.

4. Miyamoto Mataji and Sakamoto Heiichirō, *Ōsaka Kikuyachō shūshi nin-betsuchō*, vol. 2 (Tokyo: Yoshikawa kōbunkan, 1967), 182.

BIBLIOGRAPHY

ARCHIVAL SOURCES

Hanagurumachō shūmon ninbetsu aratamechō MS (Kyoto-shi Shiryokan).
Iyo-ya Kinzō genin bakuchi no ken (Bunka 7), catalogue # 109, Nakanoshima Prefectural Library, Osaka.
Minami-gumi Sadoyachō shakuyaninbetsuchō. Photocopies of MS, Kokushi kenkyūshitsu, University of Osaka.
Okeyamachi genrai shūmon aratame fumie chō (MS series 316, Nagasaki Kenritsu Toshokan).
Sanjō Koromontanachō monjo, Kyōtō Machifure Kenkyu-kaisho shashin shiryō, vol. 2 (photocopied MS).
Taishiyamachō shūmon ninbetsu aratamechō, Hanagurumacho shūmon ninbetsu aratamechō MS (Kyoto-shi Shiryōkan).
Takayama Ichi no chō shūmon ninbetsu aratamechō and *Takayama Ni no chō shūmon ninbetsu aratamechō* (MS, Takayama Kyōdōkan) .

SECONDARY WORKS IN JAPANESE

Aichi-ken gōshi shiryo kankō kai, editors. *Owari meisho zue*. Nagoya: 1973. 2 vols.
Akiyama Kunizō and Nakamura Ken. *Kyōto 'chō' no kenkyu*. Tokyo: Hōsei Daigaku shuppankyoku, 1975.
Amino Yoshihiko. *Nihon chūsei no minshū zō: heimin to shokunin*. Tokyo: Iwanami shoten, 1980.
Andō Seiichi. "Bakumatsu Nishijin kigyo no kiki." *Nihon rekishi*, 99 (1958).
Aoki Kōji. *Hyakushō ikki no nenjiteki kenkyu*. Tokyo: Shinseisha, 1966.
Araki Moriaki. Bakuhan taisei shakai no seiritsu to kōzō. Tokyo: Ochanomizu shobō, 1959.
———. "Taikō kenchi no rekishiteki zentei." *Rekishigaku kenkyū*, 163–64 (1953).
Ashikaga sen-i dōgyo kai, editors. 2 vols. *Ashikaga orimono shi*. Tokyo: 1960.
Buraku mondai kenkyūkai, editors. *Buraku no rekishi to kaihō undō*. Tokyo: 1985.
Chihōshi kenkyukai kyogikai, editors. *Nihon no toshi to machi: sono rekishi to genjō*. Tokyo: Yūzankaku, 1982.
Chikamatsu Monzaemon. *Chikamatsu jōruri shū*. Edited by Shigetomo Ki. Tokyo: Iwanami shoten, 1958.
Chikamatsu Monzaemon. *Chikamatsu zenshū*. Edited by Fujii Otō. Osaka: 1926.
Endō Motoo. *Kinsei seikatsu nenpyō*. Tokyo: Yūzankaku, 1982.
———. *Shokunin no rekishi*. Tokyo: 1958.
Fujita Gorō. *Hōken shakai no hatten katei*. Tokyo: Yūhikaku, 1952.

Fukushima-shi shi hensan iinkai, editors. *Fukushima-shi shi: Kinsei shiryō*. Fukushima, Nichirento insatsujo, 1968. 2 vols.

Harada Tomohiko. *Harada Tomohiko ronshū*. 3 vols. Tokyo: 1985.

Hashimoto Seiji, editor. *Himeji-shi shi*. Himeji: 1973.

Hayami Akira. "Kyoto machikata no shūmon aratamechō: Shijo Tateuri Nakanomachi," *Tokugawa rinsei shi kenkyūjo kenkyū kiyo*, (1980).

———. "Tokugawa kōki jinkō hendo no chiikiteki tokusei." *Mita gakkai zasshi*, 64–68 (1971).

Hayashi Reiko. *Edo tonya kabunakama no kenkyu*. Tokyo: Ochanomizu shoten, 1967.

Hayashi Reiko et al., editors. *Ibaraki-ken shiryo, Kinsei shakai keizai kan*. 2 vols. Tokyo: 1971.

Higuchi Kiyoyuki. *Nihon josei no seikatsu-shi*. Tokyo: Kōdansha, 1977.

Hirai Kiyoshi. *Nihon jūtaku no rekishi*. Tokyo: NHK Books, 1974.

Hiroshima Shiyakusho, editors. *Hiroshima-shi shi*. Hiroshima: 1922.

Honjō Eijirō, editor. *Nishijin shiryō*. Osaka: 1972.

Horie Eiichi. *Nihon no manufakuchua mondai*. Tokyo: 1949.

Hōseishi Gakkai, editors. *Tokugawa kinreikō*, vol. IV. Tokyo: 1932.

Hyogo-ken shi henshū senmon iinkai, editors. *Hyogo-ken shi*, vol. 4. Himeji: 1980.

Ihara Saikaku. *Taishaku Saikaku zenshū* 14: *Saikaku oritome*, edited by Asō Isoji. Tokyo: Meiji shoin, 1976.

Ikeda Shōichirō. *Edo jidai yōgo kosho jiten*. Tokyo: Shinbutsu ōraisha, 1984.

Ikegami Akihiko. "Kōki Edo kasō chōnin no seikatsu." In Nishiyama Matsunosuke, editor, *Edo chōnin no kenkyū*. 2 vols. Tokyo: 1974.

Inui Hiromi. "Hōreki-Tenpō ki ni okeru ōsaka machikata shakai no dōtai." *Hisutoria*, 83 (June 1979).

———. *Naniwa ōsaka Kikuyachō*. Tokyo: Yanagiwara shoten, 1977.

———. "Ōsaka chōnin shakai no kōzō: jinkō dōtai ni okeru," in Tsuda Hideo, *Kinsei kokka no kaitei to kindai*. Tokyo: 1979.

Ishida Baigan. *Ishida Baigan zenshū*, edited by Shibata Minoru. Osaka: 1972.

Ishii Ryosuke. *Edo jidai manpitsu*. 2 vols. Tokyo: Asahi sensho, 1979.

Ishii Ryosuke and Takayanagi Shinzō, editors. *Ofuregaki Kanpō shūsei*. 5 vols. Tokyo: Iwanami shoten, 1936.

Ishikawa Ken. *Sekimen Shingaku shi no kenkyu*. Tokyo: Iwanami shoten, 1942.

Ishikawa-ken Toshokan Kyokai, editors. *Kaga han shoki no samurai chō*. Kanazawa: 1942.

Kiryū-shi shi hensangakari, editors. *Kiryū-shi shi*. Kiryu: 1959.

Kitajima Masamoto. "Buke no hōkōnin." In *Edo jidai bushi no seikatsu*. Tokyo: Yūzankaku, 1984.

———. *Edo bakufu no kenryoku kōzō*. Tokyo: Iwanami shoten, 1964.

———. *Edo jidai*. Tokyo: Iwanami shinsho, 1983.

Kobata Atsushi, editor. *Sakai-shi shi*. Sakai: Sakai Shiyakusho, 1971–76.

Kōda Rohan. *Kōda Rohan zenshū*. Tokyo: Iwanami shoten, 1951.

Koda Shigetomo. *Edo to Ōsaka*. Tokyo: 1934.

Kodama Kōta. *Genroku jidai*. Tokyo: Chūo kōronsha, 1984.

Koji Ruien, 51 vols. Tokyo: Yoshikawa kōbunkan, 1981–85.

Kuranami Seiji, *Hyakumangoku daimyō*. Tokyo: 1965.

Kurowa Heijirō, editor, *Ōsaka shōgyō shiryō shūsei*. Osaka: Ōsaka shiritsu daigaku keizai kenkyujo, 1934.

Kyushū shiryo kankō kai, eds., *Kyūshū shiryō sōsho*, Nagasaki Hiradomachi ninbetsuchō. Nagasaki: 1955.

Maki Hidemasa. *Jinshin baibai*. Tokyo: Iwanami shoten, 1971.

———. *Koyō no rekishi*. Tokyo: Kobundō, 1977.

Matsudaira Sadanobu. *Uge no hito goto: Shugoroku*. Edited by Matsudaira Sadamitsu. Tokyo: Iwanami shoten, 1983.

Matsumoto Shirō. "Bakumatsu Ishinki ni okeru toshi to kaikyu tōsō." *Rekishigaku kenkyu*, supplementary volume (October 1970).

———. *Nihon kinsei toshi ron*. Tokyo: Tōkyō Daigaku shuppansha, 1983.

Minami Kazuo. *Edokko no sekai*. Tokyo: Kōdansha gendai shinsho, 1980.

———. "Edo no chūgen kyukin kō." *Nihon rekishi*, 204, 5 (May 1965).

Mitsui Rokurō et al., editors. *Shin Nagasaki nenpyō*. Nagasaki: 1974. 2 vols.

Mori Kahei. "Kinsei nōgyō rōdō jikan oyobi kyujitsu no seido." *Shakai keizaishigaku*, 16, 1 (1950).

Mutō Sadao. *Edo kobanashi jiten*. Tokyo: 1965.

Nagakura Tamotsu, "Nada no sake," in Chihoshi kenkyū kyōgikai, editors. *Nihon sangyōshi taikei*. Tokyo: Tōkyō daigaku, 1960.

Nagaoka Hakao, *Kaga Noto no seikatsu to minzoku*. Tokyo: 1983.

Nagasaki shishi nenpyō hensan iinkai, editors. *Nagasaki shishi nenpyō*. Nagasaki: 1981.

Nagasaki-ken shihenshū iinkai, editors. *Nagasaki-ken shi, hansei hen*. Tokyo: Yoshikawa kōbunkan, 1973.

Nakabe Yoshiko. *Kinsei toshi no seiritsu to kōzō*. Tokyo: 1974.

Naramoto Tatsuji. *Yomeru nenpyō, 5 Edo-hen*. 2 vols. Tokyo: Jiyukokuminsha, 1982.

Nihon keizaishi jiten, v. 2. Tokyo: Nihon hyōronsha, 1940.

Nihon meichō zenshū kankōkai, editors. *Nihon meichō zenshū*. Tokyo: 1926–69.

Nihon zuihitsu taisei kankōkai, editors. *Nihon sankai meisan zue*. Tokyo: 1965.

Nikki kōki shū. Tokyo: Yūhōdō bunko, 1929.

Nishiyama Matsunosuke. *Iemoto no kenkyū*. Yoshikawa kōbunkan, 1982.

Nishiyama Matsunosuke et al., editors. *Edo gaku jiten*. Tokyo: Kobunkan, 1984.

Noma Kenshin. "Miyako no Nishiki gokuchū gokkai," part 1, *Kokugo kokubun*, vol. 17, 8 (1948).

Oana Yoshimi. "Shomin to tojiba." In Oishi Shinzaburō, editor, *Edo to chihō bunka*. Tokyo: 1977.

Ogyu Sorai. *Nihon shisō taikei*, vol. 36: Ogyū Sorai, edited by Yoshikawa Kojirō et al. Tokyo: Iwanami, 1983.

———. *Seidan*, in *Nihon keizai taiten*, vol. 9. Tokyo: Keimeisha, 1928.

Ōkubo Toshiaki et al., editors. *Shiryo ni yoru Nihon no Ayumi*. Kinseihen. Tokyo: Yoshikawa kōbunkan, 1955.

Ōsaka-shi shi hensangakari, editors. *Ōsaka-shi shi*. 8 vols. Osaka: 1911–14.

Ōtake Hideo. *Kinsei koyō kankei shiron.* Tokyo: Yūzankaku, 1983.

Owada Tetsuo. *Shiro to jōkamachi.* Tokyo: Kyōikusha, 1979.

Saitō Osamu. "Shōka hōkōnin to zatsugyosha: Kinsei toshi rōdō shijō ni okeru nijū kōzō no keisei," *Keizai kenkyū,* 36, no. 3 (August 1985).

Sakamoto Heihachirō and Miyamoto Mataji, editors. *Ōsaka Kikuyachō shūshi ninbetsuchō.* Tokyo: 1941–73. 7 vols.

Saku Tadashi. *Echizen kuni shūmon ninbetsu go-aratamechō.* Kogawa kōbunkan, 1973.

Satō Shin'ichi and Ikeuchi Yoshimoto, editors. *Chūsei hōsei shiryō shū,* vol. 3: *Buke kahō.* Tokyo: Iwanami shoten, 1965.

Satō Ubei, editor. *Tzūzoku keizai bunko.* Tokyo: 1916.

Sekiyama Naotarō. *Kinsei Nihon no jinko.* Tokyo: Yoshikawa kōbunkan, 1958.

Shibata Kyūo. *Kyūō Dōwa.* Tokyo: Heibonsha, 1970.

Shibusawa Keizō. *Nihon jōmin seikatsu ebiki.* Tokyo: Heibonsha, 1966–67.

Shibusawa Eiichi. *Rakuō kōden.* Tokyo: 1937.

Shikitei Sanba. *Ukiyoburo.* Edited by Nakamura Michio. Tokyo: Iwanami shoten, 1957.

Shinmura Izuru et al. *Kōjien.* Tokyo: Iwanami shoten, 1981.

Shirayama Tomomasa. "Ezochi no yoseba kō." *Hōseishi kenkyū.* vol. 13 (1962).

Sumiya Mikio. *Nihon chinrōdō ron.* Tokyo: 1955.

Takagi Shūsaku. "Iwayuru 'mibun hōrei' to 'ikii' kinrei: 'samurai' wa 'bushi' de wa nai," in *Nihon kinsei shi ronsō,* 1. Tokyo: 1984.

Takahashi Masahiko. *Daiku-gashira Nakai komonjo.* Tokyo: Keiō tsūshin, 1983.

Takikawa Masajirō. *Nihon shakai shi.* Tokyo: 1948.

Tanaka Keiichi. *Sado kinzan.* Tokyo: Kyōikusha, 1980.

Tanaka Yoshio. "Kaga-han hiningoya seiritsu to jijo ni tsuite," *Nihon rekishi,* vol. 183 (August 1963).

———. *Kaga han ni okeru toshi kenkyū.* Tokyo: Bun'ichi sōgō shuppan, 1978.

———. *Kaga hyakumangoku.* Tokyo: Kyōikusha, 1980.

Tema Kenkyujo, editors. *Sadō Kinzan.* Tokyo: 1985.

Tezuka Yutaka. "Nagaoka han no yoseba to Matsuyama han no tokeisho," *Hōgaku kenkyū,* 31, no. 5 (1965).

Tokoro Rikio. "Edo no dekaseginin." In Nishiyama Matsunosuke, editor, *Edo chōnin no kenkyū.* Tokyo: 1943.

Ueda Akinari. *Ueda Akinari zenshū.* Tokyo: Kokusho kankō kai, 1917–18. 2 vols.

Wakayama-shi shi hensan iinkai, editors. *Wakayama-shi shi.* 6 vols. Tokyo: 1975.

Wakita Osamu. *Genroku no shakai.* Tokyo: 1980.

———. *Kinsei hōken shakai no keizai kōzō.* Tokyo: Ochanomizu shobō, 1963.

———. "Kinsei shoki no toshi keizai." *Nihon shi kenkyū,* no. 200 (April 1974).

Yamakawa Kikue. *Buke no josei.* Tokyo: Iwanami shoten, 1983.

Yamamoto Takeo. *Shin kenkyū Nihonshi.* Tokyo: 1979.

Yamamoto Tsunetomo. *Hagakure zenshū.* Edited by Nakamura Ikukazu. Tokyo: Satsuki shobō, 1978.

Yasuoka Shigeki. "Kyohō ki ni okeru shōka hōkōnin no seikatsu—Kōnoike no baai." *Ōsaka no kenkyu.* Osaka: 1969.

———. "Zenkiteki shihon no henshitsu katei." *Doshisha shūgaku,* 13, no. 5 (February 1962).

Yoshida Nobuyuki. "Chōnin to machi." In *Koza Nihonshi, 5: Kinsei,* 1. Tokyo: Tōkyo Daigaku, 1985.

———. "Edo machi kaisho kinkashitsuke ni tsuite." *Shigaku zasshi,* vol. LXXXVI, 1 (January 1977).

———. "Edo no hiyoza to hiyō: mibun." In Bito Masahide sensei kanreki kinen-kai, eds., *Nihon kinsei shi ronsō.* Tokyo: Yoshikawa kōbunkan, 1984. 2 vols.

———. "Nihon Kinsei ni okeru puroretaria-teki yoso ni tsuite," *Rekishigaku kenkyū,* 548 (1985).

———. "Toshi minshū no seikatsu to henkaku ishiki," *Rekishigaku kenkyū,* 534 (October 1984).

WORKS IN ENGLISH

Alcock, Rutherford. *The Capital of the Tycoon: A Narrative of Three Years' Residence in Japan.* 2 vols. New York: Harper and Brothers, 1863.

Andrews, Roy Chapman. "The Worst Slum." In Michael Wise, comp., *Travellers' Tales of Old Japan.* Singapore: Time Books International, 1985.

Arai Hakuseki. *Told Around a Brushwood Fire: The Autobiography of Arai Hakuseki.* Translated with introduction by Joyce Ackroyd. Tokyo: University of Tokyo, 1979.

Aries, Philip. *Centuries of Childhood.* Harmondsworth: Penguin, 1973.

Armstrong, Robert Cornell. *Just Before the Dawn: The Life and Works of Ninomiya Sontaku.* New York: Macmillan, 1912.

Bellah, Robert. *Tokugawa Religion: The Cultural Roots of Modern Japan.* Glencoe, Ill., Free Press, 1957.

Birt, Michael P. "Samurai in Passage: The Transformation of the Sixteenth-Century Kanto." *Journal of Japanese Studies,* 11 (1985).

Bix, Herbert P. *Peasant Protest in Japan, 1590–1884.* New Haven: Yale University Press, 1986.

Blyth, R. H. *Japanese Life and Character in Senryū.* Tokyo: Hokuseido Press, 1959.

———. *Oriental Humour.* Tokyo: Hokuseido Press, 1959.

Broom, L. and Smith, J. H. "Bridging Occupations," *British Journal of Sociology,* 14, 4 (December 1963).

Brown, Delmer M. *Money Economy in Medieval Japan: A Study in the Use of Coins.* New Haven: Far Eastern Association, 1951.

Casal, V. A. "The Yamabushi." In *Mitteilungen der Deutschen Gesellschaft fur Natur- und Volkerkunde Ostasiens,* vol. 49.

Chikamatsu Monzaemon. *Major Plays of Chikamatsu.* Translated by Donald Keene. New York: Columbia University Press, 1961.

Chikamatsu Monzaemon. *Masterpieces of Chikamatsu Monzaemon*. Translated by Miyamori Asataro. Tokyo and Kobe: Taiseido Shobo, n.d.

Cipolla, Carlo. *Before the Industrial Revolution*. New York: Norton, 1976.

Clark, Alice. *Working Life of Women in the Sixteenth Century*. New York: Harcourt, Brace and Howe, 1920.

Cooper, Michael J., S.J., translator and editor. *This Island of Japon: João Rodrigues' Account of 16th-Century Japan*. Tokyo: Kodansha International, 1973.

Crawcour, E. S. "Kawamura Zuiken: A Seventeenth-Century Entrepreneur," Transactions of the Asiatic Society of Japan, 3d ser., 9 (May 1966).

Dazai Jun, "Food and Wealth." Translated by G. Kirby. Transactions of the Asiatic Society of Japan, 35 (1908).

Dore, Ronald. *Education in Tokugawa Japan*. Berkeley: University of California Press, 1975.

Dowdy, Edwin. *Japanese Bureaucracy: Its Development and Modernization*. Melbourne, Australia: Cheshire, 1973.

Dower, John W., "E. H. Norman, Japan, and the Uses of History." In E. H. Norman, *Origins of the Modern Japanese State*. Edited by John W. Dower. New York: Random House, 1975.

Dunn, Charles J. *Everyday Life in Traditional Japan*. Tokyo and Rutland, Vt.: Charles E. Tuttle Co, 1969.

Fairbank, J. K. and Reischauer, E.O. *East Asia: The Great Tradition*. New York: Houghton Mifflin Co., 1958.

Fairchilds, Cissie. *Domestic Enemies: Servants and Their Masters in Old Regime France*. Baltimore and London: Johns Hopkins University Press, 1984.

Faulds, Henry. *Nine Years in Nipon: Sketches of Japanese Life and Manners*. New York: Scholarly Resources, 1973.

Fitchen, John. *Building Construction before Mechanization*. Cambridge: M.I.T. Press, 1986.

Foucault, Michel. *The Birth of the Prison*. New York: Random House, 1977.

———. *Madness and Civilization: A History of Insanity in the Age of Reason*. New York: Random House, 1965.

Fraser, Andrew. "Town-ward Administration in Eighteenth-Century Edo." Papers in Far Eastern History, Australian National University vol. 27 (March, 1984.

Fraser, Antonia Fraser. *The Weaker Vessel*. New York: Alfred A. Knopf, 1984.

Frederic, Louis. *Daily Life in Japan at the Time of the Samurai*, 1185–1603. Tokyo and Rutland, Vt.: Charles E. Tuttle and Co., 1973.

Fruin, Mark. *Kikkoman: Company, Clan and Community*. Cambridge: Harvard University Press, 1984.

Fukuzawa Yukichi. *The Autobiography of Fukuzawa Yukichi*. New York: Columbia University Press, 1966.

Furth, Charlotte. "Concepts of Pregnancy, Childbirth and Infancy in Ch'ing Dynasty China." *Journal of Asian Studies* 46, no. 1 (February 1987).

Garon, Sheldon. *The State and Labor in Modern Japan*. Berkeley: University of California Press, 1987.

Goldwaithe, Richard A. *The Building of Renaissance Florence: An Economic and Social History*. Baltimore and London: Johns Hopkins University Press, 1980.

Gordon, Andrew. *The Evolution of Labor Relations in Japan: Heavy Industry, 1853–1955.* Cambridge: Harvard University Press, 1985

Griffis, William Elliot. *The Mikado's Empire.* New York: Harper and Brothers, 1877.

———, ed., *Townsend Harris: First American Envoy in Japan.* Boston and New York: Houghton, Mifflin and Co., 1985.

Hall, John Carey. "Japanese Feudal Laws." Transactions of the Asiatic Society of Japan. vol., 33 (1910–12).

Hall, John Whitney. "The Castle Town and Japan's Modern Urbanization." In *Studies in the Institutional History of Early Modern Japan.* Edited by John W. Hall and Marius B. Jansen. Princeton, N.J.: Princeton University Press, 1968.

———. "Changing Conceptions of the Modernization of Japan." In *Changing Japanese Attitudes towards Modernization.* Edited by Marius B. Jansen, Princeton N.J.: Princeton University Press, 1965.

———. "Feudalism in Japan—A Reassessment." In *Studies in the Institutional History of Early Modern Japan.* Edited by Hall and Marius B. Jansen. Princeton N.J.: Princeton University Press, 1968.

———. *Japan from Prehistory to Modern Times.* New York: Dell, 1980.

———. "Kyoto as Historical Background." In *Medieval Japan: Essays in Institutional History.* Edited by John W. Hall and Jeffrey P. Mass, New Haven: Yale University Press, 1974.

Hanley, Susan. "The Material Culture: Stability in Transition." In *Japan in Transition: Tokugawa to Meiji.* Edited by Marius B. Jansen and Gilbert Rozman Princeton, N.J.: Princeton University Press, 1986.

———. "Migration and Economic Change in Okayama during the Tokugawa Period." *Keio Economic Studies,* 10, no. 2 (1973).

Hanley, Susan and Kozo Yamamura. *Economic and Demographic Change in Preindustrial Japan, 1600–1868.* Princeton, N.J.: Princeton University Press, 1977.

Haraguchi Torao et al. *The Status System and Social Organization of Satsuma: A Translation of the Shumon Aratame Jomoku.* Honolulu: University Press of Hawaii, 1975.

Hauser, William B. *Economic Institutional Change in Tokugawa Japan: Osaka and the Kinai Cotton Trade.* Cambridge: Cambridge University Press, 1974.

Hayami Akira, "Labor Migration in a Pre-industrial Society: A Study Tracing the Life Histories of the Inhabitants of a Village." Keio Economic Studies 10, no. 2 (1973).

Hearn, Lafcadio. *Japan: An Attempt at Interpretation.* Tokyo and Rutland, Vt.: Charles E. Tuttle Co., 1955.

Hecht, J. Jean. *The Domestic Servant Class in Eighteenth Century England.* London: Routledge and Paul, 1956.

Hepler, Chester W. "The Labor Boss System in Japan." *Monthly Labor Review,* January 1949.

Hill, Bridget, ed. *Eighteenth Century Women: An Anthology.* London: Allen and Unwin, 1984.

Hill, Christopher. *Change and Continuity in 17th Century England.* Cambridge, Mass.: Harvard University Press, 1975.

Hill, Christopher. "William Perkins and the Poor." In *Puritanism and Revolution*. London: Mercury Books, 1958.

Hilton, R. H. "A Crisis of Feudalism." In *The Brenner Debate: Agrarian Class Structure and Economic Development in Pre-industrial Europe*. Edited by T. H. Aston and C. H. E. Philpin. Cambridge: Cambridge University Press, 1985.

―――. "Feudalism." In *A Dictionary of Marxist Thought*. Edited by Tom Bottomore. Cambridge, Mass.: Harvard University Press, 1983.

―――. "Introduction." In *The Brenner Debate: Agrarian Class Structure and Economic Development in Pre-industrial Europe*. Edited by T. H. Aston and C. H. E. Philpin. Cambridge: Cambridge University Press, 1985.

Hironaga Shuzaburo. *The Bunraku Handbook*. Tokyo: Maison des Arts, 1976.

Holton, R. J., ed. *The Transition from Feudalism to Capitalism*. New York: St. Martin's Press, 1985.

Honey, William Bower. *The Art of the Potter*. New York: Beechhurst Press, 1955.

Hooper, Wilfred. "The Tudor Sumptuary Laws." *English Historical Review*, 30, 1915.

Horie Yasuzō. "An Outline of the Rise of Modern Capitalism in Japan." *Kyoto University Economic Review* 11, no. 1 (July 1936).

Hoston, Germaine A. *Marxism and the Crisis of Development in Prewar Japan*. Princeton, N.J.: Princeton University Press, 1986.

Hughes, Charles, ed. *Shakespeare's Europe: Unpublished Chapters of Fynes Moryson's Itinerary*. London: Sharratt and Hughes, 1903.

Innes, Robert LeRoy. *The Door Ajar: Japan's Foreign Trade in the Seventeenth Century*. Ph.D. diss., University of Michigan, 1980.

Isaku, Patia R., *Mountain Storm, Pine Breeze: Folk Song in Japan*. Tucson: University of Arizona Press, 1981.

Ishida Baigan. *Dialogues of City and Country*. Translated by Matsuo Akira. Osaka: Osaka Kyoiku Tosho, 1985.

Ishino Iwao. "The Oyabun-Kobun: A Japanese Ritual Kinship Institution." *American Anthropologist* 55 (1953).

✓ Jacobs, Norman. *The Origins of Modern Capitalism and East Asia*. Hong Kong: Hong Kong University Press, 1958.

Jansen, Marius. "Tosa in the Sixteenth Century." In *Studies in the Institutional History of Early Modern Japan*. Edited by John W. Hall and Marius Jansen. Princeton N.J.: Princeton University Press, 1968.

Kaempfer, Englebert. *The History of Japan*. 3 vols. Glasgow: J. MacLehose and Sons, 1906.

Kaplow, Jeffrey. *The Names of Kings: The Parisian Laboring Poor in the Eighteenth Century*. New York: Basic Books, 1972.

Kawatake Mokuami, *The Love of Izayoi and Seishin: A Kabuki Play*. Translated by Frank T. Motofuji. Tokyo and Rutland, Vt.: Charles E. Tuttle Co., 1966.

Keene, Donald. *World Within Walls: Japanese Literature of the Pre-modern Era, 1600–1867*. New York: Grove Press, 1976.

Kirkwood, Kenneth P. *Renaissance in Japan: A Cultural Survey of the Seventeenth Century*. Tokyo and Rutland, Vt.: Charles E. Tuttle Co., 1970.

Koda Rohan. *Pagoda, Skull and Samurai*. Translated by Chieko Irie Mulhern. Tokyo and Rutland, Vt.: Charles E. Tuttle Co., 1985.

Kodansha Encyclopedia of Japan. Tokyo: Kodansha, 1983.

Koschmann, J. Victor. *The Mito Ideology: Discourse, Reform, and Insurrection in Late Tokugawa Japan, 1790–1864*. Berkeley: University of California Press, 1987.

Kussmaul, Ann. *Servants in Husbandry in Early Modern England*. Cambridge: Cambridge University Press, 1981.

Lehmann, Jean-Pierre. *The Image of Japan: From Feudal Isolation to World Power, 1850–1905*. London: Allen and Unwin, 1978.

Leutner, Robert W. *Shikitei Sanba and the Comic Tradition in Edo Fiction*. Cambridge: Harvard University Press, 1985.

Lu, David John. *Sources of Japanese History*. 2 vols. New York: McGraw-Hill, 1974.

McClain, James. *Kanazawa: A Seventeenth-Century Japanese Castle Town*. New Haven: Yale University Press, 1982.

McEwan, J. R. *The Political Writings of Ogyu Sorai*. Cambridge: Cambridge: University Press, 1981.

Maruyama Masao. *Studies in the Intellectual History of Tokugawa Japan*. Princeton, N.J.: Princeton University Press, 1974.

Marx, Karl. *Capital*. 3 vols. New York: International Publishers, 1984.

———. *Grundrisse: Introduction to the Critique of Political Economy*. Translated by Martin Nicolaus. New York: Vintage, 1973.

Matsumoto Shigeru. *Motoori Norinaga, 1730–1801*. Cambridge, Mass.: Harvard University Press, 1970.

Maza, Sarah. *Servants and Masters in Eighteenth-Century France: The Uses of Loyalty*. Princeton, N.J.: Princeton University Press, 1983.

Minami Ryoshin. *The Economic Development of Japan*. Tokyo: Oriental Economist, 1986.

Mitford, A. B. *Tales of Old Japan*. Tokyo and Rutland, Vt.: Charles E. Tuttle Co., 1966.

Mori Hideto, "The Longshoremen of Kobe Harbor." In *The Japanese Image*. Edited by Maurice Schneps and Alvin D. Coox. Tokyo and Philadelphia: Orient/West, 1965.

Munsterberg, Hugo. *The Arts of Japan: An Illustrated History*. Tokyo and Rutland, Vt.: Charles E. Tuttle Co., 1957.

Murdoch, James. *A History of Japan*. 3 vols. Kobe and London: K. Paul, Trench, Trubner and Co., 1926.

Nagahara Keiji and Yamamura, Kozo. "Shaping the Process of Unification: Technological Progress in Sixteenth- and Seventeenth-Century Japan." *Journal of Japanese Studies* 14, no. 1 (1988), 73.

Najita, Tetsuo. *Visions of Virtue in Tokugawa Japan: The Kaitokudo Merchant Academy of Osaka*. Chicago: University of Chicago Press, 1987.

Nakamura Hajime. "Suzuki Shōsan, 1579–1655 and the Spirit of Capitalism in Japanese Buddhism." Translated by William Johnson, *Monumenta Nipponica* 22, no. 1. 1967.

Norman, E. H. *Andō Shōeki and the Anatomy of Japanese Feudalism*. Transactions of the Asiatic Society of Japan. 3rd ser., vol. 2. Tokyo: Kenkyusha Press, 1949.

Norman, E. H. *Origins of the Modern Japanese State: Selected Writings of E. H. Norman.* Edited by John W. Dower. New York: Random House, 1974.

Papinot, E. *Historical and Geographical Dictionary of Japan.* Tokyo and Rutland, Vt.: Charles E. Tuttle Co., 1972.

Pompe van Meerdervoort, L. C. *Doctor on Desima: Selected Chapters from JHR J. L. C. Pompe van Meerdervoort's Vijf Jaren in Japan [Five Years in Japan] (1857–1863).* Translated and annotated by Elizabeth P. Wittermans and John Z. Bowers. Tokyo: Sophia University, 1970.

Porter, Ray. *English Society in the Eighteenth Century.* Harmondsworth: Penguin, 1982.

Rainey, Ronald E. *Sumptuary Legislation in Renaissance Florence.* Ph.D. diss., Columbia University, 1985.

Roche, Daniel. *The People of Paris: An Essay in Popular Culture in the 18th Century.* Translated by Marie Evans in association with Gwynne Lewis. Berkeley: University of California Press, 1987.

Rozman, Gilbert. "Edo's Importance in the Changing Tokugawa Society." *Journal of Japanese Studies* 6, no. 1 (Autumn 1974).

———. *Urban Networks in Ch'ing China and Tokugawa Japan.* Princeton, N.J.: Princeton University Press, 1973.

Sadler, A. L. *The Maker of Modern Japan: The Life of Tokugawa Ieyasu.* London: Allen and Unwin, 1937.

Saitō Osamu, "Changing Structure of Urban Employment and Its Effects on Migration Patterns in Eighteenth- and Nineteenth-Century Japan." Institute of Economic Research Discussion Paper, no. 134 (Hitotsubashi University March 1986).

———. "The Labor Market in Tokugawa Japan: Wage Differentials and the Real Wage Level, 1727-1830." *Explorations in Economic History* 15 (1978).

Sakanishi Shio. *Japanese Folk-Plays: The Ink-Smeared Lady and Other Kyogen.* Tokyo and Rutland, Vt.: Charles E. Tuttle Co. 1960.

Sansom, George B. *A History of Japan, 1615–1867.* Stanford: Stanford University Press, 1963.

———. *Japan in World History.* New York: Institute for Pacific Relations, 1951.

———. *Japan: A Short Cultural History.* Stanford: Stanford University Press, 1952.

Sasaki Junnosuke with Ronald P. Toby. "The Changing Rationale of Daimyo Control in the Emergence of the Bakufu State." In *Japan Before Tokugawa: Political Consolidation and Economic Growth.* Translated by John Whitney Hall et al. Princeton, N.J.: Princeton University Press, 1981.

Sheldon, Charles David. *The Rise of the Merchant Class in Tokugawa Japan, 1600–1868.* New York: Institute for Pacific Relations, 1958.

Shively, Donald. "Bakufu versus Kabuki." In *Studies in the Institutional History of Early Modern Japan.* Edited by John W. Hall and Marius Jansen. Princeton, N.J.: Princeton University Press, 1968.

————. "Sumptuary Legislation and Status in Early Tokugawa Japan." *Harvard Journal of Asiatic Studies* 25 (1964–65).

Smith, Henry D. "The Edo-Tokyo Transition: In Search of Common Ground." In Marius B. Jansen and Gilbert Rozman, *Japan in Transition: From Tokugawa to Meiji*. Princeton, N.J.: Princeton University Press, 1986.

Smith, Neil Skene, ed. "Materials on Japanese Social and Economic History: Tokugawa Japan (1)." Transactions of the Asiatic Society of Japan, 2d ser., 14 (1937).

Smith, Thomas C. *The Agrarian Origins of Modern Japan*. Stanford: Stanford University Press, 1959.

————. "The Japanese Village in the Seventeenth Century." In *Studies in the Institutional History of Early Modern Japan*. Edited by John W. Hall and Marius B. Jansen. Princeton, N.J.: Princeton University Press, 1968.

————. *Nakahara*. Stanford: Stanford University Press, 1977.

————. "Peasant Time and Factory Time in Japan." *Past and Present*, vol. 111 (May 1986).

————. "Pre-modern Economic Growth: Japan and the West." *Past and Present*, vol. 60 (August, 1973).

Solomon, Howard M. *Public Welfare, Science, and Propaganda in Seventeenth Century France: The Innovations of Theophraste Renaudot*. Princeton, N.J.: Princeton University Press, 1972.

Sombart, Werner. *The Quintessence of Capitalism: A Study of the History and Psychology of the Modern Business Man*. New York: E. P. Dutton and Co., 1915.

Spencer, Daniel Lloyd. "Japan's Pre-Perry Preparation for Economic Growth." *The American Journal of Economics and Sociology* 17 (1958).

Spufford, Margaret. *Small Books and Pleasant Histories: Popular Fiction and Its Readership in Seventeenth Century England*. Cambridge: Cambridge University Press, 1981.

Stone, Lawrence. *The Family, Sex and Marriage in England, 1500–1800*. Abridged edition. London: Penguin, 1979.

Strayer, Joseph R. "The Tokugawa Period and Japanese Feudalism." In *Studies in the Institutional History of Early Modern Japan*. Edited by John W. Hall and Marius B. Jansen. Princeton, N.J.: Princeton University Press, 1968.

Sugimoto Etsu. *Daughter of the Samurai*. Tokyo and Rutland, Vt.: Charles E. Tuttle Co., 1955.

Sumiya Mikio and Taira Koji, eds. *An Outline of Japanese Economic History, 1603–1940*. Tokyo: University of Tokyo Press, 1979.

Sussler, Bernard. "The Toyotomi Regime and the Daimyo." In *The Bakufu in Japanese History*. Edited by Jeffrey P. Mass and William B. Hauser. Stanford: Stanford University Press, 1985.

Taira Koji. *Economic Development and the Labor Market in Japan*. New York: Columbia University Press, 1970.

Takeda Izumo, Miyoshi Shōraku, and Namiki Senryu. *Chūshingura (The Treasury of Loyal Retainers)*. Translated by Donald Keene. New York: Columbia University Press, 1971.

Takekoshi Yosaburō. *Economic Aspects of the History of the Civilization of Japan*. 3 vols. London: Allen and Unwin Ltd., 1930.

Takizawa Matsuyo. *The Penetration of Money Economy in Japan and Its Effects upon Social and Political Institutions*. New York: Columbia University Press, 1927.

Tawney, R. H., *Religion and the Rise of Capitalism*. New York: Harcourt, Brace and World, 1926.

Tawney, R.H. and Power, Eileen, eds. *Tudor Economic Documents*. 3 vols. London: Longmans, Green, and Co., 1924.

Thompson, Edward P. *The Making of the English Working Class*. New York: Vintage, 1963.

Tilly, Louise A. and Scott, Joan W. *Women, Work and Family*. New York: Holt, Rinehart and Winston, 1978.

Toyoda Takeshi. *A History of pre-Meiji Commerce in Japan*. Tokyo: Kokusai Bunka Shinkokai, 1969.

Toyoda Takeshi and Sugiyama Hiroshi, with Morris, V. Dixon. "The Growth of Commerce and the Trades." In *Japan in the Muromachi Age*. Edited by John W. Hall and Toyoda Takeshi. Berkeley: University of California, 1977.

Tsukahira, Toshio G. *Feudal Control in Tokugawa Japan: The Sankin Kotai System*. Cambridge: Harvard East Asian Monographs, 1966.

Vaporis, Constantine N. "Post Station and Assisting Villages: Corvee Labor and Peasant Contention." *Monumenta Nipponica 41*, no. 4 (1986).

Varley, H. Paul. "Samurai." In *Kodansha Encyclopedia of Japan*. vol. 7. Tokyo: Kodansha, 1983.

Veblen, Thorstein. *The Theory of the Leisure Class: An Economic Study of Institutions*. New York: The Modern Library, 1931.

von Siebold, Philipp Franz and others. *Manners and Customs of the Japanese in the Nineteenth Century from the Accounts of Dutch Residents in Japan and from the German Work of Dr. Philipp Franz von Sielbold*. Tokyo and Rutland Vt.: Charles E. Tuttle Co, 1973.

Vlastos, Stephen. *Peasant Protests and Uprisings in Tokugawa Japan*. Berkeley: University of California Press, 1986.

Wakita Haruko with Hanley, Susan B. "Dimensions of Development: Cities in Fifteenth- and Sixteenth- Century Japan." In *Japan Before Tokugawa: Political Consolidation and Economic Growth, 1500 to 1650*. Edited by John Whitney Hall, Nagahara Keiji and Kozo Yamamura. Princeton, N.J.: Princeton University Press, 1981.

Walthall, Anne. *Social Protest and Popular Culture in Eighteenth-Century Japan*. Tucson: University of Arizona Press, 1986.

Webb, Sidney and Beatrice. *English Local Government. English Poor Law History: Part I: The Old Poor Law*. London: Longmans, Green and Co., 1927.

Weber, Max. *Economy and Society*, 2 vols. Edited by Guenther Roth and Claus Wittich. Berkeley: University of California Press, 1978.

———. *General Economic History*. New York: Greenberg, 1927.

———. *The Protestant Ethic and the Spirit of Capitalism*. New York: Charles Scribner's Sons, 1958.

Wiesner, Merry E. *Working Women in Renaissance Germany*. New Brunswick, N.J.: Rutgers University Press, 1986.

Wigmore, John Henry, ed. *Law and Justice in Tokugawa Japan, Part I: Introduction*. Tokyo: Kokusai Bunka Shinkokai, 1969.

Wilson, John Dover, comp. *Life in Shakespeare's England: A Book of Elizabethan Prose*. Cambridge: Cambridge University Press, 1956.

Yamamoto Tsunetomo. *The Book of the Samurai: Hagakure*. Translated by William S. Wilson. Tokyo: Kodansha, 1978.

Yamamura, Kozo. *A Study of Samurai Income and Entrepreneurship*. Cambridge: Harvard University Press, 1974.

Yanagita Kunio. *Japanese Manners and Customs in the Meiji Era*. Tokyo: Kinen Bunka Jigyokai, 1957.

Yazaki Takeo. *Social Change and the City in Japan: From the Earliest Times through the Industrial Revolution*. Tokyo: Japan Publications, 1978.

(

INDEX

abscondence, 7, 72, 86–87; by *fudai*, 15–16
Aikawa, 11, 138; miners' strike in, 153
Ainu, placed in workhouses, 174
Aizawa Seishisai, 107
Alcock, Sir Rutherford, 133
Andō Hiroshige, 153
Andō Shōeki, 107
apprentices, apprenticeship, 16, 47, 85
Arai Hakuseki, 76, 131
arson, 99
artisans, 13, 123, 125; guilds, 141
Asahi Bunzaemon, 93–95
Asai Ryōi, 132
Asakawa Zen'in, 153

bakuhan system, 9–10
bantō. See head clerks
Banzuiin Chōbei, 142
baths, public, 90, 115
beggars, begging, 154, 156, 216; control of,
    159–61
bonuses, to servants, 103–4
Bureau d'Adresse, 164–65

capitalism, emergence of, 28, 156, 183
carpenters, 16, 134, 136, 144, 148, 150;
    high quality of, 136; strikes by, 153;
    working hours, 146–47
carters, 127
castle-towns, 10, 16, 183; construction of,
    155; manual laborers numerous in, 15
chambermaids, 46, 50–51, 53, 55, 87–89,
    103, 121
Chikamatsu Hanji, 115
Chikamatsu Monzaemon, 73, 94, 97, 108–
    9, 113–15, 117, 120, 130, 132, 145, 151,
    153, 180; on organization of packhorse-
    men, 145, 151
children: as day laborers, 139; as servants,
    60–61, 67–68
China, 13, 16, 24, 138, 198
Chōsokabe Motochika, 14
Christianity, 9, 18, 177–79
chūgen. See valets
clerks, 47, 50, 102, 106
concubines, 92

conspicuous consumption, 10
construction workers, 27, 134; types of,
    134–37
contracts: of laborers, 130; of servants, 100
corvee labor, 13, 15–17, 129, 131, 135

daimyo, 9
daki-uba. See nannies
day laborers, 4, 16–17, 27; populations of,
    4, 123–26; samurai as, 126; types of,
    124–38. *See also* laborers
Day Laborers' Registry, 161–65
Dazai Shundai, 16–17, 23–24, 121, 136,
    155; on lack of day laborers in China,
    23–24; on novelty of wage-labor, 17;
    against short-term service, 24
dekawaribi. See servants: replacement days
detchi. See apprentices
dock workers, 133–34

Edo, 18, 21, 28, 30, 36, 38–39, 44, 49, 55–
    57, 66–67, 69, 74, 76, 78, 82–83, 91, 94,
    108, 114–15, 123, 125, 128, 133, 135;
    carpenters of, 137; Day Laborers' Regis-
    try in, 162–65; fire-fighters of, 135;
    Isedana shops, 48, 61, 63; population of,
    11; riots in, 151–52, 159; Shirokiya
    shop, 88, 117–18; workhouse in, 169;
    working class neighborhoods in, 148
Edo Castle, 99, 108
Edo *yoseba*, 170–74; Matsudaira Sada-
    nobu on, 173; rules in, 171–73. *See also*
    workhouses
Ejima Kiseki, 50, 56, 74, 121, 153; on
    maidservants' vanity, 121
employers: populations of, 191–92; tenants
    as, 50, 69; types of, 25–27, 38
employment agencies, 69–72; as sites for
    trysts, 97

famines, 151, 159, 170
feminization of service, 62
feudalism, 7, 184
fire-fighters, 135–36, 153; gang violence
    among, 142
footboys, 42–45, 47–48, 55, 119